Suicide Voices

Labour Trauma in France

Studies in Modern and Contemporary France   8

Studies in Modern and Contemporary France

Series Editors

Professor Gill Allwood, Nottingham Trent University
Professor Denis M. Provencher, University of Arizona
Professor Martin O'Shaughnessy, Nottingham Trent University

The Studies in Modern and Contemporary France book series is a new collaboration between the Association for the Study of Modern and Contemporary France (ASMCF) and Liverpool University Press (LUP). Submissions are encouraged focusing on French politics, history, society, media and culture. The series will serve as an important focus for all those whose engagement with France is not restricted to the more classically literary, and can be seen as a long-form companion to the Association's journal, *Modern and Contemporary France,* and to *Contemporary French Civilization*, published by Liverpool University Press.

Suicide Voices

Labour Trauma in France

SARAH WATERS

Liverpool University Press

First published 2020 by
Liverpool University Press
4 Cambridge Street
Liverpool
L69 7ZU

British Library Cataloguing-in-Publication data
A British Library CIP record is available

ISBN 978-1-78962-223-2 cased

Typeset by Carnegie Book Production, Lancaster
Printed and bound by CPI Group (UK) Ltd, Croydon CR0 4YY

Contents

Acknowledgements   vii

Introduction   1

1.   Capitalism, Work and Suicide   25

2.   Suicide as Testimony   71

3.   Going Postal   107

4.   Orange on the Inside   139

5.   Fast Cars and Vital Exhaustion   171

Conclusion   215

Bibliography   223

Index   239

Acknowledgements

Suicide is a deeply personal, traumatic and complex act and a book that sets out to study suicide and real-life suicide cases runs the risk of transforming this most singular of human acts into a mere object of academic enquiry or a topic like any other, to be analysed, dissected or read about. In his series of essays on suicide, Holocaust survivor Jean Améry, observed that this is ultimately an unknowable experience and that a consideration of suicide should start with the unique experiences of suicidal individuals themselves in the period 'before the leap' (1999, 1). I would like first and foremost to acknowledge the employees whose cases are described in this book and who experienced such unimaginable suffering in their working lives that they chose suicide as a desperate means of escape. Suicide has a ripple effect and its consequences extend far beyond the suicidal individual, often triggering immense pain and distress for families, colleagues and friends. I would also like to acknowledge this wider network of family and friends whose lives were profoundly affected by the cases described in this book.

Work-related suicide is a highly contentious phenomenon and remains a source of deep-seated controversy over its nature, meaning and causes. A suicide that takes place at the workplace or because of work is a private tragedy but also a public act that holds considerable legal, financial and ethical implications for all those concerned. Many of the cases studied in this book have been the focus of litigation in the courts, where families and colleagues of a deceased individual have challenged companies and managers regarding the causal factors surrounding a suicide. While recognising the polemical nature of these suicide cases, I have chosen in this book to focus squarely on the perspectives of suicidal individuals themselves, examining the words that they have left behind in the form of letters, emails, texts or formal documents. Suicide is a sensitive phenomenon that is fraught with ethical dilemmas. Yet work-related suicide is also a social phenomenon that is on the rise, and I believe that it is crucial to open it up to scrutiny, analysis and critical debate. Indeed, the risks of not talking about suicide and of turning away, may outweigh the dangers of analysing its significance and listening to what suicidal individuals have to say.

I owe a debt of gratitude to the many people who supported my research and shared their knowledge and experiences. I am very grateful to Martin McKee at the London School of Hygiene and Tropical Medicine, who was a source of tremendous support, encouragement and practical help from the beginning. Martin exemplifies the very best qualities of an academic researcher, someone who produces cutting-edge research but also uses his work to challenge social injustices and speak truth to power. At the LSHTM, I'm also grateful to Marina Karanikolos for her help and support. I am very grateful to colleagues at the Observatoire national du suicide in Paris, who were very generous in allowing me to present my work and meet French specialists there. I would like to thank Valérie Ulrich, Imane Khireddine and Laurence Chérié-Challine. I am grateful to researchers in France who met me and shared their knowledge, in particular Christophe Dejours, Noëlle Burgi, Duarte Rolo and Danielle Linhart. Lawyers Rachel Saada and Jean-Paul Teissonnière generously gave their time to discuss the legal dimensions of work suicides. Thanks also to Jean-Claude Delgènes at Technologia, who discussed recent cases with me. The following trade union representatives allowed me to interview them for my research and gave invaluable insights into the links between changing working conditions and suicide: Patrick Ackermann at France Télécom, Régis Blanchot and Philippe Charry at La Poste, and Dominique Perrot and François Baudlot at Renault.

In the UK, I am extremely grateful to Rory O'Neill at *Hazards* for his ongoing support and his tireless work to help raise awareness of work suicides in the UK and to push for legal recognition. Rory has been a mine of knowledge, useful contacts and activism. I am very grateful to my colleagues at Leeds University who inevitably held the fort when I went on periods of research leave. Thanks to those colleagues who read draft chapters at various stages, in particular Max Silverman, David Platten, Claire Launchbury, Di Holmes and Margaret Atack. Thanks to Chloe Johnson at Liverpool University Press and to the two anonymous readers for their helpful comments.

I am grateful to the AHRC for awarding me a research fellowship (AH/N004299/1) that allowed me the invaluable time to undertake research for this book. Thanks to Carmina Gustrán Loscos and Matthew John, who worked as postdoctoral researchers on this AHRC project. I am grateful also to my PhD student Martin Goodman for pointing me towards interesting fictional texts on the French workplace. I am grateful to the Wellcome Trust for supporting the early stages of my research through Seed Award funding. Thanks to the School of Languages, Cultures and Societies at Leeds, which awarded me the precious teaching relief needed to reach the finish line with this book. My greatest acknowledgement is to my family and friends based in Leeds, Dublin, Rotselaar and Rouen. Thanks for putting up with my obsession with work suicides over the past few years, for keeping me sane and for making me smile.

Introduction

> Suicide is an accusation brought against the organization
> of society when society becomes incapable of guaranteeing
> the happiness of its members.
>
> Minois, *History of Suicide*, 326

Suicide Controversies

Work suicide or work-related suicide[1] is a phenomenon that punctuates
contemporary French public life with all the force of the banal and
the sublime. Suicides now occur with such frequency that they have
become a routine event, one that barely elicits widespread shock or
consternation. Newspapers report on the human toll: engineers, nurses,
teachers, assembly-line workers, checkout assistants, farmers, managers,
postmen, *gendarmes* who, in the face of extreme pressures at work,
choose to take their own lives. Suicide 'waves' have affected a wide

---

1   In this book, I use the generic term 'work suicide', rather than the more
scientific categories 'work-related' or 'occupational suicide', in order to express
the broad, complex and indeterminate nature of this phenomenon. In France,
work-related suicide is recognised in jurisprudence and is recorded in official
statistics, albeit to a limited extent. French public authorities have actively
sought to improve the mechanisms for recording these suicides. In the UK by
contrast, no data is collected on work-related suicide and the phenomenon is
not recognised in legislation (see footnote 7 below).

range of companies, including France Télécom (Orange), La Poste, gas and electricity providers, car manufacturers (Renault and Peugeot), Disneyland,[2] banks, supermarkets, schools and research centres. Approximately half of the employee suicides reported to the authorities (the Sécurité sociale) for investigation are officially recognised as being work-related (ONS 2014, 69). Occupations including the police and social care have experienced an alarming rise in suicide cases in recent years.[3] Meanwhile, farming is experiencing a 'quiet suicide epidemic', with one farmer taking his own life every two days in France (*New York Times*, 20 August 2017). Commentators often minimise the importance of the suicides, seeking to normalise them, individualise them or treat them as an unremarkable occurrence. When French politicians have intervened publicly on the question of work suicides, it has often been to downplay their significance and portray them as an unexceptional phenomenon by national standards. For instance, Claude Guéant, then president of the Elysée, seeking to assuage public opinion following a wave of suicides at France Télécom, hinted that suicides were a personal matter rather than an issue of broader social concern: 'these are often personal dramas and we must bear this in mind' (*Challenges*, 16 September 2009).[4] Meanwhile, certain experts have denied the existence of work suicides and suggested that the issue is driven by a media frenzy in response to a small handful of cases (Vatin 2011, 410). Reacting to reports of a suicide epidemic in the workplace, sociologist

2 In November 2013, a Disneyland Paris worker poured petrol over himself and had to be restrained from setting himself alight after he was summoned to a meeting with bosses. This followed two earlier suicides by employees in 2010 which trade unions have linked to poor working conditions. These events inspired Sylvain Levey's play *Au pays des* (2011), which is set in a theme park where an employee, a victim of bullying by his colleagues, shoots himself.

3 In January 2019 alone, 11 police officers took their own lives and there were 68 suicides by police officers in France in 2018, leading some to compare this with the 'année noire' of 1996, during which 70 police officers died by suicide (*Le Monde*, 12 April 2019). Some claim that suicide poses a greater threat to police officers than criminals (*Le Monde*, 8 December 2017). There have been incidents of suicide amongst nurses, with five cases in 2016 and in one case a nurse left a letter blaming working conditions.

4 In a similar line, Laurence Parisot, head of the employers' union MEDEF observed that French work suicides were not remarkable by international standards, noting that 'some countries have much higher rates' (*Challenges*, 16 September 2009).

François Vatin argued that work suicide was a 'fake concept' and stemmed from 'a collective paralysis of rational analysis in the face of overwhelming emotions' (2011 410–11). In a similar vein, statistician René Padieu remarked that concerns about work suicide were rooted in a 'collective delirium' that was gripping the nation and obfuscating people's critical faculties (*La Croix*, 20 October 2009).

Yet, conversely, suicides are also an object of perverse fascination, configured in the media as human tragedies of epic proportions: tales of life cut short, wasted talent, blighted careers and bereaved families. Work suicides have been subject to a 'hypermediatisation' that has exaggerated, distorted and misrepresented their significance (*Les Echos*, 29 September 2009). Such media stories often invite readers to pore over lurid details of a personal tragedy, as private pain is transformed into public pleasure. Early newspaper reports of work suicides tended to sensationalise individual cases, dwelling on details of personal lives or the dramatic mode of suicide, reproducing extracts from suicide letters or family testimonies, while occluding the structural context in which the suicides took place. Meanwhile, suicides have been an object of intense interest for cultural producers, who often tend to aestheticise the suicidal act, transforming it into a unique dramatic device.

Recent novels, films, documentaries and theatre give represen-tation to work suicide as a singular dramatic episode and often draw on real-life suicide cases at particular French companies. There have been at least 15 French or Belgian fictional films that represent work suicide since 2000, in which self-killing is either the core dramatic event around which the plot is centred or a marginal tragedy in a broader workplace drama (O'Shaughnessy 2018). In *Corporate* (2016), directed by Nicolas Silhol, which draws closely on events at France Télécom, self-killing constitutes the opening act and is an irrevocable and brutal act of violence which forces the leading character to reassess herself, question her professional values and dramatically change the course of her life. The film presents the act of suicide as an explosive and visceral act of violence that intrudes on the slick, ordered and hierarchical spaces of the multinational corporation. In Stéphane Brizé's *En guerre* (At War, 2018), suicide is the film's closing scene and represents a final, desperate and tragic act of protest by the trade union leader and main character Laurent, played by Vincent Lindon. Despite the heroic struggle of Laurent and his colleagues, suicide symbolises the failure of conventional trade unionism to defend jobs and livelihoods in the face of the implacable economic decisions made by distant corporate bosses.

Meanwhile, scholarship has not kept up with this new and violent social reality. While media reports of suicide are characterised by their spectacular immediacy, statistical data takes a long time to collect and may be published years after the deaths that it records. Few existing studies can explain why work suicides are taking place, why they are taking place now and what this phenomenon signifies in social, cultural or economic terms. Although work suicides in France have been the focus of intense media attention and political debate,[5] research has so far lagged behind and is hampered by two significant obstacles. On the one hand, statistical data is patchy and often inconsistent, and there are no official statistics at national level that systematically record the number of work suicides and how these have evolved over time. We know that French suicide rates are amongst the highest in Europe at 16.7 suicides per 100,000 inhabitants, against an average of 11.7 per 100,000 inhabitants for the 28 countries of the EU (ONS 2016). France stands out amongst post-industrial nations for its high suicide rate, compared with the US at 10.4, Germany at 13.5, Sweden at 13.4 and England at 7.5. Mortality rates for suicide in France are three times higher than those for road accidents and this is the second cause of death amongst those aged 25 to 45. In 2015, there were nearly 9,000 suicides in France, two thirds of which were among the working-age population (Delézire et al. 2019).

However, data pertaining to suicide that takes place in work or because of work is less readily available. In France, national statistics are extrapolated from a regional study carried out in Normandy in 2003, from which a national figure of 400 cases per year has been estimated (Gournay, Lanièce & Kryvenac 2004). Yet some specialists argue that this figure grossly underestimates the scale of the problem, and one psychologist has estimated a national average of 6,500 cases per year

---

5   The notion of suicide is also evoked as a metaphor for national and civilisational decline, particularly amongst right-wing commentators who use it to appeal for national renewal. In *Le Suicide français* (2014), Eric Zemmour argues that France's national traditions and social fabric have been destroyed by its own elites in the period since 1968, in a form of national self-harm and cultural sabotage that has resulted in all of the social, cultural and moral ills of the present. In an American equivalent, Jonah Goldberg in *Suicide of the West* (2018) decries the assault on liberalism and capitalism by emerging forms of populism in the United States.

(Michel Debout, president of the National Union for the Prevention of Suicide, quoted in *La Croix*, 29 July 2009). One recent study based on a qualitative analysis of statements by survivors of suicide in a French hospital reported that work-related issues were identified in 40 per cent of cases (Géhin & Raoult-Monestel 2013). Another French study found that suicidal risk was disproportionately high amongst young adults working in unstable or unfair conditions (Daglish et al. 2015). Meanwhile, work is a significant cause of suicidal thoughts or 'ideation' within the French working-age population, with over one third of those surveyed in a recent study stating that work was the determining factor (Delézire et al. 2019). Moreover, those who cited work as the cause of their suicidal thoughts increased between 2010 and 2014 from over a third (37.1%) to just under half (44.8%) of those surveyed.[6] In France there have been concerted efforts at national level to improve the mechanisms for recording workplace suicides, and a recent pilot study drew on data from a multiplicity of sources – death certificates, labour inspectorate, social insurance and autopsy reports (Bossard et al. 2016). Yet the findings of this research are undermined by the scarcity of reliable data sources. Death certificates do not always record the details of the suicide or the profession of the suicidal individual.

On the other hand, work suicide is a highly controversial phenomenon that is subject to a discursive battle over its causes, nature and meaning. To define a suicide as work-related implies that it is no longer a voluntary, intended or self-inflicted act, but a potential crime for which an external agent may be responsible. Both business and political elites in France have sought to minimise or individualise suicides taking place within companies, and this has impeded independent research on the phenomenon (Baudelot & Gollac 2015). Suicides damage the reputational and financial interests of businesses, and where liability is established, a company may be obliged to pay large sums in financial compensation to the family of a victim. Work suicides have been the focus of a number of high-profile legal cases that have pitted families against company representatives. In July 2019, the criminal trial closed

---

6   According to the same study, in 2017, 3.8 per cent of the working population stated that they had experienced suicidal thoughts over the previous 12 months, compared with 4.7 per cent amongst the general population (including employed and unemployed). Women present a higher rate of suicidal thoughts (4.5%) than men (3.1%) amongst the working population (Delézire et al. 2019).

in the case of the former chief executive and six other executives of France Télécom, who were charged with driving their employees to suicide as a consequence of their management policies. In a landmark criminal case, the bosses were accused not of personally targeting individuals, but of pursuing management practices across the whole company based on 'harcèlement moral' or psychological harassment. Prosecutors brought 19 suicide cases before the criminal court, along with 12 attempted suicides and eight cases of employees with severe depression or other work-related illnesses. Because suicide is legally recognised in France as a 'workplace accident',[7] there have been scores of successful litigation cases won by families of suicidal individuals against companies. For instance, 49 suicides by France Télécom employees were officially recognised as being work-related in 2008 (*Le Monde*, 17 September 2009).

Work suicides also jeopardise the vested interests of political elites. In France, suicides have taken place predominantly in large, former state-owned companies[8] which are seen as national champions that embody state-defined values and project French economic power in the world (Baudelot & Gollac 2015). In several of these companies, the state was still the main shareholder and was represented on the

7   Suicide is recognised in French jurisprudence as a workplace accident. The Social Security code defines as work-related any accident that takes place 'because of or during work' ('par le fait ou à l'occasion du travail'; art. L.411-1 of the Code de la Sécurité sociale). Any fatality that occurs in the workplace, including suicide, is immediately investigated as a workplace accident and the burden of proof is on the employer to prove that the suicide is not work-related. Even in cases where a suicide takes place outside of work, it is still investigated as a work-related accident where the individual (in the case of an attempted suicide) or the family can prove a causal link to work (in the form of a suicide letter, a work uniform or use of a work implement). This presumption of causality is meant to protect the employee (in an attempted suicide) or his or her family and circumvent the need for them to engage in legal action in the aftermath of a tragic incident, in order to prove the employer is liable (Lerouge 2014). In the UK, by contrast, work suicides are not recorded in statistics or recognised in legislation. In fact, suicide is explicitly excluded from the list of work-related accidents that need to be reported to the Health and Safety Executive for further investigation. See Waters (2017a).
8   One report lists the 11 companies and sectors in which work-related suicides have been most prevalent. Of the 11 listed, nine are or were in the public sector: France Télécom, Renault, La Poste, EDF-GDF, Fnac, ONF (Office national des forêts), police, banks, hospitals, Thalès, agricultural companies (Blaize 2011).

company's board of executives when the suicides were taking place. In some cases, their chief executive was appointed by the state and was a former member of government or joined a government ministry after leaving the company. In 2007, at a time when suicides were beginning to rise at France Télécom, its chief executive Didier Lombard was awarded the Légion d'honneur by the French state, France's highest decoration. Political elites could not claim to be innocent bystanders in the face of global economic forces that were outside their control. Work suicide has been the object of intense controversy, as the government has sought to contain, manage and limit the crisis. The high stakes involved mean that the whole question of work suicide has been subject to a 'rule of silence' or to 'states of denial' that tend to keep it hidden from public view (Dejours & Bègue 2009; Waters 2017b). Because of a lack of rigorous statistical data and the sheer contentiousness of this phenomenon, current research cannot yet provide us with answers as to why there are rising work suicides in France and what these suicides mean in economic, social or political terms.

Aims and Context

Work suicides do not reveal exceptional social conditions on the margins, but express extreme suffering within the everyday structures of social life. Indeed, the spectacular and tragic nature of each act of self-killing contrasts with the mundane, quotidian and functional setting in which it takes place: the call centre, the corporate office, the post office, the assembly line. Suicide is a phenomenon that shocks, unsettles, perturbs and forces us to ask questions of ourselves. It challenges a veneer of everyday normality and a belief that everything will turn out fine in the end. It disrupts the social order and cannot be easily reintegrated or ordered within our familiar terms of reference. In the words of Frédéric Zanati, 'suicide spoils everyone's fun' and threatens the social equilibrium, making us all feel guilty, uncomfortable or under accusation (Zanati quoted by Minois 1999, 324). This book is intended to contribute to our understanding of the emerging social phenomenon of work suicide, examining its complex social, economic and historical determinants in the French context.

The book complements a number of other recent studies that examine the social and psychological causes of work suicide (Dejours & Bègue

2009; Clot 2015; Baudelet & Gollac 2015; Clot & Gollac 2017). Written by psychologists and sociologists of work, these studies are concerned with how suicides reflect changing management methods and organisational practices within the specific setting of the French workplace. Few if any critics examine work suicide from the broader social and historical perspective of neoliberal restructuring, investigating how structural transformations at international and national level register on lived and localised experiences. Why are work or conditions of work increasingly pushing some workers to take their own lives? What does this tell us about conditions of human labour at the present historical juncture? Does neoliberalism condition a desire for suicide? Writing at the close of the nineteenth century, Emile Durkheim argued that suicide was a mirror held up to society that reveals the fundamental tensions and dysfunctions of the social order at a given historical moment. For Durkheim, an analysis of the nature, frequency and causes of suicide, could help shed light on fundamental and underlying tendencies affecting society as a whole. This book investigates the complex causal connections that link the singular, embodied and extreme act of suicide with the systemic, disembodied and rational economic processes that underpin contemporary neoliberalism. My aim is to interrogate the economic order from the vantage point of the suicidal act, looking at what this tells us about the values, processes and imperatives on which contemporary economics is based. Looking at economics from the prism of experiences of intense human suffering gives us a very different picture compared with top-down macro-economic perspectives that often eclipse the experiential dimensions of work. Such a perspective also subverts an order of value that measures costs and benefits according to abstract mathematical criteria and ignores the human effects of economic processes. It allows us to question the values of a system that subjects workers to such intolerable pressure that some choose to take their own lives. What are the circumstances in which work makes life unliveable? I treat suicide as an exceptional and subjective human phenomenon that can help make visible the complex, generalised and often unseen processes that underpin the contemporary economic order (Sassen 2014).

Work suicides are not random or isolated phenomena, but have taken place at a particular historical juncture at a time of profound economic restructuring linked to the transition to a neoliberal order. Work suicide is a new phenomenon in historical terms and documented cases prior to the 1990s are rare (Bourgoin 1999; Dejours & Bègue 2009). For some critics, the shift to neoliberalism has been marked by a transformation in the relationship between workers and employers, so that labour has been subordinated to the interests of capital in unprecedented ways (Boltanski & Chiapello 1999; Peters 2011). The economic processes of liberalisation, privatisation, deregulation and financialisation that have underpinned neoliberal restructuring have triggered a sharp deterioration in working conditions across the international stage (Danford, Richardson & Upchurch 2003; Benach et al. 2014). Work suicides are not unique to France and are on the rise across societies internationally in the context of a generalised deterioration in working conditions. Studies carried out in the United States (Tiesman et al. 2015), Japan (Kawanishi 2008; Yamauchi et al. 2017), Australia (Hazel Routley & Ozanne-Smith 2012), China (Chan & Pun 2010) and India (Merriott 2017) point to a steep rise in suicides at a time of neoliberal restructuring. In the United States, workplace suicides decreased between 2003 and 2007, but then rose sharply in the following years. In Japan, *karo-jisatsu*, or suicide by overwork, is treated as an urgent public health issue and, under a 2014 law, the government is obliged take measures to prevent it from happening. In the UK, a 2017 national survey found that suicides in England were disproportionately high for men in the construction sector, and for women in nursing and primary school teaching (ONS 2017). The media reported in March 2019 on a 'suicide wave' at US Amazon warehouses, where at least 189 instances of suicide attempts, suicidal thoughts and mental health episodes were recorded between October 2013 and October 2018 (*Newsweek*, 11 March 2019). If France's workplace suicide crisis has been particularly acute,[9] this is linked to its specific experiences of neoliberal restructuring where economic transformations came into conflict with a particular historically defined model of work. French suicides emerged in the fault lines between two models of work, a Fordist model of stable and protected employment underpinned by a deeply rooted workplace culture and identity and a post-Fordist and neoliberal model of flexible and insecure labour with limited social

---

9   Some critics assert that France and Japan have the highest work-related suicide rates in the world (Alemano & Cabedoche 2011), yet without comparable international statistics recording work suicide rates in each country, it is difficult to substantiate this claim.

protection and rights. It was in France's extensive former public service companies that the clash between these two opposing models of work was most keenly felt and where suicides were at their highest (Baudelot & Gollac 2015).

Work suicide can be situated within changing patterns of labour conflict in the neoliberal juncture and in particular the rise of extreme, violent and corporeal forms of dissent or 'bodily resistance' in which the individual body has become a site of political intervention (Puggioni 2014, 563). Instead of positing a collective structure or class identity, some workers turn to their own bodies, enacting forms of violence against the self or others. For some critics, the new labour radicalism reflects a shift in the model of social conflict with a decline of class-based collective mobilisation and a shift to more fragmented and individualised forms of protest (Boltanski & Chiapello 1999; O'Shaughnessy 2007). Hence there has been a 'radicalisation of social conflict' in the contemporary period with a rise in more extreme and unconventional forms of protest (Kaspar 2010). Others situate this radicalism within an established repertoire of protest that stretches from trade union militancy to sporadic acts of illegal protest (Hayes 2012; Parsons 2012; Béroud 2018).

The French workplace has been the site of an unprecedented wave of labour protest in recent years that pits workers and trade unions defending economic conditions and social rights against political and business elites. Labour reforms implemented under the Hollande and Macron governments have sought to loosen rules on hiring and firing, restrict trade union influence and increase employers' decision-making autonomy. Hollande's efforts to push through reforms to employment law met with the 'the strongest and longest social protest under a left-wing government under the Fifth Republic', as school pupils barricaded their *lycées*, lorry drivers blocked roads and protestors occupied public spaces in a series of cities in the Nuit debout movement (Béroud 2018, 180). Emmanuel Macron's executive rulings on labour reform provoked further mass protest that culminated in the *gilets jaunes* movement which led the longest-running protest in France of the post-war period.[10] As an individual act of self-inflicted violence,

10   Mobilised by lower-income groups from rural and semi-urban areas, the *gilets jaunes* expressed the social and economic difficulties of those on low salaries who struggled to reach the end of the month on their wages. The symbol of the

suicide may appear to be the very antithesis of conventional and organised forms of social protest. Yet, like other recent forms of labour radicalism, it expresses a deep-seated sense of rage and hopelessness in the face of the growing asymmetries of power between labour and capital (Hayes 2012).

This book focuses on 66 cases of suicide across three large French companies during the period 2005–15: 35 suicide cases at the telecoms giant France Télécom (rebranded Orange in 2013), 21 cases at French postal service La Poste, and ten at car manufacturer Renault. Suicides in these companies took place at a particular historical moment, when each company was restructuring in response to extraneous neoliberal imperatives. Suicides reached a peak at a time when each company was radically reorganising the value and parameters of work. The NExT[11] plan (2005–8) at France Télécom set as its strategic priority to cut 22,000 jobs in the space of three years in order to reduce costs and improve financial performance. As its chief executive made clear, mass job cuts would be achieved by whatever means necessary, either by encouraging staff to leave or by forcing them out. At Renault, Contrat 2009 set a target to increase car production by 800,000 new cars and to launch 21 new models in three years, without expanding the existing workforce. This required an unprecedented increase in the productivity and workload of each employee. At La Poste, strategic plans focused both on extensive job cuts and on transforming the company from a public service entity to a commercial enterprise capable of generating economic profits.

Suicide Voices situates work suicides in the context of specific and localised workplace restructuring processes driven by wider international and structural transformations in the neoliberal economy. The book examines a corpus of 40 testimonies linked to the above suicide cases, consisting of 32 suicide letters and eight testimonies written by

---

gilet jaune was intended to give voice and visibility to groups who felt forgotten, abandoned and humiliated by the direction of France's economic reforms. All motorists are required under a 2008 French law to keep a yellow vest in their vehicle in case of an emergency, and this is therefore a readily available, cheap and easily identifiable item of clothing that has been adopted by protesters as a way of making themselves symbolically visible.

11   Next (Nouvelle Expérience de Télécommunications / New Experience in Telecom Services) was a restructuring plan that aimed to vastly reduce staff costs and merge products and services under a single brand name, Orange.

family members or colleagues of a suicidal individual. Of the 32 letters, 13 were written by employees at France Télécom, ten by employees at La Poste and three at Renault. In addition, I draw on six suicide letters by employees who worked at other companies and which were written during the same period. The letters vary considerably in content and form and consist of detailed letters, brief notes, emails, audio recording, video clips and in some cases a detailed dossier of documents. Twenty-one consist of full letters or detailed documents, five of brief notes and six of emails, three of which were sent to a series of recipients, including family members, colleagues and in one case the chief executive of the company.[12] The brief notes are often emotional and express words of love to family members, whereas the more detailed letters may contain material that is intended to be used in a legal case against the company. A senior technician at the nuclear power station at Chinon who took his own life on 21 August 2004 left a brief note before throwing himself under a train near his place of work: 'J'embrasse mes enfants' (I kiss my children). By contrast, a former shop supervisor who worked at a branch of the Tati discount store in Paris left a ten-page letter for her step-son that outlined with precise dates and events, the bullying to which she had been subjected on a daily basis. This letter, which was read out in court, was part of the evidence used to convict her manager in a Paris correctional tribunal on 11 July 2018 (*Le Parisien*, 11 July 2018).

Critical Approaches

Suicide has long been a central question in social, political and philosophical debates in France, and it is inextricably bound up with wider questions about the social order and its relationship with the individual (Crocker 1952; Giddens 1971; Minois 1999). To determine

---

12   Of the 32 suicide letters, 26 were written by individuals who took their own lives and six by those who attempted to commit suicide. Twenty-six letters were written by men and six by women. The majority of cases involve male white-collar workers in their fifties and include senior managers, middle managers, engineers, technicians and postal workers. Among the female suicides, the age group is younger, with three women in their thirties, two in their forties and one in her fifties.

whether suicide is a legitimate and morally acceptable act is to define the nature of free will, the role of political authority and the limits of religious morality. During the Enlightenment, most of the *philosophes* wrote extensively on suicide, including Rousseau, Voltaire, Montesquieu, Mme de Staël and Holbach. Suicide was a subject at the centre of a project to define an enlightened and rational society and to affirm individual liberty and self-determination in the face of religious mysticism and state tyranny: 'Never before had people talked so much about voluntary death, never before had as much been written about it. Many thinkers hastened to take a stand on it; and entire treatises were written, pro or con' (Minois 1999, 210). This rich philosophical tradition has persisted in the modern context in the work of writers such as Albert Camus, for whom the question of suicide was essential to defining the parameters of meaningful existence. At the beginning of the *Myth of Sisyphus*, Camus famously observed, 'there is but one truly serious philosophical problem and that is suicide' (1955, 3). Similarly, Holocaust survivor Jean Améry wrote a series of reflective essays on the meaning of death and the human capacity for suicide before taking his own life. His book is a defence of the freedom of individuals to define their own destiny and an appeal for understanding and recognition of the humanity of their situation. Whereas in the concentration camp, death was systemic and the greatest denial of personal freedom, suicide is the most extreme affirmation of one's freedom and personal dignity: 'At the moment when a human being says to himself he can throw away his life, he is already becoming free, even if it is in a monstrous way. The experience of freedom is overwhelming' (Améry 1999, 133).

Yet, as critics have shown, in the twentieth century, medicine won the battle over the meaning of suicide in the western context and disciplines such as psychology and psychiatry have become the authoritative discourses about suicide. These discourses locate the causes of suicide in the mind and see it as a manifestation of a psychological disorder, leading to a silencing of free debate about the meaning of suicide (Minois 1999; Taylor 2015). A library search at the Bibliothèque nationale de France, undertaken as part of this study, for entries under 'suicide' published between 2000 and 2018 found 307 non-fiction works identified, of which 141 texts came under medical approaches, 90 came under the category of philosophy, religion or morality and 16 under the social sciences. Of the 141 medical works listed, 78 were in the discipline of psychology or psychiatry.[13] In his Foucauldian analysis of the discursive construction of suicide, Ian Marsh shows how self-killing is almost always read as a tragedy caused by pathological processes internal to the individual that require specialist diagnosis and management. This 'regime of truth' tends to marginalise alternative approaches for understanding suicide. He suggests that reframing suicide as a self-determined act and a form of agency might open up possibilities for considering suicide in political terms as a form of resistance, refutation or protest (Marsh 2010, 65). The dominance of the medical sciences has meant that the individual is often treated as a passive victim to pathological forces beyond his or her control and is stripped of autonomy. In her sociology of mortality, Zohyreh Bayatrizi notes 'The modern Western imperative to subject suicide to scientific objectification stripped the self-killer of any claim to subjective meanings and intentions: if he killed himself, he was merely driven by social or psychological forces' (quoted by McGuire 2012, xi). Although some suggest that claims regarding the extent of this medicalisation have been exaggerated, it is clear that the tendency to pathologise suicide has led to a 'depoliticising medical model' that treats suicide as a matter of individuals rather than societies (Taylor 2015, 12). If suicide is located in the body, then there is no need to question the wider social structures and power relationships in which the individual is embedded.

Engaging with this rich critical tradition, this book reaffirms the importance of suicide as a question that lies at the centre of the social order and determines wider conceptions of individual freedom, social belonging, subjectivity and moral value. The book draws not on philosophical or psychological approaches, but on a sociological tradition with its roots in the nineteenth century and the work of Emile Durkheim. In *Le Suicide* (1897), Durkheim challenged the individualist and medicalised approaches of the nineteenth century and argued that suicide was a social phenomenon that transcended the individual and found its causes in society. Drawing on an analysis of national statistics across different countries, he argued that each society had a collective tendency towards suicide that determined the number of suicides taking place:

13   This library search was carried out by Carmina Gustrán Loscos, postdoctoral researcher on the AHRC fellowship that underpinned this book.

At any given moment the moral constitution of society establishes the contingent of voluntary deaths. There is, therefore, for each people a collective force of a definite amount of energy, impelling men to self-destruction. The victim's acts, which at first seem to express only his personal temperament are really the supplement and prolongation of a social condition which they express externally. (Durkheim quoted by Giddens 1971, xiii)

Durkheim saw suicide as a subject on which to define sociology itself, as an autonomous discipline, with its own theories and concepts.

In *Les Causes du suicide* (1930), Maurice Halbwachs used more recent statistics to refine and deepen Durkheim's approach. For Halbwachs, suicide was a consequence of an interaction between internal forces and the social milieu and the individual factors that determined suicide were shaped by wider social forces:

Thus suicides are always to be explained in terms of social causes. But sometimes these manifest themselves as collective forces proper – such as family and religious practices or great political and national movements – and sometimes in the form of individual motives, more or less numerous and distributed in varying fashion according to the degree of complexity of the society itself. (quoted by Giddens 1971, 34–5)

While Halbwach, like Durkheim, emphasised the social causes of suicide, he believed the main determinant was urbanisation and the social alienation linked to city life, rather than the impact of religion. In their magisterial study of suicide in the nineteenth and twentieth centuries, Christian Baudelot and Roger Establet reaffirm Durkheim's sociological approach, arguing that suicide is a social phenomenon: 'it is not society that elucidates suicide, but suicide that elucidates society' (2006, 15). They argue that suicide reflects fundamental inequalities in society and that the experience of poverty is a key determinant of suicide in modern societies. My aim in this book is to draw on this rich sociological tradition in order to examine suicides in the French workplace as a prism for understanding the impact of abstract economics on lived and everyday experiences of work.

My methodological approach lays emphasis on subjective, lived and narrated experiences, as a means of shedding light on the social causes of suicide in the workplace. While treating suicide as a socially determined phenomenon, my aim is to bring the individual back in, examining how the individual interprets, narrates and communicates the social conditions that pushed him or her to such violent extremes. Writers such as Améry caution us against theorising about suicide and imposing scientific or moral categories on this most deeply personal and singular of acts. In his series of essays, Améry aims not to make 'a bold description of the act', but rather to strive for 'a gentle and cautious approach to it' that starts with the suicidal individual and the perspective of his or her own interior world (1999, 28). For Améry, an understanding of self-killing begins where psychology and sociology end, with the situation of the suicidal individual before he or she takes the leap. My aim in this book is to take seriously the individual's own interpretation of suicide and investigate carefully who or what they see is to blame for their self-killing. In his post–Durkheimian analysis of suicide, Jack Douglas argues that suicide has no abstract or predefined meaning other than that given to it by the suicidal individual him or herself. He criticises the determinism of Durkheim's sociology for reducing the individual to a passive victim in the face of overwhelming social forces. Douglas calls for a new sociological approach that situates subjective and narrated meanings at the centre of an analysis of the social meanings of suicide. To examine the meaning of suicide, we need to start with the motivations and interpretations given to it by suicidal individuals themselves:

> Since there are no specific meanings imputed to all (or even most) suicidal actions, the meanings of such actions must be *constructed* by the individuals committing them and by others involved *through their interactions with each other.* Just what meanings are realized or actually imputed will depend on the intentions of the various actors, the *socially perceived* ways in which the actions are committed, the specific *patterns of suicidal meanings* [...] which are realized, and the whole *argument processes*, before, during and after the 'suicidal actions'. (Douglas 1971, 135)

Using the suicide letter as a form of narrative voice, I will examine the shared social meanings attributed to this act across a wide range of recent cases.

Suicide Voices

French work suicides have been marked by an intensive production of texts in which suicidal individuals ascribe meaning to their own death and interpret it for others. Suicidal individuals have left letters, notes, audio recordings, emails, texts and, in some cases, detailed portfolios of documents. They have addressed their letters to family members, colleagues, trade union members, the media or to their bosses. Far from being a silent retreat from the world or a quiet act of self-effacement, suicide is a desperate howl of protest against working conditions that are deemed to be unbearable. Some of these letters have been published in detail in the French and international press. Others have been made public by family members or colleagues of the suicidal individual in order to draw attention to deteriorating conditions of work. In some cases, survivors of suicide have written autobiographical books that describe how work pushed them to attempt to take their own lives (Dervin 2009; Selly 2013). Some letters have been published in books by journalists investigating suicides at particular companies including France Télécom (Decèze 2008; Du Roy 2009a), Renault (Moreira & Prolongeau 2009), Peugeot, IBM and Renault (Coupechoux 2009). Others have been made public in film documentaries such as Jean-Robert Viallet's *La Mise à mort du travail* (The Killing of Work, 2009) and Samuel Bollendorff and Olivia Colo's interactive web documentary *Le Grand Incendie* (The Great Fire, 2013). Others still have been examined in scholarly publications (Dejours 2005; Clot 2015). Such testimonies convey stories of immense human suffering by those who find themselves in situations of 'unimaginable extremity' within the ordinary setting of today's workplace (Chambers 2002, 6). Suicide letters also have an important legal and political function: the causal links between work and self-killing are highly contested and a work suicide is often only recognised as such after a lengthy process of reconstruction in order to establish the causes of death. Personal testimonies have been used in a number of high-profile legal cases taken by families against French companies in order to establish their responsibility in a suicide.[14]

14 The book also draws on a small number of testimonies from unpublished sources and I have had access to legal dossiers in prosecution cases and trade union sources. All of the suicide letters in this book have been anonymised, but

The suicide note is a unique document that contains an unsolicited account of the victim's thoughts and emotions regarding the intended act and who or what they thought was responsible in the moments before their death (Jacobs 1967). Suicide is an act of communication in which the individual transforms their self-killing into a form of enunciation that aims to convey meaning, apportion blame or challenge a social injustice. In this book, I treat suicide as a form of communication in both its written and performative dimensions. In his study of narrative forms, Barthes notes that a story is a system where everything, including the form, has a meaning. This implies that the act, the circumstances, the choice of location and the form of suicide carry a significance that is open to interpretation (Barthes 1966). Work suicides are often spectacular public acts that are performed in front of others and are intended to be witnessed. Although rare and extreme, cases of suicide by self-immolation have risen in France in recent years and are increasingly used as a desperate mode of protest against social conditions. In many of the cases studied here, suicidal individuals chose to kill themselves in the workplace in order to make clear the connections between work and their own violent actions. At the Renault Technocentre, where few letters were recovered, suicides were characterised by their dramatic and visible nature, as six employees jumped from a suspended walkway above a busy lobby in the main building during working hours. Indeed, the horror of each act of self-killing contrasts with the banality of the context in which it is situated within the everyday spaces of working life.

My aim is to examine patterns of meaning that recur across the letters, by focusing on 'suicidal argument processes' and the forms of explanation and legitimation that are used to frame the act of self-killing and its connections to work (Douglas quoted by Giddens 1971, 140). I draw on insights from testimony studies and the work of scholars who have used testimony as a means to gain insight into the lived experiences of epochal historical events. Recent letters by suicidal individuals document experiences of suffering that are so extreme that death is presented as an inescapable solution: 'The problem is thus seen to be as absolute as life and must be resolved by something no less

the date and location of each suicide have been retained, as I consider this an important element in establishing a historical record of the suicides that took place within the time period under study.

absolute than death' (Jacobs 1967, 66). Yet the causes of suffering are rarely attributed to individual circumstances of an emotional, psychological or familial nature. Instead, they consistently and explicitly blame external social factors, and more specifically conditions of work, as the cause of their actions. A key purpose of these letters is to bear witness to the destructive effects of economic transformations in the workplace that are linked to a company's restructuring. They point to a profound deterioration in working conditions stemming from ever increasing productivity rates, chaotic restructuring, tyrannical management practices, forced redeployment, constant surveillance and mass redundancies. My analysis of suicide letters focuses on three key questions: (i) Who or what is to blame according to the suicidal individual? We will see that the suicide letter becomes a means to reverse power relationships as the victimiser is forcing those deemed responsible to account for their actions and explain themselves in the face of this accusation; (ii) How are the social and subjective experiences of work narrated and described? We will see that normalised, rational and necessary economic processes are often transposed onto lived experience in terms of intense pain, trauma and suffering; (iii) Why is self-killing deemed the only recourse available? I examine why, in the face of social conditions of work, the extreme subjective act of suicide, rather than other conventional forms of political intervention (via trade unions, collective action or negotiation with management), is perceived to be the only response possible.

For centuries in France, suicide has been an object of strict censorship, repression and taboos. During the medieval period, the bodies of suicides were dragged through the streets face down and then hung by their feet. Their property was confiscated and they were denied a Christian burial (Minois 1999). Writing about suicide and about suicide letters continues to raise considerable moral and ethical dilemmas in the present day. As the final statement of someone who has chosen death over life, a suicide letter has the quality of a 'haunted text' that casts a shadow over the living and exerts control beyond the author's death (Chambers 2002, 95). A suicide letter often communicates the sense of an injustice that has gone unrepaired and that has pushed a person to unimaginable extremes. As the author of the letter isn't here to explain or interpret its meaning, we bear the responsibility of speaking on their behalf and of confronting the injustice of which they speak. How do we speak of the dead in a way that is fair, that avoids being too theatrical or theoretical and that steers clear of the lurid or the rhetorical? To what extent is it morally appropriate to textualise dead bodies and turn them into something one reads? Patricia Yaeger speaks of the risks of 'consuming trauma' and of turning death into an object of academic discussion or debate. Yet, as she makes clear, the risks of not talking about suicide, of not listening to the dead or of turning away, outweigh the risks of listening to what they have to say and giving them our attention: 'In calling out to the spectre we encounter a new kind of nightmare – not the gothic terror of being haunted by the dead, but the greater terror of not being haunted, of ceasing to feel the weight of past generations in one's bones' (Yaeger 2002, 35).

Chapter Outline

This book draws on insights from a wide range of disciplinary perspectives in economics, testimony studies, history, sociology and suicidology in order to analyse recent suicide cases across three French companies. A first chapter places the phenomenon of work suicide in the contemporary context, by drawing on both histories of suicide and historical studies of industrial labour. To what extent does work suicide constitute a new phenomenon reflecting the historically specific conditions of neoliberalism? Despite the physical hardship and poor material conditions of labour during the period of industrial capitalism, there are few recorded cases of work-related suicide. In nineteenth-century France, suicide was characterised as a marginal phenomenon that affected the most impoverished social groups: the jobless, the destitute or the infirm. There is little documented evidence that work or labour conditions pushed workers to take their own lives. The chapter goes on to examine the structural transformations that have precipitated a rise in work suicides in the contemporary juncture. I argue that the shift to a finance-driven economic order has transformed the status and perceived value of the worker in a system of capital accumulation. From a source of productivity and therefore profit under industrial capitalism, labour has become, in the contemporary context, an obstacle to rational and extraneous financial goals that often needs to be removed from the workplace. Suicides are the product of differential neoliberal management regimes. On the one hand, suicides have affected workers who were pushed to their very limits by management in a bid to increase their individual productivity, economic worth and therefore maximise profits. On the other, suicides have affected workers who were pushed out of the workplace as a form of surplus cost. Within large French companies, suicides rarely affect underperforming or unskilled workers, but are the preserve of professional elites, highly skilled and productive employees who identified their own goals with those of the company. These employees seemed to be most affected by management tactics that reconfigured labour as costly, superfluous and excess to requirements.

Chapter 2 outlines the book's methodological approach, which examines suicide letters as a mode of testimony that bears witness to extreme suffering in the contemporary workplace. In an economic order that conceals the labour relationships that bring services and products to us, suicides push human suffering to the surface and force it out into the open. Drawing on testimony studies, I situate suicide letters at a juncture between the everyday and the extreme that unsettles the boundaries between the two and forces us to confront extremity in the everyday. Whilst these letters give expression to exceptional trauma, they are located within the quotidian, routine and functional spaces of work. Some recent critics have depicted the contemporary workplace as a site of extremity, drawing on the historical metaphor of the Holocaust to describe forms of managerial brutality and violence (Dejours 1998). Films of the workplace also invoke images of the concentration camp to depict the exceptional injustice of the present. Contrary to these representations, I suggest that the workplace is best understood in terms of its everydayness. This is a space governed by order, discipline and routine, where working life is subject to endless repetition and reiteration. Yet this everydayness has a unique quality: work suicides make visible extreme suffering, not as an exceptional phenomenon, but one that is embedded within the universal and everyday spaces of social life.

Chapter 3 examines work suicides at La Poste, situating them in relation to a restructuring strategy that sought to transform the company from a public service entity, underpinned by a notion of the general interest, to a commercial entity driven by product sales and profit margins. Whereas earlier reforms had modified external working methods and practices, the new phase of restructuring sought to transform workers themselves, targeting their ways of being, seeing and thinking. I draw on Michel Foucault's conception of disciplinary surveillance to examine the management methods that were imposed across the company following its liberalisation. While the company was freed of regulatory controls and administrative constraints, the individual employee was subject to intensified surveillance of daily working activity. The chapter goes on to discuss a corpus of suicide letters in which postal workers explain the causes and motivations of their self-killing. Beyond a piecemeal structural reform or change in matcrial circumstances, many employees experienced restructuring as a cultural assault that undermined the values, meanings and ideals by which they had defined themselves and their place in the world. The case of La Poste shows that when company strategy transcends external working activity and targets the intimate, subjective and vulnerable resources of the person, it can have deleterious consequences for lived experiences of work.

In Chapter 4, I examine the suicide crisis at France Télécom, situating it in the shift to a new finance-driven management model following the company's privatisation, whereby the search for shareholder value became the overarching strategic goal of the company. I draw on scholarship on financialisation and, in particular, the rise of shareholder value, examining its impact on the changing status and conditions of labour. The suicides were not an aberration in an otherwise smoothly functioning system, but the consequence of systemic processes that sought to remove labour from the workplace as an obstacle to financial imperatives. The chapter examines the structural transformations of the company which altered the perceived value of the individual worker, and considers the new expulsionary management tactics that characterised the NExT restructuring plan. The chapter draws on testimonial material, including suicide letters and witness statements drawn from a legal case brought against the company by a work inspector in 2010, which culminated in the recent criminal trial against the company's former bosses. An analysis of this testimonial material allows us to reconstruct the causal connections that link structural transformations in the company to the acute suffering that triggered the act of self-killing.

Chapter 5 examines a series of suicides at car manufacturer Renault, situating them in the transition from an industrial model to a knowledge economy, in which value is expropriated from the resources of the mind. Suicides did not take place in the emblematic spaces of the factory, where cars were once mass-produced, but in a state-of-the art research centre where cognitive workers conceptualised and designed cutting-edge cars of the future. In the knowledge economy, the mind is treated as an endlessly productive resource that reproduces itself continuously and is unencumbered by the physical limitations of the body. I argue that suicides were the end point of a form of vital exhaustion that transcends the corporeal defences of the physical body and depletes the mental and emotional resources of the self. Suicides do not necessarily reflect a deterioration in the formal or material conditions of work, but rather a transformation in forms of constraint, as the individual worker internalises modes of discipline and becomes his or her own boss. Suicides affected workers who experienced a phase of chronic overwork in which the quest to achieve productivity targets pushed them to work continuously and obsessively. Unlike the experience of Fordist labour during the post-war era, when home offered a physical and symbolic refuge from the exigencies of the factory, in the contemporary knowledge economy, work consumes both professional and private life and there are few opportunities for escape.

In the Conclusion, I consider whether work suicides reflect the emergence of necropower in the workplace whereby capital increasingly extends control over the conditions of both life and death. In an economic order based on necropower, it becomes profitable to categorise, segregate and eject groups of workers in order to maintain the vitality and productivity of the whole. A system of necropower may generate extreme and violent forms of corporeal resistance in which the individual assumes control over the power to live or die. In the absence of collective channels for externalising and mediating individual grievances, suicide has, for some workers, become a desperate and extreme mode of protest or a form of necroresistance against deadly workplace practices.

Chapter 1

Capitalism, Work and Suicide

> Finance reveals itself as an ideal form of crime, actively establishing suicide at the core of the social game.
>
> Berardi, *Heroes: Mass Murder and Suicide*, 89

This chapter aims to trace the complex causal connections that link the singular, embodied and extreme act of suicide to systemic, disembodied and rational economic processes. My aim is to look outwards from the individual act of self-killing towards the neoliberal order as a whole and investigate its effects on lived experiences of work within the localised spaces of the French company. I treat suicides as a symptomatic eruption that makes visible generalised, unseen and systemic tendencies that define the neoliberal economic order. As noted in the Introduction, since Durkheim's *Le Suicide* (1897), we know that suicide acts as a mirror held up to society that reveals the fundamental tensions and dysfunctions of the social order at a given historical moment. This chapter engages with critical work that connects the rise of extreme forms of subjective violence with the structural conditions of contemporary capitalism (Žižek 2008a; Sassen 2014; Berardi 2015). For these critics, individual acts of violence take place against the background of a deeper systemic violence exerted by capitalism on the individual whether within or outside the workplace.

To observe the economic order from the perspective of the deeply traumatic and subjective act of suicide presents a radically different viewpoint on economics to that of conventional 'top-down' approaches. Orthodox economics measures value in terms of calculable metrics including productivity targets, performance indicators and shareholder value. Yet how do we measure the value of economic processes that subject workers to such intense pressure that some choose to take their own lives? How do we evaluate economic results that are achieved at the cost of immense human suffering? Are workers' lives expendable in the interests of overarching financial goals?

I situate work suicides within one of the core structural dynamics that characterise the shift to neoliberalism, that of financialisation and the rise of abstract money as the key source of capital accumulation. Financialisation is recognised as a distinctive historical phase in the development of capitalism that has generated new forms of profit, exacerbated crises and reordered social relationships (Lapavitsas 2013). In the finance-driven economy, profits are no longer derived solely from material production and the physical act of making things or providing services, but are accrued increasingly from speculative flows of finance on international markets. For some critics, finance sets itself against the real and productive economy as a 'predatory' formation that expropriates value and is inherently destructive: 'finance is an extractive sector: once it has extracted what there is to extract, it moves on, leaving behind destruction' (Sassen 2017, 4).

I suggest in this chapter that the rise of finance as the driving force of economic profit has transformed the status and perceived value of the individual worker within the economic system. Whereas under industrial capitalism, the worker was an agent of production and therefore a source of economic profit, in a finance economy, where profits are derived from extraneous financial transactions, the worker has diminished economic value and may even be seen as an obstacle to rational profit-making goals. We will see that in some French companies, these suicides were not an aberration of an otherwise smooth-running system, but a tragic consequence of rational and logical processes pursued in the interests of overarching economic goals. Work suicides might be seen as a manifestation of absolute capitalism, a system in which the quest to accumulate profits now takes precedence over a notion of the common good or other human considerations (Berardi 2015).

Different critics have pointed to the expulsionary dynamics that underpin contemporary neoliberalism and that seek to eject people from the core spaces of social and economic life (Sassen 2017; Christiaens 2018; Haskaj 2018). Whereas industrial capitalism sought to bring labouring bodies into the fixed spaces of the factory as a source of production and therefore profit, finance capitalism seeks to push them out as a surplus cost. Saskia Sassen describes the rise of contemporary capitalism in terms of 'new logics of expulsion' that eject people from the core spaces of society (2014, 1). Similarly, Zygmunt Bauman describes a new era of liquidity that is driven by a logic of waste disposal that consigns people and things to the rubbish bin:

> In a liquid modern society, the waste-disposal industry takes over the commanding positions in liquid life's economy. The survival of that society and the well-being of its members hang on the swiftness with which products are consigned to waste and the speed and efficiency of waste removal. In that society nothing claims exception from the universal rule of disposability, and nothing can be allowed to outstay its welcome. (2005, 3)

For Bauman, the economic order has produced a new stratum of 'wasted humans' who are rendered superfluous, functionless and redundant (ibid., 147). In a similar vein, Henry Giroux and Brad Evans argue that the contemporary economic order is driven by a politics of disposability that consigns humans to excess and subjects them to hidden forms of violence and brutality. Workers are dehumanised and treated as factors of adjustment, to be disposed of when economic interests require (Giroux & Evans 2015).

In the French workplace, the shift to neoliberalism was characterised by a 'managerial revolution' from the 1990s onwards and the integration of new methods and practices that redefined the individual's relationship to work (De Gaulejac & Hanique 2015, 95). Economic pressures derived from global competition and financial markets were transposed from the company onto the individual employee in the form of new techniques of discipline, coercion and control. In the restructured French company, workers were subject to differentiated management dynamics that sought to reduce costs and maximise profitability (Christiaens 2018). The first dynamic sought to intensify individual productivity, pushing each person to work harder and achieve raised economic targets: as the individual worker has less intrinsic value in a finance-driven system, they are obliged to increase their profitability by devoting themself more fully to the company's objectives. The second sought to monetise all dimensions of working activity, converting material work into abstract financial forms and codified signs. The new management model is 'disinterested in concrete production and in workplace organisation, it is obsessed by financial results and real activity escapes it' (De Gaulejac & Hanique 2015, 117). Forms of working activity that cannot be converted into abstract financial indicators are often dismissed as worthless. The third dynamic seeks to push workers out of the workplace in order to eliminate the superfluous costs linked to a salaried workforce. For some critics, finance seeks to dissolve labour and its material existence by converting it into a liquid asset that can be used by financial investors to calculate share value (Bauman 2005; Berardi 2015). Some workers are subject to forms of programmed mistreatment that aim to make their lives so miserable that they will choose to leave the company of their own accord (Burgi 2012). This is not to suggest that suicides were a deliberate or intended outcome of management strategies, rather they were what Zygmunt Bauman describes as a form of 'collateral damage', the victims of the unintended, but nevertheless devastating, consequences of normalised economic processes and their social effects (Bauman 2011).

This chapter draws on a wide range of multidisciplinary sources to analyse the relationship between suicide and capitalism in the French workplace, combining histories of suicide with critical texts on capitalism, suicidology, neoliberalism and labour. As is the case in the other chapters, I draw on examples of cultural production including novels, documentaries and fictional films that give representation to work suicides and elucidate particular dimensions of the phenomenon. A first section examines the historical conditions in which work suicides have emerged at the contemporary juncture, by exploring the broad historical connections between capitalism and suicide. If work suicide is a new phenomenon in historical terms, then what are the specific structural dynamics that have given rise to it? The second section examines how the status of the individual worker has been transformed by neoliberal financialisation. In a third section, I consider suicides in relation to expulsionary management practices that pressurise workers to either intensify their individual productivity or leave. The chapter goes on, in a fourth section, to consider the sociocultural specificities of French work suicides. Those who take their own lives are characterised as professional elites, privileged employees who hold well-paid, protected and desirable jobs. As the fifth section shows, neoliberal restructuring goes beyond the material conditions of work and is experienced by many as an assault on the values, meanings and forms of identity by which they define themselves and their place in the world. Suicides seem to manifest Emile Durkheim's notion of 'anomie' and stem from the disruption of a moral and social universe that conferred identity, meaning and social belonging. The final section considers the rise of suicides as a mode of extreme protest that reflects the collapse of collective structures of organised protest in the workplace. In the absence of conventional channels that can articulate, mediate and externalise individual grievances, these grievances may be internalised and manifest themselves in the form of extreme violence by the self against the self.

Suicide and Capitalism

While research on work suicides remains limited and this is a 'hugely under-researched' area, some recent studies suggest that work suicide constitutes a new phenomenon in historical terms that reflects the specific features of capitalism at the present historical juncture (Cullen 2014, 42). For Christophe Dejours, work suicides are a sign of an 'unprecedented historical evolution' that has laid bare changed power relationships in the workplace and, in particular, the effects of new forms of domination and servitude (Dejours & Duarte 2018, 239). He points out that documented cases of work suicide prior to the 1990s are rare and are generally confined to the agricultural sector and linked to factors of social isolation (Dejours & Bègue 2009). The significance of rising suicide rates, Dejours argues, transcends the workplace and represents a broad civilisational crisis signalling a transition to a new era of decadence (Dejours 2008). Other critics also attribute suicides and the social suffering that gives rise to them to the emergence of new and dangerous forms of work organisation under neoliberalism and their catastrophic effects on mental health (Rolo 2015; Clot 2015; Clot & Gollac 2017). For others, contemporary economic transformations have destroyed the workplace as a site of social integration and generated increasingly precarious and insecure forms of work which exacerbate suicidal tendencies (Baudelot & Establet 2006).

However, it is difficult to say with certainty whether work suicide is a new phenomenon historically or is new as a 'subject of knowledge' that reflects a changed understanding of the connections between suicide and work (Foucault 2002). The question of work suicides became a major social, political and cultural concern in France during the 2000s, dominating media headlines, triggering political intervention and represented widely in cultural production. Some suggest that suicides are as much an objective social reality as a discursive construct that reflects the outcome of political struggle by trade unions and also the rise of medicalised discourses for describing labour conditions (Lallement et al. 2011). The statistical evidence remains fragmentary and incomplete and tells us little about how the phenomenon of work suicides has evolved over time, across different historical periods. Although statistics on suicide, including suicide by occupation, have been collected in France since the close of the nineteenth century, data on work-related suicides, where work or working conditions are the suspected cause, has only been gathered since the 2000s, and the data is largely speculative.

Researchers rarely turn their attention to the long-term historical context that preceded and shaped the current suicide crisis.[1] Few studies can explain why work suicides have emerged now, at the present time, and not during earlier periods of capitalism when material conditions of work were arguably far worse. This section aims to contribute to debates about the historical specificity of work suicides by examining the broad historical connections between suicide and capitalism over time. Histories of suicide and studies of capitalism provide two rich sources that are neglected in recent debates but that shed light on the impact of working conditions on suicide during different historical periods of the nineteenth and twentieth centuries.

1   There are media reports of suicide waves affecting specific economic sectors in France during the 1990s, including care workers in 1995 and police officers in 1996–7, with one national newspaper reporting that 70 police officers killed themselves in 1996 (*Le Monde*, 12 April 2019). Yet these are generally isolated cases that attracted limited attention from the media, scholars or political leaders. One study shows how the notion of work-related suicide is constructed discursively over time through the role of trade unions who push management to confront the links between suicide and work. Hence, Marlène Benquet, Pascal Marichalar and Emmanuel Martin examine the changing nature of discourse on work suicide at the French gas and electricity company EDF-GDF during the period from 1985 to 2008, by analysing the minutes of meetings of the health and safety committee. They show how through insistence by trade unions, management moved from a position of denial to one of grudging recognition of cases of employee suicide at the company (Benquet, Marichalar & Martin, 2010).

The emergence of historical studies of suicide in recent decades reflects a growing recognition of the importance of suicide as a window onto wider social and cultural dynamics and, in particular, how daily existence, class relationships, questions of morality and public attitudes shape a propensity towards suicide at a given period. Historians of suicide tend to establish a correlation between suicide and conditions of daily life and, in particular, the impact of poverty as a social determinant of suicide. In his study of the labouring classes in Paris in the nineteenth century, Louis Chevalier examines why suicides seem to be prevalent amongst the working classes. Drawing on suicide statistics which divide deaths by occupational categories,[2] he shows that suicide was on the increase in France particularly in the first half of the nineteenth century, more in Paris than elsewhere and more amongst the working classes than any other classes. For Chevalier, suicide was inseparable from other forms of violent crime, in particular murder, each finding their common causes in poverty, immiseration and economic destitution. He draws on the observations of Jean-Baptiste Mercier and his portrait of Parisian life in the late 1770s: 'Those who kill themselves when they have no notion how they are to survive the next day are anything but philosophers; they are the indigent, the wearied, those worn out by life because merely to subsist has become so difficult, nay sometimes impossible' (Mercier quoted by Chevalier 1973, 281). Whilst demonstrating the links between suicide and social class, Chevalier does not address the impact of work or working conditions on the propensity towards suicide. Indeed, in examining suicide statistics, he shows that the highest rates of suicide per occupation were amongst those who were identified as 'persons without occupation or occupation unknown', in other words, the jobless (1973, 291–2). In 1876, per million persons in each category, there were 120 suicides in agriculture, 190 in industry, 130 in trade, 290 in domestic service, 550 in the liberal professions and 2,350 among persons without occupation or of occupation unknown. For Chevalier, suicide is a reflection of profound social inequalities and this was a prerogative of the 'misérables', those who were driven into poverty by joblessness or by the worst-paid jobs, and for whom suicide offered an escape from misery.

2   Statistics on suicide including details of occupation became available in France during the period from 1875 to 1885. The official statistics for France divided suicides into ten occupational categories (Chevalier 1973).

Similarly, historian Jean-Claude Chesnais argues that suicides during this period came from groups at the margins of society: the jobless, the mad, criminals, vagabonds and prostitutes. However, for Chesnais, suicide is not simply a consequence of material deprivation, but reflects wider social factors and, in particular, the social alienation of urban life. The vast majority of new workers in Paris were young men, newly arrived from the countryside, who had been uprooted from their family and communal ties and struggled with the alienation of city life: 'It was not misery in itself that these young countrymen experienced, but rather the shock of disorientation and atomisation that triggered this wave of despair' (Chesnais 1981, 268–9).

Other historians reaffirm the strong correlation between poverty and suicide. Richard Cobb's *Death in Paris* (1978) analyses police records of violent deaths in Paris at the turn of the nineteenth century and provides a rich insight into the social circumstances of those who took their own lives. Of the 274 suicides recorded in the archives, the vast majority were poor people who died by drowning, having thrown themselves into the Seine. They came from the poorest and least-skilled sections of the working population: porters, stable hands, transport workers and carters, rivermen, seamstresses, washerwomen and police officers: 'In general terms, suicide seems to have owed as much to purely personal causes as to biting poverty or to sudden economic failure, debt, bankruptcy, or fear for the immediate future' (Cobb 1978, 14). Examining the rich archival details concerning their clothing, he notes that this was generally of poor quality and was typical of people in occupations that required long hours, great physical effort, allowed very little sleep and involved appalling conditions. In many cases, those who jumped into the river were wearing several layers of clothing even in summer, as these constituted the sum total of their worldly possessions that they wished to take with them to their watery grave.[3]

---

3   Historical studies of suicide in England point to similar connections between suicide and conditions of poverty. In *Sleepless Souls*, Macdonald and Murphy (1990) note that large numbers of reported suicides in the early modern period were poor labourers, servants and workers in menial trades. Suicide rates soared in periods of financial crisis and following poor harvests. Pauper suicides were frequently reported and many chose self-killing as a means to escape destitution. Macdonald and Murphy observe that whilst newspapers expressed shock when wealthy individuals decided to take their own lives, poverty was so obvious a motive for suicide that it was rarely elaborated on.

Historian Georges Minois challenges the perception that in eighteenth-century France, suicide was the preserve of aristocratic elites. Newspapers reported on noble suicides in great detail, often presenting them as a heroic act, but suicides by common people aroused little enthusiasm and were either criticised or ignored: 'stories of love in thatched huts could not be taken as seriously as ones that took place in castles' (Minois 1999, 289). Far from the salons and their speculations about the meaning of life, common people continued to take their lives in large numbers because of the 'vicissitudes of a harsh, even merciless daily life' (ibid., 287). While Minois is interested in the connections between social class and suicide, he only gives limited attention to the question of work and he identifies only two cases where occupation was a direct cause of suicide. The first concerns children or adolescents pushed into domestic service, where they were separated from their families at an early age and often subject to mistreatment. The second concerns military men who at the end of the nineteenth century were twice as likely to kill themselves as civilians in France, using their own weapons. Yet, in these cases, suicides are linked to conditions pertaining uniquely to these occupations (early separation from the family and access to arms) rather than reflecting generalised social conditions, and Minois does not extend his analysis to the broader connections between work and suicide.

Historical studies of suicide point to a strong correlation between suicides and the periodic transformations of capitalism and, in particular, the impact of economic crises at different periods. For Durkheim, suicide is a historically contingent phenomenon that reflects systemic changes in the economic order at a given period: 'the evolution of suicide is composed of undulating movements, distinct and successive, which occur spasmodically, develop for a time, and then stop only to begin again' (1971, 11–12). Suicides rise during periods of economic crisis when the social order is destabilised and the individual becomes socially isolated. Hence, suicides increased steadily in France throughout the nineteenth century during a period of rapid industrialisation and social upheaval. Suicide was not a consequence of the material or economic circumstances of the individual, according to Durkheim, but reflected the nature of the social relationships that bound the individual to society. Indeed, strong social integration based on family, religion or community could mitigate the effects of material deprivation and he famously argued that 'poverty protects against suicide' (Durkheim 2002, 214). This argument was contradicted by later theorists including Maurice Halbwachs, who reaffirmed the link between poverty and suicide, showing that suicides tend to rise only during periods of economic decline and not during periods of growth. More recently, Baudelot and Establet have shown that despite the deep-seated social transformations linked to the *trente glorieuses* period of economic growth in post-war France, suicide rates remained stable throughout this period and only increased in the aftermath of the economic crisis of the 1970s. They argue that while, on the one hand, modernisation disrupts traditional forms of social belonging and leaves the individual isolated, it also lifts the individual out of poverty and the daily struggle for survival and therefore mitigates against suicidal tendencies: 'suicide decreases with growth' (Baudelot & Establet 2006, 258). More recently still, a range of international studies have pointed to a rise in suicides in the aftermath of the 2008 economic crisis, and one comparative study showed that after 2008, France was the country with the strongest connection between rising suicides and rising unemployment rates (Laanani & Rey 2015).

Historians of suicide rarely identify work or working conditions as a direct cause of suicide, and work is generally seen to protect the individual from the social alienation that leads to suicide. For Durkheim, work is an idealised form of social integration where the individual is bound to others by relationships based on a shared occupation, common identity and moral purpose and it is here that suicide is least likely to occur: 'Since it consists of individuals devoted to the same tasks, with solidary or even combined interests, no soil is better calculated to bear social ideas and sentiments. Identity of origin, culture and occupation makes occupational activity the richest sort of material for a common life' (2002, 346). Indeed, in the concluding chapter of *Le Suicide*, Durkheim suggests that the solution to a relentless rise of suicides in the late nineteenth century could lie in improved forms of work organisation. While he gives limited attention to the connections between occupation and suicide, Durkheim notes that industrial and commercial sectors had the highest rates of suicide, as these were most vulnerable to market instability and therefore to social upheaval. He notes that employers are more prone to suicide than workers because 'the possessors of most comfort suffer most' during periods of crisis and lack the self-restraint of the lower classes (ibid., 219).

Olive Anderson's study of suicide in Victorian and Edwardian England seems to confirm Durkheim's arguments about a loss of social integration as the key determinant of suicide. Drawing on statistics on suicide and occupation in the late nineteenth century, she notes that suicide rates were highest not in industrial occupations where material conditions were the most difficult, but in professional, artisanal and service occupations. The lowest rate of suicide amongst men across all occupations in the years 1878 to 1883 was that of miners, followed by railway workers, engine drivers, navvies, road labourers, fishermen and shipbuilders. Soldiers had the highest suicide rate and Anderson attributes this to the rigours of military life and the availability of weapons, but rates were also high amongst the liberal professions including doctors, lawyers, chemists and teachers. She suggests that suicide rates were lowest in the occupations where group solidarity is strong, despite difficult material conditions (Anderson 1987).

If histories of suicide give scant attention to the links between suicide and work, analyses of capitalism that focus on the impact of labour on social conditions under industrial capitalism might provide richer insights. In the *Condition of the Working Class in England* (1845), Friedrich Engels documents in exhaustive detail the effects of factory work on all aspects of the daily life of the industrial working class in the factories of Manchester and other English cities during the 1840s, describing its impact on health, mortality rates, sanitation, housing and living conditions. He describes labour conditions that ravage the bodies of workers through physical injury, starvation, poverty, accidents and disease. For Engels, the conditions imposed by the bourgeoisie in industrial England constituted a form of 'social murder' that cut short the lives of workers:

> I have now to prove that society in England daily and hourly commits what the working men's organs, with perfect correctness, characterize as social murder, that it has placed the workers under conditions in which they can neither retain health nor live long; that it undermines the vital force of these workers gradually, little by little, and so hurries them to the grave before time. (2009, 127–8)

Whilst documenting the types of mortality that afflict workers, Engels only gives passing attention to suicide. In a brief reference, he presents suicide as a desperate moral choice by workers:

Want leaves the working man the choice between starving slowly, killing himself speedily, or taking what he needs where he finds it – in plain English, stealing. And there is no cause for surprise that most of them prefer stealing to starvation and suicide. True, there are, within the working class, numbers too moral to steal when reduced to the utmost extremity, and these starve or commit suicide. For suicide, formerly, the enviable privilege of the upper classes, has become fashionable among the English workers, and numbers of the poor kill themselves to avoid the misery from which they see no other means of escape. (ibid., 143)

For Engels, death is a fate imposed on the worker by external forces and in particular conditions of factory labour, while the individual worker himself is engaged in a desperate struggle for survival in the face of such brutal social forces: 'This battle, a battle for life, for existence, for everything, in case of need a battle of life and death' (ibid., 111). The worker is conditioned to struggle for his or her existence, to fight to stay alive, rather than cede voluntarily to an early death.

Marx wrote a brief article about suicide which was published in a German socialist journal in 1846 and consists of a commentary and translation of an extract from the memoirs of the police adminis-trator Jacques Peuchet, who had examined suicide cases in the police archives in early nineteenth-century Paris. Marx's interest in suicide may have been sparked by reports of suicides by English and French workers in the 1840s. Hence Walter Benjamin makes passing reference to French and English workers' suicides in the 1840s and suggests, 'Around that time the idea of suicide became familiar to the working masses' (Benjamin quoted by Plaut & Anderson 1999, 7). Yet the focus of Marx's article on suicide is not social conditions, not least working conditions in the factories, but rather the miseries of private life and, in particular, the tyranny and oppression inflicted on women within the confines of the bourgeois family. Only one of the six case histories he presents in his article was directly related to economic circumstances; the other five involved women who were driven to suicide by the mistreatment inflicted upon them by their family. One of the cases involves a woman driven to suicide to escape the violent jealousy and brutality of her husband, and Marx observes:

The unfortunate woman was condemned to unbearable slavery and M. de M. exercised his slaveholding rights, supported by the civil code and the right of property. These were based on social conditions which deem love to be unrelated to the spontaneous feelings of the lovers, but which permit the jealous husband to fetter his wife in chains, like a miser with his hoard of gold, for she is but a part of his inventory. (quoted in Plaut & Anderson 1999, 57–8)

Marx's interpretation of suicide is clearly shaped by his wider analysis of capitalism, the labour theory of value and in particular, the notion of commodification that reduces a person to an object or a form of property to be disposed of by others. Yet, in Marx's analysis, suicide results not from the impact of society on the individual, but rather from an absence of society that leaves the victim vulnerable to the hidden tyrannies of the domestic sphere: 'suicide becomes the most extreme refuge from the evils of private life' (ibid., 67). Marx did not return to the subject of suicide in his subsequent work and it is absent from his analysis of capitalism and industrial working conditions in the three volumes of *Capital* that were completed with Engels.

The historical sources examined here rarely document or address the relationship between capitalist transformations, labour conditions and suicide. Despite the brutalising conditions of factories in the nineteenth century, workers did not appear to take their own lives or at least this only documented in a limited number of cases. Where suicides did occur, these were linked to general conditions of poverty or destitution that defined everyday existence, but not to material conditions of work specifically. Statistical data from the late nineteenth century shows that suicides were prevalent amongst the working classes, as these experienced the worst social conditions in their daily lives, so that self-killing became an escape from a quotidian struggle for survival. Although historical sources provide little concrete evidence of the connections between work and suicide, they do provide an important critical perspective for framing the dynamics that have given rise to suicides in the contemporary context. We know, since Durkheim, that work provides an idealised form of social belonging that protects the individual from the social isolation that leads to suicide. As Olive Anderson's analysis of suicide statistics in late nineteenth-century England show, suicide is rarely connected to material conditions of work, but is shaped instead by forms of social integration in the workplace. Hence, the most physically arduous jobs in the industrial sector had the lowest rates of suicide historically because the worker was protected by relationships of solidarity and class identity. *If suicides are shaped by the nature of social relationships in the workplace, how and why have these relationships been transformed in the contemporary era of neoliberalism? Why does work no longer protect the individual from suicide, but instead generate the social conditions that can lead to self-killing?*

Finance and the Flesh

The rise of work suicides can be situated in the context of other emerging forms of extreme individual violence. Some critics have examined the social roots of rising violence in contemporary society, situating this in relation to forms of systemic violence exerted by capitalism on the individual. For Slavoj Žižek, subjective violence such as crime, terror, civil unrest or international conflict emerges against the background of a deeper systemic violence that is inherent to the structures of capitalism. Subjective violence is a response to the 'speculative dance of capital' which pursues its goal of profitability in blind indifference to its catastrophic effects on social and economic life (Žižek 2008a, 11). Although subjective violence is visible and performed by a clearly identifiable agent, systemic violence is anonymous, hidden and part of the normal state of affairs, so that we do not always see it or recognise it: 'systemic violence is thus something like the notorious "dark matter" of physics, the counterpart to an all-too-visible subjective violence. It may be invisible, but it has to be taken into account if one is to make sense of what otherwise seem to be "irrational" explosions of subjective violence' (ibid., 2). Žižek urges us not to be distracted by the mystifying or spectacular nature of subjective violence, but to look at it 'sideways' by taking into account the legitimate order of things from which it emerges. Similarly, for Franco Berardi, acts of murderous suicide which disrupt the social order are not isolated, random or atomised phenomena, but emerge from the devastation wreaked by pathologies of late capitalism and the corrosive ideology of neoliberalism. Those who engage in such violence are victims of an absolute capitalism that reduces everything to financial abstraction and destroys the concrete materiality of social life. Acts of violence are committed by 'heroes' who engage in a perverse search for meaning, status and self-assertion in the face of capitalism's eviscerating and nihilistic effects (Berardi 2015).

Like the forms of subjective violence described above, recent work suicides have their roots in the systemic transformations that mark the transition to neoliberalism. Suicides can be situated at a juncture between the subjective and the structural, the rational and the extreme, the abstract and the embodied. The 'financialisation' of the economy, in other words, the rise of financial markets as the driving force of all economic activity, is widely recognised as the major feature of the shift to neoliberalism since the early 1980s. Marxist economists Gérard Duménil and Dominique Lévy (2011) interpret neoliberalism as the restoration of the hegemony of finance. Financialisation is identified as the first stage in a phase of neoliberalism that has progressively freed finance of territorial and material constraints, creating a system of international finance in which 'the movement of money capital has become a fully autonomous force vis-à-vis industrial capitalism' (Chesnais quoted by Harman 2009, 293). The rise of a finance-driven economy has been marked by the dominance of 'disconnected capital' that is increasingly generated not by human activities, such as the production or sale of physical commodities, but by manipulation of stock markets and complex financial transactions on international markets, including leveraged buyouts, derivative contracts, mergers, acquisitions and so forth (Thompson 2003). Financialisation is a form of 'profiting without producing' and is characterised by an asymmetry between the sphere of production and a ballooning sphere of circulation (Lapavitsas 2013).

The rise of finance has transformed modes of capital accumulation, as profits are generated from immaterial exchanges of money on distant financial markets and from activities that are 'increasingly abstract from specific forms of economic production' (Hardt & Negri 2006, 281). Capital is no longer necessarily grounded in specific territories or tied to heavy machinery or material objects, but takes flight and flows through exchanges that may seem to operate outside of the physical and material world. This model is marked by the rise of shareholder value as the primary measure of a company's economic performance and in which an ideology of finance rooted in slick mathematical efficiency dictates the conditions of human activity in the workplace As Costas Lapavitsas makes clear, finance is not necessarily located in a separate nebulous sphere, but permeates the real productive economy and reorganises it to suit its own interests. Finance takes on the guise of a predatory force that extracts value from productive activities, as large companies behave increasingly like financial institutions orientated towards making profits on external financial markets: 'This, the systematic extraction of financial profits out of the revenue of workers and other social layers constitutes a new set of relations that has been called financial expropriation' (Lapavitsas 2013, 800).

Recent French documentary films have captured the changing logics of power and capital accumulation that characterise the shift to a new globalised and finance-driven order. They portray a world marked by 'the irruption of finance capital into the driving seat' in which abstract money has become the *sine qua non* of economic progress (Moulier Boutang 2011, 16). If in the cinema of earlier decades, the car or the television were symbols of affluence and progress, these have been replaced in recent films by financial instruments, such as hedge funds, private equity or stock bonds, monetary forms that are often divested of connections to the material world. Jean-Robert Viallet's three-part documentary, *La Mise à mort du travail* (The Killing of Work, 2009) sets out to provide a forensic examination of the modern French company, looking at the connections that link the nebulous world of the New York Stock Exchange to the localised spaces of the French factory floor. The third film in the series, *La Dépossession* (Dispossession), follows the lives of workers within the French manufacturing company Fenwick. Once a small family-based firm created in the late nineteenth century, Fenwick underwent rapid expansion during the *trente glorieuses* to become a world leader in the production of fork-lift trucks. The film follows the fortunes of the company after its takeover in 2006 by the American private equity firm Kohlberg Kravis Roberts & Co., contrasting images of workers in the present day with those of workers during the company's industrial heyday. Hence we see archive footage of workers in a factory during the 1960s standing proudly beside a gleaming forklift truck, presented as a symbol of economic progress and of all their physical endeavours. We see close-up shots of pairs of hands at work as they expertly attach machine parts, tighten screws or adjust knobs, honing their manual skills to the tasks of material production. This is contrasted with footage in the present day, where we see Fenwick salesmen as they traipse into an annual board meeting where they are invited, over the course of several hours, to gaze at financial graphs and stock market figures that chart the company's position on the international stock exchange. In the boardroom, all traces of the product have disappeared and the abstract mathematical formulae that signify shareholder value are presented as the culmination of all productive activity in the workplace.

Kristin Ross notes that France's industrial expansion of the 1950s and 1960s was marked by 'a coming of objects' and that products increasingly determined the terms of human existence: 'a space where objects tended to dictate to people their gestures and movements' (Ross 1995, 5). In recent films, we glimpse a very different order in which abstract financial formulae determine the terms of productive activity and work is no longer circumscribed by the finite materiality of the object. Fenwick's workers are dispossessed, as the film's title suggests, in that their working activity is now channelled exclusively towards repaying the debts incurred by financial investors in purchasing their company through a leveraged buyout.[4] The second part of the documentary is based at a Fenwick factory in Cenon-sur-Vienne where production is being reorganised to meet the exigencies of finance capital and, in particular, the vastly increased productivity targets imposed by outside financial investors. A new Japanese model of production is being introduced (*kaizen*) which requires workers to speed up their activity, improve efficiency and eliminate all unproductive time ('le temps mort'). We witness a workforce subject to intense and relentless pressure, forced to carry out robotic gestures at high speed. One expert comments that each worker is now expected to reach the performance level of an elite athlete whilst being paid the minimum wage. We learn that two years after the company's takeover, this financial logic reaches its ultimate goal, as the factory announces over a hundred redundancies in order to reduce costs.

Each of the three companies examined in this book were former state-owned companies that underwent a process of privatisation or liberalisation during the 1990s that profoundly reoriented their company strategy – from producing commodities or providing services

---

4   Kohlberg Kravis Roberts & Co., like other private equity firms, purchases companies using leveraged buyout, a financial transaction that combines equity and debt, so that a company's cash flow is the collateral used to secure and repay the borrowed money.

on the domestic market, they became multinational corporations that were geared towards meeting exogenous financial indicators defined by international markets. Companies opened up their shares to international financial markets and were assigned credit ratings by financial agencies such as Standard & Poor's, Moody's or Fitch Ratings. According to one study, the credit rating system has reshaped the strategy of French companies and their relationship with their workforce. The study found that 32 per cent of French companies whose credit rating was downgraded by Standard & Poor's had, within a year of this credit rating, initiated restructuring measures in the form of mass lay-offs and redundancies (Faverjon & Lantin 2011). Here the causal connections between finance and material labour is made clear, as decisions and transactions made on remote financial markets are transposed into the localised spaces of the workplace, with often devastating effects on labour. France Télécom exemplifies this transformation from a state-owned service provider to a global player in 'the vast planetary monopoly of telecommunications' whose value was determined by international financial markets (Du Roy 2009a, 79). Following its privatisation, the company increasingly turned from the state to equity markets to finance its operations. One testimonial account by a former employee describes the shift to a finance-driven ethos and its impact on the workforce:

> What now motivates business leaders is managing share value. The ultimate goal of management is henceforth not to lead an industrial strategy or orientate the workforce in the development and production of telecommunications services, but to create share value [...] Instead of negotiating with those who produce value, that is, the company's employees, and pursuing a common strategy, France Télécom's leadership collaborates with external operators who determine share prices and for whom the company has become a cash cow. (Diehl & Doublet 2010, 52–3)

Soon after floating its shares, France Télécom merged its department of human resources with finance to make a new department of human and financial resources, placing these two economic instruments side by side.

The rise of a finance-driven economic model has redefined the perceived value of the individual worker as he or she is increasingly seen as a potential factor of adjustment that can be removed from the workplace in order to improve a company's financial standing. Economists have shown how corporate restructuring for shareholder value has a negative impact on labour, as efforts to increase returns to capital are made at the expense of the internal workforce (Froud et al. 2000). Financialisation has been linked to a deterioration in labour conditions through practices such as downsizing, outsourcing, intensifying output through lean production practices and negotiating more flexible wage agreements (Peters 2011). The strategy of many French multinational companies was now to 'dégraisser' the workforce (trim off the excess fat) in order to reduce costs and satisfy international investors. The phenomenon of *licenciements boursiers* (stock market redundancies), whereby a corporation that is otherwise profitable, announces mass redundancies in order to shore up further profits and defend share prices, is one of the perverse consequences of this new logic. Hence French companies such as Danone, Moulinex, Continental and Michelin have been the focus of controversy following decisions to lay off workers, despite each company being in a situation of profit. In 2014, workers at American tyre company Goodyear in Amiens took two company executives hostage in an act of 'boss-napping' in response to the decision to close the factory and lay off 1,173 workers, despite the company's profits and rising sales internationally. Following the introduction of Emmanuel Macron's labour reforms, which made it easier for multinationals to hire and fire workers, PSA, the maker of Peugeot and Citroën, announced in January 2018 that it would take advantage of the reforms by offering 1,300 voluntary redundancies in order to create a more attractive and flexible business climate for investors.

Philippe Claudel's novel *L'Enquête* (The Investigation, 2010) presents the modern French company as a senseless, inhumane and perverse entity that has become detached from all human norms and moral considerations. The novel follows an inspector who has been sent to investigate a series of employee suicides at an anonymous company ('l'Entreprise') in a nameless town. He finds himself plunged into a fantastical universe where the company is omnipotent, controlling the entire local town, yet is driven by absurd and illogical impulses. Inspired by Kafka's absurdist fiction, Claudel's novel is intended as a parody of the modern company, its immeasurable power, dehumanising effects and senseless logic. In the novel, all of the characters are reduced to nameless functions: the security guard, the manager, the guide, the policeman, the waiter. The security guard who works for the company reflects on the nature of modern corporate power:

This is no longer an age in which we take to the streets to guillotine kings. There are no kings left any more. Today's monarchs have neither a head nor a face. They are complex financial mechanisms, algorithms, projections, speculations on risks and losses, endless equations. Their thrones are immaterial and consist of screens, fibre optics and circuit boards. Their blue blood is encrypted information that travels at a speed faster than light. Their castles are data banks. (Claudel 2010, 137–8)

The inspector's every attempt to enquire about the suicides is met with countless obstacles in the form of absurd bureaucracy or the ignorance and confusion of the employees he meets. His journey is a struggle to preserve his sanity, identity and individuality in a world that crushes the individual under a weight of meaninglessness and economic abstractions. We never find out why the suicides happened, and this is merely a side story in the company's bizarre operations. The company has become an organisation underpinned by absurdity, inhumanity and an abasement of reason, and the inspector's search for truth, justice and meaning leads to nothing.

Management par la terreur

On the night of 14 July 2009, a 51-year-old technician employed by France Télécom in Marseille, killed himself at his home. He left a letter addressed to his family and colleagues in which he explained his motives: 'I am killing myself because of my work at France Télécom. It is the only cause. Constant pressure, work overload, absence of training, a company in complete disarray. Management by terror. It has completely destabilised and traumatised me. I've become a wreck, it is better to end things' (*Le Point*, 13 June 2019). His suicide took place in the context of a restructuring plan which sought to cut jobs massively across the company, pushing one in five employees to leave in the space of two years. The technician was described in the legal proceedings that followed as a high-achieving professional whose working life had been rendered dysfunctional by incessant restructuring. He had previously spoken to his sister about being bombarded with messages from managers suggesting that he find work elsewhere and, in one instance, proposing that he open a rural guesthouse. In a post scriptum at the end of his suicide letter, seeking perhaps to pre-empt any arguments to the contrary, he reiterates once again that it is work rather than personal factors that have pushed him to such extremes:

> I know that lots of people are going to say that there are causes other than work (I am alone, unmarried, childless, etc.). Some suggest that I can't adjust to growing old. But, no. I've always been fine with all of that. It is work which is the sole cause. (ibid.)

His case was one of three suicides by France Télécom employees in the month of July 2009 and the eighteenth recorded employee suicide at the company over the course of the previous 18 months (Rabatel 2010). His suicide letter, which was widely published in the press, brought to public attention the use of management methods across the company based on *harcèlement moral* or psychological bullying that were designed to coerce, pressurise and intimidate employees to leave. Testimonies by employees evoked a widespread use of terror tactics across the company and a climate of fear and intimidation that prevailed over daily working life. The notion of 'management by terror' has since become a familiar term in French public life that is used to evoke the deep-seated trauma and distress experienced by many workers at the hands of their managers.[5] It denotes abusive forms of management practice that transcend external working activity or individual performance and instead target the intimate mental and emotional resources of the person, exploiting a worker's subjectivity for economic ends.

The rise of neoliberalism has been marked by expulsionary dynamics (a 'tipping into radical expulsion') that seek to push out of the workplace those who are deemed to be unprofitable or surplus to requirements (Sassen 2014, 1). In the French workplace, these explusionary dynamics were confronted by a seemingly insurmountable obstacle: a highly regulated and protected workforce whose job security, working hours and rights were rigorously defined in the French Labour Code. While companies sought to adapt rapidly to changing market conditions and create a flexible, mobile and disposable workforce, they lacked the

---

5   In a suicide case in March 2017, management terror was used to explain why a 42-year-old rail worker threw himself under a train at Saint-Lazare station, where he worked (*Libération*, 15 March 2017).

formal and legal means to do so. This conflict between two opposing models of labour was particularly intense in France's large public service companies, where the workforce was composed of a majority of public service employees or *fonctionnaires* who held protected employment status and couldn't be legally fired.[6] Studies have shown that fonctionnaires were the primary targets of abusive management practices and had become the 'placardisés de la République' (the Republic's rejects) who were subject to an assault on their social status, psychological well-being and moral values. Louis Balthazard contrasts the image of fonctionnaires as privileged, well-paid public servants enjoying job security and considerable benefits with a reality of intense pressure, intimidation and bullying: 'One of the striking paradoxes of psychological bullying in work is that it affects employees who have protected status and takes place mainly in public service and social care organisations' (2007, 56). France Télécom exemplifies this conflict between a regulated, protected and stable workforce and a neoliberal strategy bent on evicting workers from the company by every means possible. Stéphane Richard, chief executive of France Télécom since 2010, makes explicit the connections between the company's new management practices and work suicides:

> Even though the firm's suicide rate is in line with the national average, France Télécom says that it was partly to blame. Because of the group's former status as part of government, 66,000 or 65 per cent of its employees are classed as civil servants, with guaranteed tenure. Unable to fire them, France Télécom instead subjected them to a system called 'Time to Move', in which they were obliged to change offices and jobs abruptly every few years […], but the company underestimated the consequences. (quoted by Clegg et al. 2016, 400)

6 Although traditionally *fonctionnaires* could not be legally fired, successive legislation has sought to make their employment status more flexible. According to the 'loi de mobilité sur la fonction publique' (mobility law for public service) of July 2008, a fonctionnaire can be dismissed if he or she refuses three successive job offers presented by the employer: 'un fonctionnaire qui refuse successivement trois postes […] peut être licencié'. At France Télécom, the NExT strategic plan was designed to make it easier to fire public servants by forcing them into redeployment, often offering them a succession of jobs that were either beneath their career level or located hundreds of miles from their home. They were then fired when three different job offers were refused.

The recent criminal case against France Télécom rested on the systematic use of psychological techniques across the whole company that were intended to demoralise, intimidate and harass employees for strategic economic ends.

While all European workplaces underwent a transition to neoliberalism, the French management model was distinguished by a form of governance by psychology ('gouverner par la psychologie') that operated outside a formal legal or disciplinary framework and used manipulative tactics against employees (Clot & Gollac 2017, 45). The French workplace is recognised as a site of psychological violence where power is exerted through subtle coercive means that target a person's subjectivity (Dressen & Durand 2011). The government has responded by putting in place legislative measures designed to curb forms of psychological violence and protect employees' mental health. In 2002, the French Labour Code was modified to include an article that protects the employee from *harcèlement moral* or violence exerted against their mental or psychic health. This is defined as 'repeated acts having as their object or effect a degradation of an employee's working conditions likely to infringe on their rights and dignity, alter their physical or mental health or compromise their professional future'.[7] The harasser who is found to be in breach of this law may be sentenced to two years in prison and fined up to 30,000 euros. The government also introduced measures that oblige companies to assess 'psychosocial risks' in the workplace that might endanger workers' mental health. In a report commissioned by government to identify and prevent emerging psychological risks, these are identified as 'risks to mental, physical and social health engendered by working conditions and organisational and relational factors likely to interact with mental functioning' (Gollac et al. 2011, 13).

A key catalyst for government intervention was the suicide crisis at France Télécom, which reached a height in the summer of 2009 and transformed the question of workplace violence into an urgent political question. The media coverage of the suicides created a national climate

---

7   Loi n° 2002-73 du 17 janvier 2002 de modernisation sociale, Titre II, Chapitre IV Lutte contre le harcèlement moral au travail. When the law on sexual harassment was enacted on of 6 August 2012, the maximum criminal penalty for moral harassment was raised from a 15,000 euro fine and one year's imprisonment to a 30,000 euro fine and two years imprisonment.

of anguish and fear, resulting in a frenzied effort to contain, manage and predict instances of workplace violence. The French Minister of Work, Xavier Darcos, introduced an 'Emergency plan for the prevention of stress at work' in 2009 which required all large companies to launch negotiations on how to tackle workplace stress. It also included an initiative to name and shame companies which appealed to bosses to put stress prevention measures in place or face the risk of reputational damage. Yet the discourse on psychosocial risk and its use as a management tool has attracted considerable criticism from those who see it as a means to depoliticise labour conflict and medicalise workplace grievances. For Yves Clot, the notion of psychological risk tends to pathologise workplace ills, seeking to eliminate unfavourable aspects of a worker's personality in the same way as a doctor might eradicate bacteria from the body. Grievances arising from working conditions that might otherwise be situated on a register of social conflict are reconfigured as medical problems that can be diagnosed and healed by medical experts (Clot 2015; Clot & Gollac 2017).

One widely documented, yet illegal management technique is known as 'mise au placard' or 'placardisation' (literally closeting or sidelining) whereby an employee is pushed out, shelved or consigned to the waste bin in an effort to get him or her to leave the company. Typically, employees retain the formal dimensions of their contract, salary and employment status, but their working activity is taken away from them, so that they experience a form of exclusion from inside the company (Lhuilier 2002). Legal agencies advertise their services online to those who fall victim to this treatment and advise their clients on how to recognise the subtle signs that they have been *placardisés*: 'Your mobile, computer or office have been removed; you are no longer invited to attend meetings; you are no longer asked to help make decisions; you are isolated from colleagues; you are insulted; you are sanctioned'. For an employer, this can be an effective strategy and a means of getting rid of an employee without having to invoke formal dismissal procedures (*rupture conventionnelle*) and pay out the hefty financial compensation that this involves. It allows an employer to bypass strict laws pertaining to formal dismissal, which is only permissible when an employee has breached his or her contract or where economic circumstances necessitate it. One study showed that 80 per cent of *placardisation* cases involve managers in their forties or fifties with strong employment security, but who are expensive for the company and seen as inflexible or immobile. Yet, for the individual employee, this treatment can be a source of considerable distress, humiliation and trauma. In June 2016, a manager at the perfume company Interparfums took his employer to a tribunal claiming he had been *placardisé*, which he described as 'an insidious descent into hell, a nightmare'. He recounts how over a period of four years, he was stripped of his managerial role and given menial, dull, clerical tasks which left him feeling depressed, bored and humiliated. The trauma he experienced made him physically ill and he was diagnosed with ulcers, insomnia and depression. He pursued a claim for 360,000 euros from Interparfums in compensation and damages (*Les Echos*, 2 May 2016).[8]

These management methods are represented in Nicolas Silhol's fictional film *Corporate* (2016), whose leading character Emilie (Céline Sallette) is a human resources manager in the finance department of a slick Paris-based corporation, Esen. Emilie is recruited as a *killeuse* (cost killer) who is entrusted with the task of pushing employees to leave the company by making their lives so miserable that they eventually decide to leave of their own accord. We see Emilie at the start of the film in an interview with an employee, as she uses subtle violence, persuasion and veiled threats to persuade the employee to accept that redeployment is in fact in her own interests. One of the employees she targets, Didier Dalmat, the finance director of the department, who has already been redeployed by Emilie ten months previously, jumps from an office window onto an inner courtyard and dies instantly. A formal investigation into the suicide is launched and the film proceeds with a forensic examination of the management methods that led to his self-killing. Inspired by real-life cases of work suicide, the director makes his intentions clear in the opening lines of the film: 'the characters in this film are fictional, but the management methods are real'. In fact, the film gives representation to the methods that were used at France Télécom as part of its 'Time to Move' strategy that set out to destabilise the workforce. We learn that Emilie is tasked with removing 10 per cent of employees as part of the company's Ambition 2016 strategy, by using psychological strategies such as the 'grieving curve' that is

---

8   On 3 November 2010, the Cour de cassation decided that employees have the right to end their employment contract if they are no longer given work by their employer. According to the labour code, an employer is obliged to supply an employee with work and the employee is obliged to carry it out.

designed to exploit an employee's emotional and mental vulnerabilities for strategic ends. We see secret footage of Emilie at a training seminar where she is in a role play situation, demonstrating to colleagues how she would persuade an employee whose mother is sick to accept a transfer to another city. The film contrasts the hidden and subtle psychological violence used by management with the physical, direct and corporeal violence embodied by Didier's act of suicide.

Alongside the use of psychological methods to push employees out of a company, these techniques are also used to motivate workers to increase their productivity and work far beyond the regulated working hours that contractually limit labour time. This is achieved through motivational discourses and strategies that appeal to workers to give fully of themselves and identify their own goals with those of the company. Employees are enjoined to *dépasser les normes* or surpass expectations, not only during a period of exceptional need, but on a routine and permanent basis. In her book, *Les managers de l'âme* (Managers of the Soul, 2008), Valérie Brunel examines the integration into French management practice of psychological and behaviouralist techniques during the 1990s, based on principles of personal autonomy, responsibility and creativity. These draw on an individualist conception of the person, with its origins in American organisational practice, that contrasts with the French and European conception of the individual as a social being, bound to a collectivity and having shared rights and obligations. For Brunel, these methods are characterised by an internalisation of constraint in which the individual becomes his or her own source of authority and relationships of domination are thereby concealed:

> Constraint is internalised by the individual who feels free, responsible and keen to acquire the necessary traits that are useful to the functioning of the system. Because of this internalisation of social constraint and the injunction to manage oneself, the manager is less inclined to exert authority than to fill the role of coach who helps the individual to acquire the necessary competences. The forms of power are therefore disguised. (Brunel 2008, 16)

The suicides at Renault's Technocentre manifest the insidious effects of management strategies that encourage employees to become their own boss and internalise objective economic goals. Suicides were linked to a phase of chronic overwork in which employees worked themselves into a state of physical and mental exhaustion in order to meet the strategic goals set by the company's chief executive. While the police investigation into the first suicide showed that the employee was working excessively long hours, the company argued in the court case that this was an individual choice and he was not forced to work overtime.

Suicidal Elites

The international media reacted with shock and puzzlement to suicide waves across French companies. They questioned why French workers, who enjoyed some of the best labour rights in the world and benefitted from strong social protection and seemingly idyllic working conditions, could possibly be driven to take their own lives. Unlike their Anglo-American counterparts, the French were protected from the cutting edge of economic globalisation and market competition by rigorous laws codified in the Labour Code and supplemented by collective bargaining agreements, company-wide agreements and case law. French employees enjoyed strong representation in company decision-making with delegates sitting on the board of directors and represented in work councils and health and safety committees. A *New York Times* article evoked a popular image outside of France of 'a cosseted workforce protected from lay-offs by near-hermetic job security and pampered by a 35-hour workweek' (29 September 2009). Another article presented suicides as a shocking anomaly in 'a country with never-ending vacations and long leisurely lunches' (*Guardian*, 12 February 2014). Although these responses often played on stereotypes of pampered French workers compared with their tough Anglo-American counterparts, they also pointed to a paradox at the heart of the French labour model. Suicides did not emerge amongst low-paid workers in precarious jobs with limited social protection, who were the primary victims of neoliberal restructuring. Rather, suicides emerged in the interstices of two worlds of work, the first marked by a Fordist social compromise, a public service culture, job security, an attachment to a *métier* or skilled profession, organisational continuity and strong collective identities and a second, marked by a neoliberal model of labour based on flexible employment, short-term economic returns and individual autonomy.

French work suicides constitute a unique phenomenon in sociocultural terms that defies statistical patterns for suicide amongst the general population. Suicide in France's large companies was a preserve of 'les nantis' (the well-off), a privileged stratum of professional elites in well-paid, protected and desirable jobs who experienced few economic or material difficulties in their daily lives (*Le Figaro*, 5 February 2014). Those who took their own lives were typically 'ideal employees', hard-working and conscientious, who devoted themselves to their profession and to their company: 'workers who were fully implicated in work, appreciated by their colleagues and managers and benefitting from strong emotional stability in their private lives' (Dejours & Bègue 2009, 28). Few suicides had a pre-existing history of mental illness or depression: 'Many suicides involve subjects who present no pathological symptoms and attain excellent levels of professional performance [...] On the question of psychological vulnerability, it cannot be considered to be a determining cause' (ibid., 28–9). In the general working population, suicide rates increase as the level of income decreases and the highest rates are amongst the lowest-paid occupations. One French study of suicide patterns amongst men in active employment, during the period from 1976 to 2002, shows that suicide amongst manual workers (*ouvriers*) was three times higher than amongst managers (*cadres*). Suicide rates are highest amongst those out of work and the unemployed have a suicide rate that is double that of those in active employment (Institut de veille sanitaire 2010). Similarly, general suicide rates reflect the level of educational attainment. Suicide increases as the level of education decreases and 'intellectual professions' have a low rate of suicide compared with low-skilled occupations (Bourgoin 1999). Statistics on suicide also show that depression is a risk factor in suicide. While death may be a great equaliser, the chances of suicide or early death from other causes are generally shaped by inequalities experienced in life.

Public service companies reveal this disparity between a stratum of *fonctionnaires*, older workers in well-paid, secure jobs who were affected by suicides, and the ranks of younger, newly recruited workers on short-term contracts (*contrats à durée déterminée*), who were less affected by suicides.[9] For instance, at the Chinon nuclear power plant in the

9   Public service companies are France's largest employers, providing 19.8 per cent of total employment and one in five employees is a *fonctionnaire* (OECD 2013). Despite reforms to reduce the number of public service employees,

Loire Valley in central France, which produces electricity for EDF, there were three suicides in close succession in 2006 and 2007. The deaths did not occur amongst the ranks of low-paid seasonal workers who undertake the most dangerous and menial jobs and who are exposed to 90 per cent of the ionised radiation emitted from EDF's power plants. Instead the three suicides were *agents statuaires*, workers who held public-sector contracts and had excellent salaries, social protection and generous benefits.[10] Elisabeth Filhol's debut novel, *La Centrale* (The Reactor, 2010), which is set at the Chinon nuclear plant in the aftermath of the suicides, makes clear this stark division of labour between statutory employees and seasonal workers. It is narrated by Yann, who ekes out a meagre existence as a seasonal worker and whose life is characterised by a succession of precarious jobs, social isolation and the deep-seated fear that he will exceed the maximum radiation dose, regularly checked by safety inspectors, and therefore be forced out of his job. He undertakes the most dangerous work and is responsible for decontaminating the plant by going inside the reactor where he is exposed to radiation for a controlled period. The novel opens with a description of the recent suicides, which are presented as a portentous event that overshadows the entire narrative:

> Three employees have died in the last six months, statutory employees who each had a role in management or supervision and who were meant to be taken very seriously. Because of their gesture, they are spoken of as comrades in arms even though they barely knew each other, all three victims of the nuclear reactor, fallen on the same front. (Filhol 2010, 11)

The author describes the suicides as an implosion of a delicate chemical balance that had previously given stability to their lives, an excess of

France still had 5.64 million fonctionnaires at the end of 2014. Fonctionnaires are inculcated in a public service culture and enjoy life-long jobs in exchange for modest salaries compared with their private sector counterparts and limited opportunities for career advancement.
10   These suicides were linked to transformations in their working conditions with intensified pressure, a devaluing of their professional skills ('a loss of meaning') and increased workload. The shift towards cheaper subcontracted workers meant that statutory workers were assigned management functions that no longer drew on their professional skills, yet their jobs were highly stressful as they were responsible for ensuring safety within the nuclear plant.

pressure, with catastrophic human consequences. Their lives are seen to mirror that of the nuclear plant itself, as it is suspended precariously in its surrounding natural environment, posing an ever-present threat of environmental destruction that belies its calm exterior: 'this moral pressure that has no equivalent in any other industry. So, yes the dangers of nuclear power. Behind the walls, a pressure cooker' (ibid., 33). The novel culminates in a description of the suicide of Yann's friend and co-worker, Loïc, who is also a seasonal worker and whose act constitutes an anomaly in the pattern of suicides at the plant. His suicide is a desperate act following an accident which exposed him to excessive radiation and meant that he faced the prospect of being prohibited from working.

Christophe Dejours presents a fascinating case history of a suicide that typifies the profile of an exceptional, high-performing and devoted employee who becomes the target of extreme management bullying. The case involves a 43-year-old female manager who worked in the human resources department of a multinational and took her own life by jumping from a bridge nearby. She was distinguished by a brilliant career and was recognised by her colleagues and managers as an outstanding employee who was highly intelligent, conscientious and energetic:

> This was a woman of extraordinary intelligence, considered by everyone as above the norm. She was even thought to be gifted. This brilliant intelligence is matched by an exceptional energy and capacity for work. When she undertakes a project, she does it with all guns blazing. Every task is crowned with success. She is completely at ease in her professional environment, where she is not only a considerable strength, but someone to be trusted. For her colleagues, loved ones and friends, she has an extremely solid and stable personality, is always available to others and generous. (Dejours 2005, 60)

Prior to her suicide, she continued to receive excellent performance evaluations. Her difficulties began when she requested to change to a part-time contract in order to allow her time to begin a process of adoption with her husband (she had three other adult children). This request was extremely badly received by her new line manager, who believed that work should take precedence over family or private life. The new manager initiated a vicious campaign of harassment against her, taking away her work, allocating her basic clerical tasks, insulting her and successively demoting her to roles far beneath her career level. In her suicide letter, she makes evident her moral repugnance regarding the treatment she received, her refusal to comply with her line manager's demands and her attachment to ethical values:

> This lack of human intelligence: do we have to be brutal for the company to function better, to gain respect and recognition by human resources? Why this lack of respect? Why humiliate someone? [...] So I say no, I will not come back. Some accept the humiliation or become submissive, others escape to other roles [...] I'm stopping everything because I don't think an improvement is possible. I appreciate my colleagues and my work far too much to accept these conditions. (ibid., 59–60)

For Dejours, the management abuse that led to the suicide was not derived from the victim's inadequate professional performance, but because she was insufficiently servile, refusing to capitulate to her managers, to replicate their treatment or accept their moral authority. For her managers, the need to make her servile, docile and submissive took precedence over any concerns with the quality of her work or with economic performance. Dejours suggests that her suicide makes visible new forms of power relationship in the workplace, pointing to practices of domination and submission.

Work suicides more typically affect middle-aged professional men, reflecting gendered suicide patterns in the general population, in which male suicide rates are three times higher than among women, both in France and internationally. These gender patterns may reflect the differing importance of work as a dimension that defines male and female identity. Whereas occupation is considered a major factor in defining masculine identity and tends to determine social status, independence and economic well-being, female identity may be less bound up with work and influenced by other factors including family relationships, parenthood and community. Hence, the impact of job loss is a key factor in rising suicide rates amongst men, but only has a minimal impact on female suicide rates (Bourgoin 1999). In cases of attempted suicide, professional or educational failure is stated as the main reason for men, whereas family problems are cited as the main factor for women (ibid.). Women, according to studies of suicide, are more closely integrated into social networks that protect the individual from the socially marginalising effects of unemployment. For Pascale Molinier, gender is a critical factor in explaining why recent work suicides have been transformed from a question of statistical and demographic interest into a major societal and political concern. If suicides have attracted intense media and political interest, this is because they concerned white, highly educated, male professionals working for France's largest multinational corporations. Increasingly, the male manager or public servant has come to embody the figure of workplace suffering, and this dominance tends to minimise or occlude the suffering of others including women, precarious workers and undocumented workers. Work suicide has become synonymous with masculine suffering and a male identity crisis (Molinier 2012).

This notion of suicide as a crisis of masculinity is given representation in Benoît Delépine and Gustave Kervern's film *Near Death Experience* (2015) which follows Paul (played by Michel Houellebecq), a middle-aged, world-weary call centre worker and father of two who walks out of his life and takes to the mountains on his bike, with the intention of taking his own life. As he wanders through the mountains, he reflects on the futility of his existence and his failings as a worker, husband and father. In long Hamlet-like monologues, he contemplates his own life and ruminates on whether or not to kill himself, in a film that has been described as a 'metaphysical poem' (*Le Monde*, 9 September 2014). Paul has been utterly debased by his job, where he is forced to recite scripted commercial lines to customers. He re-enacts this daily ritual now, reciting his lines to an imaginary customer alone on the mountain, as a way to express the depths to which his life has sunk. He is crushed by the meaninglessness of his daily existence and by the relentless demands and expectations that are placed on him as a man. The pressure to be exceptional, virile, creative and passionate have left him feeling empty, obsolete and suicidal. In one monologue, he compares his sorry position to that of his grandfather at a similar age, who was lucky enough to have been allowed to grow old:

> Obsolete. That's it. I'm 56 and I'm obsolete. Fifty-six. My grandfather's age when I was seven. It used to be old, a grandpa's age. You waited peacefully for retirement. You were not expected to meet objectives. To surpass them. You weren't expected to be seductive. To dress like a young man, to be virile, to still have sex, to do sport, to eat well, to love your wife like on the first day you met, to be your children's best friend. You weren't expected to be creative, to have humour and passions. You were lucky, grandpa. You had the right to be a grandpa.

Paul is an anti-hero who decides not to kill himself and comes down from the mountain, not because he has reached an inner resolve or experienced a philosophical revelation, but because he misses home comforts and the company of others: 'It's simple [...] I can no longer bear nature's harshness. My body craves soft leather'. While the film explores how the modern workplace has generated a loss of masculine identity and purpose, it does not seek to restore a sense of meaning or purpose to Paul's life. In a last-minute change of heart, he jumps onto the road from the passenger seat of the car that is bringing him home after his spell on the mountain and the film's final scene is of Paul lying unconscious on the road.

Neoliberal Anomie

For Emile Durkheim, the individual is a social and ethical subject who requires a higher moral purpose outside of the self to give meaning and purpose to everyday existence. Work or occupation, for Durkheim, confers on the individual a form of social integration and moral regulation based on shared identity, social bonds and collective purpose. When this social order is profoundly disrupted through an external crisis or social upheaval, the individual is left destabilised and isolated and may be prone to suicidal tendencies. Durkheim describes a type of anomic suicide that is derived from a breakdown of social relationships that leaves the individual in a state of disorientation, meaninglessness and hopelessness:

> Man's characteristic privilege is that the bond he accepts is not physical but moral; that is, social. He is governed not by a material environment brutally imposed on him, but by a conscience superior to his own, the superiority of which he feels. Because the greater, better part of his existence transcends the body, he escapes the body's yoke, but is subject to that of society. But when society is disturbed by some painful crisis or by beneficent but abrupt transitions, it is momentarily incapable of exercising this influence; thence come the sudden rises in the curve of suicides which we have pointed out above. (Durkheim 2002, 213)

Durkheim suggests that anomie is a modern form of suicide triggered by ceaseless economic deregulation and a weakening of traditional forms of social cohesion based on family, religion or community. Suicides are triggered by economic forces external to the individual and manifest a loss of social integration and 'society's insufficient presence in individuals' (Durkheim, quoted by Giddens 1971, 26).

In France's former public service companies, neoliberal restructuring came into conflict with a deeply ingrained workplace culture that was steeped in national tradition and collective values that defined the meaning of work. The rise of neoliberalism did not simply mark a shift from the state to the stock market as the source of company finances, but engendered a profound transformation of the culture that underpinned everyday work. Restructuring was characterised by the construction of a 'new normative order' attuned to the exigencies of financial markets that redefined the value of work and the status of the individual worker (Burgi 2014, 298). For Noëlle Burgi, neoliberalism has created conditions of social anomie in which the worker is no longer able to give meaning to the present or project into the future and is therefore placed in a situation of 'existential uncertainty' (ibid., 298). For others, suicide is the consequence of a destruction of 'human communities of work' and the reduction of the company to a purely economic and functional role (Clegg et al. 2016, 406). The restructuring of the French postal service, La Poste, which redefined itself as a 'private enterprise' in 2010, exemplifies this conflict between two models of work. The majority of La Poste's workforce were public service employees imbued in public service culture whose everyday work was harnessed, at least in principle, to a higher collective purpose: to deliver an equitable postal service to all citizens across the national territory. Ethnographic studies at La Poste show that restructuring was experienced by some as a source of deep-seated anxiety and distress. Some refused to comply with the new commercial logic and would not sell products, despite overarching imperatives to do so. Others would cheat the system, passing products on to family or friends to meet sales targets. Others still experienced a crisis of their subjective identity and sense of self (Hanique 2014).

If neoliberalism came into conflict with a public service culture, it also challenged the notion of *métier* or an attachment to a skilled profession, and a conception of work that is rooted in values of professionalism, shared expertise and social tradition. De Gaulejac and Hanique describe a new economic model driven by quantifiable results and short-term profits that undermined a culture of skill and expertise (2015, 60). A concept of abstract work defined by financial criteria, market flows and performance indicators disrupted the experience of concrete qualitative work with all its complex human realities:

> Gradually finance imposes its law, codes, norms and language on the entire economic and social system [...] This leads to a growing dissociation between the financial economy and the real economy, between the world of finance and the world of work. Measuring profitability becomes the main performance indicator for evaluating every company. (ibid., 60)

A report by a college of experts commissioned by the French Ministry of Work to identify psychosocial risks in the workplace pointed to a 'conflict of culture' as a key risk to mental health (Gollac et al. 2011, 157). This situation of conflict emerged when the exigencies or imperatives of management clashed with an employee's professional values and standards. Such a conflict, according to the report, was a source of deep-seated 'ethical suffering' which endangered mental health and, in extreme cases, triggered suicide (ibid., 157). The report detailed two instances where such forms of conflict have emerged. The first is in the health and social care sector, where constraints regarding efficiency that limit the time spent with a patient force professionals to deliver an inadequate service or even harm the patient. Employees experience anguish as they are obliged to contravene their own professional standards and provide a poor-quality service. The second case is based on a case study of a biscuit factory where, following the company's takeover, the ingredients of the product were changed so that it could be produced more cheaply. This cost-cutting measure interfered with workers' visceral attachment to the quality of the product, and to a shared industrial past. Although management tried to convince workers that the product was of the same quality, workers knew that it looked and smelt differently.

In suicide letters, workers tend to invoke collective values and professional ideals rather than material difficulties in explaining the motives of their suicide. For instance, in September 2013, before the start of a new school year, a 55-year-old teacher who taught electronics in a school in Marseille took his own life, leaving a detailed letter entitled 'Evolution of the teaching profession'. His colleagues who released his letter to the media noted that he was a teacher with 'a deep professional conscience and a vast erudition'.[11] The opening lines of the letter make his motivations clear: 'I am letting you know of my decision not to return for the 2013 school year. In effect, what has become of the profession, at least in my discipline, is no longer morally acceptable to me'. He goes on to trace his professional career and his decision to become a teacher later in life: 'Although demanding and difficult, the profession suited me when I felt I was doing useful work and had a legitimate role'. He goes on to describe how a 2010 educational reform which was 'imposed brutally and in a panic' by government had rendered it impossible for him to teach properly and to maintain his own high standards. He complains that the new assessment criteria are completely arbitrary and bear no relationship to the subject taught, remarking that the new curriculum 'violates the spirit of the *baccalauréat* [...] I consider it an infamy and I refuse to continue'. It may seem extraordinary that an educational reform that is external to an individual's personal life, that does not affect his financial or material circumstances and that concerns the profession as a whole, would provoke a state of such immense distress as to trigger suicide. Yet in this case the reform was experienced as an attack on intimate, complex and deep-seated values and professional standards by which this teacher defined himself. To violate these values by working in conflict with professional standards was to violate a part of himself. Yves Clot and Michel Gollac suggest that suicides are connected to a crisis of 'professional conscience' that affects the most conscientious and devoted employees, those who hold the highest professional standards. When restructuring comes into conflict with those values, it is not only working life, but the person's entire identity and sense of self that is compromised: 'to speak of professional conscience is to evoke what is most subjective, intimate in work, but also a social history that goes beyond each person' (Clot & Gollac 2017, 81–2).

11   This suicide letter was made public by the teacher's colleagues and extracts were published in the media (*Libération*, 21 September 2013). For a discussion of this suicide, see Clot and Gollac (2017, pp. 81–4).

Suicide as Protest

Work suicides might be seen as a symptomatic eruption that makes visible a broad crisis in the relationship between capital and labour in the context of neoliberal transformations in the French workplace. For some critics, the shift to neoliberalism has subordinated the interests of labour to those of capital in unprecedented ways (Boltanksi & Chiapello 1999; Danford, Richardson & Upchurch 2003; Peters 2011). Work suicides can be situated within changing patterns of labour conflict and, in particular, the rise of radical, individualised and corporeal modes of protest in the contemporary period. Some point to a new age of violence in which extreme violence is no longer an exceptional phenomenon confined to the margins of social life, but has become a mainstream event that erupts at the centre of the social order (Bargu 2014; Berardi 2015). Banu Bargu points to a 'weaponization of life' and to the increased prevalence of corporeal and existential practices of struggle across the world which use self-destructive techniques as a means of making a political statement or advancing a political goal (2014, 14). Recent labour protest in France has pitted enraged workers and trade unionists defending economic conditions and social rights against political and business élites seeking to liberalise the Fordist social model and create a new flexible model of labour. Protest against labour reform culminated recently in the sustained movement of the *gilets jaunes* mobilising 'forgotten' lower-income groups who struggle to reach the end of the month on their limited income. The new forms of labour radicalism are distinctive in their use of the individual physical body as a site of politics and resistance. Instead of positing a collective organisation or class identity, demonstrators turn to their own bodies, enacting forms of violence directed against the self or others, through 'violent bodily reactions' (Puggioni 2014, 563).

Using the body as a means of dissent is a 'weapon of the desperate' and reflects asymmetries of power in which workers find themselves powerless and disenfranchised in the face of the implacable economic decisions affecting their lives (Kaspar 2010, 25). In a David and Goliath struggle against remote and disembodied capital, in which the odds are impossibly stacked against them, some workers may use their corporeality and physical presence as a tool of resistance (O'Shaughnessy 2007; Hayes 2012). Bodily resistance reflects a position of political weakness and is a means of asserting power in a situation of powerlessness, as 'the weapon of choice of anyone in an obviously inferior position; when you don't have anything to fight with, you can still use and "spend" yourself' (Bradatan 2015, 114). Traditionally used in rare instances as a form of extreme political protest, motivated by ideological or religious convictions, suicide has increasingly become a means to protest against perceived social or economic injustices (Biggs 2012). Hence, Greece experienced a wave of public suicides in 2011 and 2012 against the background of economic crisis and austerity politics. In a well-publicised case, a 77-year-old pensioner shot himself outside the parliament building in central Athens on 4 April 2012, leaving a handwritten note blaming the government for reducing him to poverty (Davis 2015). Similarly, a wave of public suicides by tenants evicted from their homes set off massive demonstrations in Madrid in February 2013. In the UK, welfare reforms have been linked to an increase in suicide cases in the context of austerity politics in the aftermath of the economic crisis (Mills 2018). In China, the threat of suicides has also been used by workers as a political instrument to pressure management to improve working conditions. Hence, around 150 Foxconn workers threatened to kill themselves by jumping from the roof of their production site in January 2012. Foxconn had experienced a suicide wave two years earlier at a different production site which resulted in 14 deaths (Chan & Pun 2010).

Recent studies interpret acts of extreme subjective violence as a dialectical response to conditions of capitalist violence and their impact on everyday lived experiences (Žižek 2008a; Berardi 2015; Evans & Giroux 2015). Suicide might therefore be seen as a manifestation of trauma and despair in the face of economic conditions that render life unbearable. Yet extreme violence is not simply a counterpoint to conditions of structural violence and it also reflects a collapse of the means to express dissent in relation to such violence. In his study of the nature and causes of extreme violence, Etienne Balibar defines extremity as a threshold or boundary that marks the end of the conditions of political possibility or what he defines as 'civility'. From this perspective, extreme violence is not part of a dialectic or a relationship of economic antagonism, but constitutes a form of nihilism that emerges when politics has failed, manifesting 'the annihilation of the capacity to resist' (Balibar 2015, 149). Balibar links the rise of acts of subjective violence to a disintegration of the social and civic bonds that constitute the foundation of the democratic order and a collapse of the collective channels for articulating, channelling or expressing dissent. Extremity is the recourse of those who are denied political subjectivity and are left without hope of changing the world, leading some to acts of blind and nihilistic destruction: 'It is because it is virtually impossible for the victims to imagine or present themselves in person as political subjects capable of emancipating humanity and emancipating themselves' (ibid., 57). Suicide can be interpreted as a desperate last resort, where violence that might otherwise be mediated by external collective structures is internalised by the person. According to Anthony Giddens, suicide is a desperate form of self-assertion in a situation in which the individual is left powerless:

> Suicide is a grasping towards omnipotence in a situation in which the influence of the individual, as he may realise on a conscious level, is pathetically inadequate. His world has slipped away from him, and yet in the very act of denying that world he attempts to encompass and change it as well as to change himself. (1971, 113)

The shift to neoliberalism was marked by an erosion of the structures of collective representation through which workers organised themselves and derived collective identity. In twentieth-century France, trade unions acted as a powerful vehicle for channelling individual grievances into a collective social force, leading to key moments of social conflict including 1936, 1947, 1968, 1995. The 1970s in France were recognised as a 'golden age of workers' struggle' (4,000 days lost to strike action in 1976 alone) which marked a turning point, precipitating in the decades that followed a sharp decline in forms of organised and collective social protest (Mathieu 2010). France today has the weakest union movement in the western world and according to OECD figures had a membership rate of 7.9 per cent (2014 figures), compared with 66 per cent in Sweden and 25 per cent in the UK (2014 figures). There has been a sharp decline in union membership, which has fallen by 70 per cent from 1970 to 2003 and has stagnated at a level of 7–8 per cent over the past 15 years (Milner & Mathers 2013). The decline of trade unions was partly a consequence of changing social conditions and, in particular, the impact of deindustrialisation, rising unemployment and an outsourcing of labour. Yet, for Boltanski and Chiapello, the erosion of trade unions and other representative structures was not a secondary effect of these structural transformations, but constituted a core aspect of the 'new spirit of capitalism' that underpinned neoliberalism. On the one hand, political reforms in France have weakened trade unions' capacity to represent workers effectively, to construct a collective voice and confront employers' power. Recent labour reforms have sought explicitly to weaken the capacity of trade unions to provide a collective voice and a vehicle for worker dissent. On the other hand, employers have engaged in a campaign of 'anti-union repression' that sought to break modes of collective representation in the workplace (Boltanski & Chiapello 1999, 352).

Labour reforms under the Hollande (2012–17) and subsequently Macron presidencies (2017–) have been characterised by liberalising and business-friendly policies that have reinforced employer autonomy, constrained representative structures and removed legal controls on bargaining agreements. Whilst Hollande's labour reforms aspired towards combining social protection and flexibility, the latter had taken precedence as the key policy drive by the end of the *quinquennat* (Milner 2017). The core principle of the 2016 El Khomri law was that company-level bargaining should become the norm for regulating workers' rights giving the local level precedence in determining conditions and placing unions in a relatively weak position. The law opened up the possibility for employers to bypass unions by organising direct electoral ballots of the workforce when it proved impossible to reach an agreement with unions. The series of rulings passed by Macron in September 2017 radicalised this process of labour reform, allowing firms which are experiencing economic problems in France alone, but are profitable internationally, to make staff redundant. For Susan Milner, these reforms mark a tipping point towards a 'neoliberal model of regulation' in France (2017, 440). Macron's rulings also merged existing workplace representative structures, reducing the number and range of collective structures that represent and mediate workers' interests. These reforms have 'radically individualised' labour relationships by placing responsibility on employees to reach agreements, bypassing unions and weakening their capacity to construct collective responses (Lane 2018, 254).

Tactics used by employers to repress, marginalise and weaken trade unions are well documented and may involve targeting individual trade union representatives (Lhuilier 2002). Testimonies by colleagues of a 42-year-old rail worker who took his own life in March 2017 blamed his suicide on a campaign of 'trade union repression' waged against him by management. A delegate at the union SUD-Rail, he was involved in an ongoing dispute with management and had won a case for discrimination and harassment against management in 2012 (*Libération*, 15 March 2017). These forms of intimidation are presented in the first film in the documentary series *La Mise à mort du travail* ('The Killing of Work', 2009), which follows the case of five checkout assistants who bring a case of unfair dismissal against their employer before an industrial tribunal in Nanterre, after they were successively fired from a branch of the supermarket Intermarché, where they had worked for many years. We learn that they had challenged their boss by taking sides with a colleague, Chantelle, who had decided to stand as a CGT representative in the local trade union elections. Management cancelled the elections and fired Chantelle, who subsequently won a case for discrimination against her employer. Each of her colleagues was systematically fired on spurious grounds including slander, unprofessional misconduct and theft. Two of them described how chewing gum packets were surreptitiously hidden in their bags and they were subsequently accused of theft, a tactic described by one of the lawyers representing them as a 'recurrent operating mode' in the retail sector. Another case represented in the documentary involves two senior managers who were subject to a campaign of abuse by a new manager and then fired when one of them decided to set up a branch of the CGC (Confédération générale des cadres) in the company. As in the first case, management enlisted other colleagues to isolate the two managers, forcing co-workers to sign a petition claiming that they had been harassed by the targets. This petition was used as the formal grounds on which to sack them.

Some critics have linked work suicides to a destruction of the workplace as a site of social solidarity and collective identity. For Christophe Dejours, material conditions of work have not necessarily deteriorated in the present juncture and exploitation is a phenomenon as old as capitalism itself. What have changed are the forms of social integration through which the individual confronts the daily structural conditions of work. Neoliberal management has destroyed the workplace as a social space in which collective identities might be formed, by pitting workers against each other in a ruthless competition for survival. In a climate of fear and intimidation, the individual increasingly colludes with management in perpetrating acts of cruelty and violence against others in a 'banalisation du mal' (Dejours 1998, 19). In the face of social injustice at work, the individual increasingly finds him or herself alone:

> The rise of work suicides is not only a result of injustice, humiliation or harassment. It stems principally from the atrocious experience of silence from others, abandonment by others, a refusal by others to speak out, cowardice of others. Injustice and harassment, which in the past were a difficult or painful experience, can in the present context degenerate brutally into a crisis of identity. (Dejours & Bègue 2009, 45)

Dejours calls for a new political and philosophical project based on the notion of 'le travail vivant' (living work) that would place human needs rather than economic interests at the centre of working life (2009).

In the absence of external structures for articulating, mediating and channelling individual grievances, such grievances may trigger explosions of individual violence, including violence against the self. The person no longer necessarily locates conditions of exploitation, coercion or harassment in a conflictual social relationship with an employer, but these conditions are internalised so that they become deficiencies of the self or personal inadequacies (Berardi 2015). In recent suicide cases, letters left behind by the victims refer explicitly to an absence of collective representation and channels of communication. Some workers leave documentary evidence of their repeated efforts to communicate with management and make themselves heard but which have come to no avail. Following the suicide on 17 May 2008 of a France Télécom employee who had been on sick leave for depression for two months prior to his death, his colleague of over thirty years wrote a letter to his trade union in which he remarks that 'employees experiencing difficulties are confronted by an erosion of social structures' (quoted by Décèze 2008, 31). In a different case, on the night of the 21–2 April 2013, a 35-year-old night maintenance technician at Renault took his own life, leaving two letters, one addressed to his wife and daughters, the other to management in which he referred specifically to a lack of representation: 'Thank you, Renault. Thank you for these years of pressure, of blackmail on the night shift. Where the right to strike doesn't exist. Anyone who protests will be in trouble. Fear and uncertainty about the future are part of the game, so it seems' (*Le Monde*, 25 April 2013).

This notion of suicide as an ultimate and desperate act of protest where all other forms of intervention have failed is given poignant cinematic representation in Stéphane Brizé's film *En guerre* (At War,

2018). The film follows a group of workers led by trade union leader Laurent (played by Vincent Lindon) who engage in a bitter struggle to save their jobs following the announcement that their factory (Perrin) based in Agen, in south-west France, will close because it is deemed by the multinational CEO based in Germany to be insufficiently productive. The workers throw themselves into an exhausting and heroic battle with their bosses, drawing on every means at their disposal to advance their cause and draw attention to the plight of the 1,100 workers who are faced with unemployment. In their meeting with Perrin's management, they appeal to logic, arguing that the factory is making considerable profits and that management has previously agreed to guarantee jobs in return for a salary freeze. They enlist support from the very summit of the political establishment as the President of the Republic pledges his support to the Agen factory workers. When a group of workers attacks the German CEO as he is leaving a meeting, they are virulently chastised by other trade union members who seek to prevent an escalation of violence. The film portrays how the media seizes on this act of violence, reconfiguring a previously sympathetic workers' movement as an angry and violent mob. Meanwhile, workers lose the support of political leaders who now denounce the mindless violence of the trade union movement. Laurent's final act of violence at the end of the film is presented as an expression of hopelessness and despair by a trade unionist who has remained faithful to his struggle to the bitter end but who has now exhausted every possibility available to him. After he takes his own life, by setting himself alight outside the company headquarters in Germany, management perversely agrees to restart negotiations with the unions.

Conclusion

French work suicides can be seen as an extreme human consequence of the impact of finance on the flesh, where an economic logic grounded in mathematical efficiency and financial abstraction is imposed on real, complex and embodied working lives. Recent suicides make visible a conflict between the virtual and the corporeal, as the drive to reduce human activity to immaterial codes is confronted with experiences of intense bodily suffering. The need to accumulate abstract value has within neoliberalism radically transformed conditions of work and the status of labour across contemporary workplaces. For Franco Berardi, finance is driven by an 'annihilating nihilism' that destroys the shared values and material activity created by human production and affirms the primacy of the abstract force of money (ibid., 88). This is a system in which concrete working activity must be converted into floating values that are codified in the form of metrics of productivity, economic calculus and algorithms. In the new finance-driven order, the individual worker is transformed from an agent of production and a source of profit into an obstacle to rational economic goals whose elimination may sometimes become necessary to maintain the productivity of the whole. What is at stake is not necessarily a deterioration in the formal conditions of working life but a devaluation of the individual worker him or herself, as he or she becomes an impediment to profitability.

Recent suicides are not an aberration of an otherwise smooth-running economic system, but stem from rational, logical and normalised economic processes that underpin the new modes of capital accumulation. Suicides might be seen to signal the emergence in the workplace of a form of 'necropolitics', a system of power that is no longer concerned with a regulation of life and productivity, but with a regulation of death (Mbembé 2003). The contemporary worker has been reduced to 'bare life' that must be disposed of to preserve the economic vitality of the whole (Agamben 1998). We have seen that economic strategies pursued by some French corporations are underpinned by expulsionary dynamics that seek to remove workers from the workplace as an unacceptable cost. Workers must either push themselves to work harder, become more productive and devote their whole selves to the goals of the company, or else remove themselves from the workplace altogether. In the French workplace, suicides have tended to affect the most zealous employees, those who were devoted to the company and internalised its strategic objectives (Dejours & Bègue 2009). Suicides are a form of collateral damage in a neoliberal workplace that subjects workers to such intense expulsionary pressures that some choose to take their own lives. In this respect, work suicide constitutes a threshold that marks the boundary between civility and extremity, elucidating some of the catastrophic effects of neoliberal financialisation on lived experiences of work (Balibar 2015).

Suicide might be seen as a form of extreme protest where other forms of communicating dissent have been exhausted or are no longer available. In such a context, the only means of persuasion a person can use is their own dying body and the public spectacle of their death. Suicide becomes a perverse means of asserting power and mastery in a situation where the person is powerless. Once the possibilities of dissent through collective and democratic means are foreclosed, the individual may turn their body into an extreme instrument of political voice (Puggioni 2014). In *Dying for Ideas*, Costica Bradatan suggests that suicide can be used as a means to reverse a power relationship and impose social or political change from beyond the grave:

> At first glance, it may seem as if someone performing such a gesture is in the weakest of positions, a victim's position. But we've crossed into a territory where ordinary logic is reversed: here it is sometimes the victim who has more power than the victimizer. The former controls the latter by directing his attention, shaping his behaviour, and by giving him a victim-izer's status. By choosing to die, the victim places herself in a position that is not only inaccessible to her fellow humans, but also of significant power – the uncanny power that comes from her being in the proximity of death. Paradoxically, death does not weaken her, it makes her stronger. (2015, 101)

Chapter 2

Suicide as Testimony

This chapter examines suicide letters as a mode of testimony that seeks to bear witness to external conditions of work and their impact on lived experience in the contemporary neoliberal context. Testimony provides a perspective on social processes from the inside, telling us a story of trauma from the person who lives it in the everyday through his or her intimate, subjective and material experiences. In treating suicide letters as testimony, private suffering, narrated in a space of traumatic intimacy, is transformed into public meaning and becomes a prism for interrogating the economic order as a whole: 'Testimony records a movement from individual experience to the collective archive, from personal trauma to public memory' (Miller & Tougaw 2002, 13). I situate suicide letters at a juncture between the everyday and the extreme that helps make visible extreme human suffering within the ordinary and quotidian spaces of everyday work (Rothberg 2002; Pollock & Silverman 2019). Written in the harrowing and private moments before death, suicide letters speak from a position of the utmost despair, pain and trauma. Yet these letters are not located at a radical periphery, but are embedded in structures at the centre of social life, in the ordinary, functional and ordered spaces of the call centre, corporate office or assembly line. Work is a quintessential space of everydayness and a realm of 'routine, repetition, reiteration: the space/time where constraints and boredom are produced' (Kaplan & Ross 1987, 3). Yet, this everydayness has a unique quality, as it can help to expose conditions of extremity within the normalised boundaries of social life. It points not to exceptional experiences but to universal social conditions in which we are all immersed. What do these suicide voices tell us about conditions of human labour in the neoliberal workplace? At what point do everyday structural processes tip over into the extreme? What are the dynamics in which work generates extreme subjective suffering?

This chapter examines a corpus of 40 testimonies drawn principally from three French companies during the period 2005–15. The corpus includes 32 suicide letters (in the form of brief notes, letters, emails, formal documents or testimonial accounts) written by suicidal individuals and eight testimonies by family members. Of the 32 suicide letters, 13 were written by employees at France Télécom, ten by employees at La Poste and three at Renault. In addition, I draw on six suicide letters by employees who worked at other companies and which were written during the same period. This testimonial material has been collated from media reports, trade union sources, published judicial proceedings, legal dossiers, investigative studies, testimonial accounts and scholarly texts. I treat suicide testimonies as a form of narrative voice that seeks to ascribe meaning to the act of self-killing and to interpret it for others. Drawing on Jack Douglas, I focus on the social meanings of suicide letters investigating 'specific patterns of suicidal meanings' that reoccur across the letters (Douglas quoted by Giddens 1971, 135). Who or what is to blame, according to the suicidal individual? What are the working conditions that generate subjective suffering? Why is suicide envisaged by some as an ultimate recourse in response to social conditions of work? Do neoliberal transformations condition a desire for suicide? I examine work suicides in both their narrative and performative dimensions. Alongside letters, some individuals use their suicide as a symbolic act through a 'voluntary dramatisation' in which self-killing becomes a means to make visible and push to the surface otherwise hidden management abuses or unfair practices (Rabatel 2011, 178). Self-inflicted violence becomes a means to expose an everyday violence that is inflicted by others. Some choose to kill themselves in the workplace, either during their working day or returning out of hours. Others choose spectacular means and transform their self-killing into a public act that is witnessed by others and exerts an impact on public consciousness. I examine the connections between self-killing and work that are expressed in both these written and symbolic forms.

Suicide notes are written in a contested discursive space in which the meaning and causes of suicide are fiercely disputed. In the face of an official narrative that tends to individualise suicide, attributing it either to mental or emotional flaws in the person, suicidal individuals explicitly and consistently blame work or working conditions as the unique determinant of their actions. They seek to explain that transformations in the workplace have made their lives so unbearable that they can no longer continue. Suicide is a desperate act of communication in which the individual transforms his or her self-killing into a form of enunciation that aims to communicate meaning, apportion blame or challenge a social injustice. In *Notes on Suicide*, Simon Critchley observes that in a suicide note, 'the writer is communicating a failure to communicate, expressing the desire to give up in one last attempt at expression. The suicidal person does not want to die alone, but wants to die with another or others, to whom the note is addressed' (2015, 45).

Suicide letters reconfigure normalised economic processes as a source of profound and embodied suffering. The restructuring plan that seeks to push employees out, in the interests of logical and quantifiable cost-cutting goals, is represented as an instrument of intense anguish and distress. The strategic targets that aim to raise productivity and increase financial returns are experienced in terms of agonising psychological pressure. The company rebranding that substitutes public service values for commercial goals is experienced as an assault on identity and a person's sense of self. The letters help to make visible everyday suffering in a system in which it is often fetishistically denied. Suicide letters demarcate the boundaries between the everyday and the extreme, signalling the limits of what is humanly tolerable in the pursuit of rational economic goals.

Reading Suicide Notes

As an intensely private text written in the traumatic moments before a person confronts his or her own death, the suicide note may seem inappropriate as material for analysis or as a text that can be opened up to scrutiny by others. The suicide letter occupies a terrain that is at 'the limits of tellable experience' and challenges our expectations about what is acceptable, decorous or even ethical (Miller & Tougaw 2002, 2). A suicide note is the final statement of a person who has taken his or her own life and should arguably be kept within the realm of the family or a person's immediate circle. Yet, as Marc Etkind suggests in

Or not to be, suicide notes are not necessarily private texts and should perhaps be read as 'social acts', as these are 'the last desperate attempts at communication with the wider world' (1997, vii). Similarly, Ben Fincham and his co-authors point to the social and cultural significance of suicide notes, suggesting that these are 'social documents' that can help to elucidate the impact of social forces on the individual (2011, 85). The suicide notes examined here give expression to a realm of personal suffering, but they are also turned outwards towards an external social world and, more specifically, towards a world of work. Drawing on studies in critical suicidology, I treat the suicide note as a prism for interrogating the social order and focusing our attention on some of the structural causes of extreme subjective suffering (Marsh 2010; Taylor 2015; Mills 2018).

Much like the phenomenon of suicide itself, the study of suicide notes remains the preserve of the medical sciences and in particular, psychology and psychiatry, where notes are treated as an object of psychological enquiry and a means to deepen our understanding of mental illness. Suicide notes are considered valuable documents in so far as they help to uncover a mental disorder and reveal the underlying psychological states that influence the act of suicide.[1] Suicide notes are analysed in specialist medical science publications that are concerned with testing psychological theories in relation to categories such as gender (Canetto & Lester 2002), interpersonal relations (Sanger & McCarthy Veach 2008), the negotiation of blame (McClelland, Reicher & Booth 2000) or other psychological categories (Leenaars 1988). As suicide is usually considered to be a symptom of mental illness, the suicide note is often seen to express a predetermined pathological state. For American psychologist Edwin Shneidman, who pioneered the study of suicide notes, they are a conduit into the 'suicidal mind' and the frustrated psychological needs which he believed were the root cause of suicide. While he perceived suicide notes as valuable in expressing suicidal intentions in ordinary words and plain language, suicide was ultimately a 'drama of the mind' in which a person is prey

---

1   In nineteenth-century France, when suicide was overwhelmingly perceived to be a mental disorder, the psychiatrist Brière de Boismont examined 1,547 letters in order the investigate the connections between suicide and madness. His book would go on to have a profound influence on Emile Durkheim's study of suicide (De Boismont 1856).

to psychological forces beyond his or her control (Shneidman 1996, 4). The prevalence of medical approaches means that suicide notes are rarely considered as a mode of self-expression or a form of narrative agency, but are instead regarded as a symptom of mental pathology. The author of the suicide note is not deemed capable of producing subjective meanings and intentions or even of understanding the true nature of his or her own death. Furthermore, suicide notes are treated as introspective documents, 'personal documents' that reflect individual circumstances of biological or pathological origin, rather than wider social or cultural factors (Shneidman 1976, 258). Although a small number of studies examine suicide letters from a sociological or historical perspective, these approaches remain on the sidelines of dominant medical sciences perspectives (Douglas 1967; Goeschel 2009;[2] Fincham et al. 2011). Furthermore, what is deemed to be 'social' in these studies is often limited to the individual's immediate context and personal relationships, and the impact of wider structural conditions in society in shaping suicide is not considered. For instance, in examining the social meanings of suicide notes, Jack Douglas's (1967) gaze reverts inwards, focusing on recurrent personal motivations defined in terms of the desire to transform the substantive self, to gain empathy from others or to exact revenge. Similarly, Ben Fincham and his co-authors treat suicide notes as social documents that can elucidate the impact of social factors on the individual, yet these factors are limited to relationships with partners, children and institutions (Fincham et al. 2011).

In this chapter, I develop an alternative approach to reading suicide notes that emphasises their value as a mode of testimony and of bearing witness to the effects of objective social forces on the individual. In writing a suicide note, a person moves from being a victim of structural violence to a position that entails the promise of agency and the possibility of crafting the meaning of who they are. Rather than treating the suicide note as a conduit into the hidden recesses of the mind, I consider it as a prism for looking outwards and interrogating the social order and its engagement with the individual. As testimony, the suicide note resonates beyond the personal realm and poses urgent

2   Historian Christian de Goeschel uses a corpus of suicide notes to examine the phenomenon of suicide in Nazi Germany, as a means to bring 'the individual back into history' (2009, 4).

questions, challenges indifference and forces us to ask questions of ourselves. Felman and Laub observe that although speaking from a position of solitude, testimony is an act that transcends the self and is always addressed to a wider society: 'by virtue of the fact that the testimony is addressed to others, the witness, from within the solitude of his own stance, it is the vehicle of an occurrence, a reality, a stance or dimension *beyond* himself' (1992, 3). As a form of testimony, the suicide note is characterised by a spectral quality that disrupts everyday life and forces us to confront the meaning of self-imposed death. In *Spectres of Marx* (1993), Derrida refers to the figure of the spectre or ghost as something that is not present, not real, not there, but nevertheless enters into and disrupts the enclosure of whatever is present, real and there. The ghost addresses us, interrogates us with its voice and its gaze. The spectre is an ontological presence that challenges an absolute evil of forgetting and burying the dead.

In his autobiographical novel, *Suicide* (2008), which he submitted to the publishers ten days before he hanged himself, Edouard Levé portrays suicide as a form of authorship or a final act of composition that reorders life and gives it definitive meaning and significance. The novel, which recounts the suicide of his close friend at the age of 25, has been interpreted retrospectively as an elaborate suicide note, yet it reveals few clues as to Levé's own death. Instead, the book sets out a deep philosophical reflection on the meaning of suicide and of human existence itself. For Levé, his friend's suicide was a brutally poetic act that gave a sense of meaning and coherence to his life that was missing when he was alive: 'Your suicide was of a scandalous beauty' (2008, 19). Suicide, for Levé, creates a kind of reverse biography, so that a person's whole life is reinterpreted in relation to this final act:

> Those who knew you reread each of your acts in the light of your last [...] When they speak of you they start with your death before going back in time for an explanation [...] Isn't it peculiar how this final gesture inverts your biography? [...] Your final second changed your life in the eyes of others. (ibid. 33–4)

In a similar perspective, Simone Weil placed death at the centre of her philosophical project and believed that knowing how to die was more important than knowing how to live. When she died in Kent in 1943, by starving herself to death in solidarity with those living in occupied France, many interpreted it as a straightforward act of suicide. Yet her manner of death also reflected a deeply held philosophical belief that death was a fundamentally constructive project, a form of 'decreation' which was 'to make something created pass into nothingness' (Weil 1997, 78). For Weil, death was a means to transcend the material self, to repay an ontological debt associated with life, to purify oneself and to come closer to god.

Testimony has become a ubiquitous genre that crosses multiple disciplines and historical events and is proof that we live in a unique 'era of the witness' (Wieviorka 1998) or an 'age of testimony' (Felman & Laub 1992, 113). With its origins in the study of the Holocaust as the paradigmatic event of incommensurable human suffering, testimony has since been extended to cover multiple scenes of horror or suffering. Michael Rothberg emphasises the importance of directing our attention to new sites of trauma, reminding us of the need to confront experiences of extremity in everyday life. He points, as a critical example, to the status of labour under neoliberal globalised capitalism and reminds us 'to address the mutations of power and the conditions of life' (quoted by Kilby & Rowland 2014, 4).

In examining suicide notes, I draw on three key insights from testimony studies. Firstly, the value of reading, watching and listening to experiences of extreme suffering as a means to gain insight into external structures of systemic power. Suicide letters are documents that 'bear the trace of extremity within them' and can tell us something fundamental about the impact of social conditions on human experience (Miller & Tougaw 2002, 5). Secondly, testimony lays emphasis on the value of narrated experiences, and subjectivity is 'the very structure that makes testimony possible' (Oliver 2004, 81). Testimony is a 'saying the inside from the outside' and provides insights into flesh and blood experiences of historical events that lie beyond the limits of recorded facts (Felman & Laub 1992, 249). Testimony communicates a subjective truth expressed through the emotions, thoughts and sensations of the person and is a document that transmits 'the reality of an unimaginable occurrence' (ibid., 60). In testimony, we perceive how systemic processes are transposed onto the body and mind in experiences that are grounded in the particular, yet have universal human resonance. Thirdly, testimony is a social document that transcends the individual and holds relevance for society as a whole. It is a document that contains public meaning and that raises urgent ethical and moral questions about the social world that we inhabit. Treating suicide letters as testimony can therefore re-engage with a sociological tradition of suicide with its roots in the work of Emile Durkheim and Maurice Halbwachs, for whom suicide was a prism for understanding the social order.

Drawing on this critical scholarship, I define suicide letters as a mode of testimony that is located at a juncture between the everyday and the extreme that unsettles the boundaries between the two and forces us to confront extremity in everyday social life (Rothberg 2000; Silverman 2006; Pollock & Silverman 2019). In describing the world of work under contemporary neoliberalism, some critics evoke metaphors of extremity, using the paradigmatic event of the Holocaust to capture the brutalities of the economic system or of contemporary corporate practices. Critics such as Christophe Dejours have reconfigured the everyday workplace as a space that is permeated by the extreme and that bears the traces of past historical atrocities and, in particular, the legacy of the concentration camp. Hence, he evokes the symbol of the Holocaust to represent contemporary management methods and their effects on lived experience. Drawing on Hannah Arendt's concept of the 'banality of evil' used in the context of the concentration camps, he portrays work as a site of evil and suffering: 'I should add that if there is nothing exceptional about the banality of evil, in the sense that it underpins the liberal system itself, it is also implicated in totalitarian excesses, including in Nazism' (Dejours 1998, 21). Other critics have examined the continuity of a notion of the 'concentrationary' in everyday realities, exploring its representations in film, music and contemporary social and cultural theories. For Griselda Pollock and Max Silverman, the concentrationary isn't confined to the temporal specificity of the Holocaust, but instead inhabits 'the soft humus of daily life' (Jean Cayrol quoted by Silverman 2019, 5).

Such metaphors of extremity are also prevalent within cultural representations of the workplace. The notion of the 'concentrationary' is used in cinematic representations of contemporary work in the films of Laurent Cantet, *Ressources humaines* (Human Resources, 1998) and Nicolas Klotz's *La Question humaine* (The Human Question, 2007). For Matthew John, *Ressources humaines* might be interpreted as a form of 'concentrationary realism' that makes visible a systemic violence in the workplace that enslaves bodies and imprisons minds (2019, 146). *La Question humaine*, a film adaptation of a novel with the same title, depicts an occupational psychologist drawn into revelations about his bosses' connections to the Holocaust at the Parisian branch of the chemicals multinational SC Farb. The film makes an analogy between the management techniques used in the corporation to improve productive efficiency and the eliminatory practices of the Nazi regime. The lead character, Simon, is also forced to question his own use of technocratic language in relation to the dehumanising practices of the Holocaust (Austin 2015; John 2019).

Contrary to representations of the workplace as a site of extremity, I argue here that the workplace might best be understood in terms of its everydayness and its location within a normalised, rational and quotidian economic order. The workplace is situated not at a radical periphery that lies 'outside the parameters of normal reality', but is at the centre of the social world, as a space that integrates the individual into society and defines collective norms and principles (Felman & Laub 1992, 69). The workplace does not bear ostensible hallmarks of extremity, but is a space marked by order, routine and even tedium, as workers are harnessed in endless daily reiteration towards productive activities. Work seems to epitomise what Henri Lefebvre defines as everydayness, a social order located in the space between subjective experience and reified institutions that is mundane, ordinary, yet controlled:

> the everyday imposes its monotony. It is the invariable constant of the variations it develops. The days follow one another and resemble one another, and yet – here lies the contradiction at the heart of everydayness – everything changes. But the change is programmed: obsolescence is planned. Production anticipates reproduction, production produces change in such a way as to superimpose the impression of speed onto that of monotony. Some people cry out against the acceleration of time, others cry out against stagnation. They are both right. (1987, 10)

While the everyday escapes overarching structure or form, it is, according to Lefebvre, a tightly controlled space that is organised through a linear rationality that regulates the repetitive gestures of work and consumption. For Slavoj Žižek, the power of contemporary capitalism resides in its capacity to hide the extremities that it produces behind a façade of normalised everydayness. The more capitalism extends its power, the more its violence seems to be the product of a normal, routine and common-sense state of affairs (Žižek 2008a). Similarly, for Saskia Sassen, capitalism's brutalities are obscured by its sheer complexity and abstractness. Systemic violence is hard to see, difficult to capture and therefore escapes accountability: 'Complexity is part of the condition here. The more complex a system is, the harder it is to understand, the harder it is to pinpoint accountability, and the harder it is for anyone to feel accountable' (Sassen 2014, 215).

Work suicide is a form of subjective extremity that acts as a violent usurpation, a brutal intrusion of flesh and blood that violates our expectations about the ordinary world of work. Suicide letters testify to the presence of suffering at the centre of the everyday workplace and are situated at a 'troubling conjuncture of the extreme and the everyday' (Miller & Tougaw 2002, 7). This dissonance between the everyday and the extreme that is manifested by the act of work suicide is given representation in recent films. Nicolas Silhol's *Corporate* (2016) is set in the slick, synchronous and subdued setting of the fictional corporation Esen in Paris, a space of reflective glass windows, geometrical office spaces, hierarchical order and a barely contained social violence. The lead character, Emilie, a human resources manager, played by Céline Sallette, is a master of the art of managerial persuasion and is entrusted with the task of pushing employees to leave the company voluntarily without the need for formal dismissal procedures. When one of the managers she targets, Didier Dalmart, a finance director who is no longer deemed to have a desirable profile, jumps from an upper floor of the office building onto an inner courtyard, his suicide acts as a brutal intrusion of violence in the everyday. We do not see the suicide, but it is represented by a loud thud as his body hits the ground, a noise that penetrates the offices on each floor and that cannot be ignored. It becomes an audible manifestation of the extreme in the controlled and repressed social space of the corporation. We see the efforts of the company's bosses and PR team to restore order and reconfigure the suicide as a personal and familial tragedy with no connections to work. At a video conference, Emilie helps to frame the suicide as a 'drame personnel' by mentioning that Dalmart had recently separated from his wife and was living on his own. Yet the key message of the film is that the act of suicide cannot be symbolically contained, rationalised or smoothed over. As a form of exceptional violence, it spills over into everyday work and indelibly transforms this social space, destabilising relationships and forcing employees, and Emilie in particular, to ask profound moral questions of themselves.

Reading suicide notes as testimony raises important moral and ethical considerations. Whereas for survivors of historical atrocity, testimony can serve as a means of rehabilitation, of retelling events and of coming to terms with the past, the suicide letter is a final, irrevocable utterance before a person chooses death. For Jacques Derrida, testimony is inextricably bound up with the experience of survival, and it is the possibility of bearing witness following a threat of annihilation symbolised by the metaphor of ashes that leaves no traces or readable archive. Those who have confronted death and survived, speak of their experience both for themselves and as a debt paid for those who haven't survived. Testimony is the act 'of surviving in dying, of surviving, living on, before and beyond the opposition between living and dying' (Derrida 2000, 181). Yet, in the case of the suicide letter, testimony serves not to bear witness to the act of survival in the face of death, but to explain why death seemed the only recourse possible in the face of traumatic events. Reading suicide notes requires a form of ventriloquism whereby we speak on behalf of a dead person and interpret their words, as the author is not here to qualify our interpretation of them. As Patricia Yaegar observes, in reading testimony we therefore run the risk of commodifying death, by transforming someone's death into an aesthetic gesture or using it for rhetorical ends to advance academic arguments: 'And yet – how do we narrate or speak for the dead? What allows this speech to grant them proper weight, substance, dignity? If this weight is too heavy, can we go on writing? Do we want to? If the weight is too light, can we do justice to the injustices endured by the spectre?' (2002, 28). Yet, along with Yaegar, it seems that the risks of not listening or turning away carry far greater risks still, as we cease to feel the weight of the dead in our lives. In this chapter, I treat the suicide letter as an urgent posthumous form of writing that has critical testimonial value and that deserves to be collectively listened to and heard.

A Communicative Act

The majority of French work suicides appear to share a profoundly communicative, symbolic and performative dimension and are intended to transmit a spectral social message to others. Far from being a silent retreat from the world or a quiet act of self-effacement, suicide acts as a final, noisy and desperate act of communication with an audience very much in mind (Critchley 2015). Suicide is a form of 'communicative suffering' or 'strategic dramaturgy' in which self-inflicted violence is used to symbolise a perceived violence inflicted by others (Biggs 2012, 3 and 30). Costica Bradatan notes that since Antiquity, suicide has been used as an act of self-sacrifice that serves to draw attention to a cause, signal an injustice and exert social or political power. The individual becomes a 'martyr', a word that is etymologically derived from the Greek word for witness, meaning someone with first-hand knowledge who has seen how things happened and gives an account of them (the verb *martyrein* is 'to give testimony'). The suicidal individual uses his or her own dying body as a unique form of rhetoric:

> The body speaks, often persuasively, but the dying body is more convincing because it delivers its performance under the most difficult of circumstances. You can always ignore speech-makers, even the most entertaining of them, but you cannot take your eyes away from a dying body with something to say. What I've been trying to do here is to sketch a hermeneutic able to make sense of a unique rhetoric: that of the dying flesh. (Bradatan 2015, 124)

Suicide notes are 'acts of communication' that seek to justify the violent act of self-killing, elucidate its causes and communicate these reasons to others (McClelland et al. 2000, 225). Recent work suicides have been marked by an intensified production of texts, including letters, emails, texts, audio recordings and legal documents. Suicide letters are addressed to family, trade unions, bosses or the general public. In some cases, several letters are left for different recipients or the person requests that their letter is shared publicly with others. These letters have been widely published in the media, both national and international, printed in books by investigative journalists or reformulated as scripts in novels and films. In some cases, suicidal individuals communicate in other ways, by phoning someone just before their suicide, so that they have a witness and interlocutor to their act. Some survivors of suicide have written autobiographical books that recount how working conditions pushed them to attempt self-killing (Yervin 2009; Selly 2013).

The cultural practice of writing a suicide note emerged in eighteenth-century England, at a time when the press was expanding and newspapers for the first time indulged their readers in the 'luxury of grief' by publishing suicide notes (Parisot 2014, 277). Suicide notes were written when they could be read by others and newspapers gave access to a mass public audience. Newspapers also helped potential suicides to craft their notes, providing a distinctive convention characterised by the use of polite and literary language (Macdonald & Murphy 1990).[3] The desire to transform suicide into a form of publicity that reaches a broad audience is highlighted by recent cases, such as the attempted suicide of a France Télécom technician who swallowed a bottle of pills in a company car parked near a seaside resort in Brittany on 6 January 2009, having sent an email entitled 'End of me' to over a hundred employees at his company including managers, company executives and clients: 'My name is … I'm 50 years old and I'm ending my life today. Why? Because of harassment and humiliation' (Catala 2010, 48). He goes on to blame five managers whom he deems to be responsible for making his life a misery. He complains of humiliating treatment by one of his managers and of being subject to video and audio surveillance, without his knowledge.

In their letters, individuals seek to communicate to others, experiences of deep-seated trauma and anguish in their everyday working lives: 'I've become a wreck' (France Télécom, 2 July 2008); 'My job is making me suffer' (France Télécom, 10–11 August 2009); 'This life has become unbearable' (La Poste, 29 February 2012). They describe their work in terms of insufferable and unremitting torment, as a 'place of death' (France Télécom, 2 July 2008); a 'descent into hell' (Tati, 5–8 January 2012); or a 'psychological hell' (CPAM, 29 February 2012). Suicide is portrayed as a form of escape from an unbearable working life for which no other reprieve seems possible. They find themselves in a state of extreme psychological distress and lack the reserves or will to carry on. In December 2005, a 45-year-old senior manager at La Poste left a letter for his family that stated: 'Not seeing any way out of a situation that is getting worse each day, I decided to take my own life' (Barba 2013, 7). On 16 February 2007, a 38-year-old draughtsman working for Renault took his own life at home leaving a scribbled note that stated,

---

3   In France, by contrast, where suicide was subject to censorship during this period and newspapers rarely discussed it, suicide notes were very rare and most people perished without leaving one (Liberman 1991). In his study of 274 cases of suicide registered in Paris court records between 1795 and 1801, historian Richard Cobb (1978) finds evidence of only six suicide notes and observes that the suicide letter was a privilege of the wealthy and educated.

'I can't take it any more, this job is too much for me, they are going to fire me and I'm finished' (*Europe 1*, 19 May 2011). A 54-year-old France Télécom technician who threw himself under a train on 2 July 2008, left a letter for his partner that stated, 'I could no longer stay in this hell' (*Le Figaro*, 7 July 2016). Following her attempted suicide at the postal centre where she worked in Marseille, a postal worker stated in a subsequent investigation into her case: 'I was distraught. Killing myself was a way to stop everything, to end my problems. To continue working like this for the next 20 years is too painful' (Fontenelle 125). A 52-year-old manager who hanged himself in his workplace left a detailed email in which he presented his suicide as a means to bring an end to interminable pain: 'Of course, in putting an end to my daily torture and anguish this evening, I am sorting the problem'. He goes on: 'I can no longer bear to be left to die slowly without any attempt to listen to my cries for help or explain why' (*Midi Libre*, 1 March 2012).

Suicide also indicates a failure of communication and is a last attempt to make oneself heard, where all other efforts have failed. When the manager of a postal depot in Finistère, Brittany hanged himself in his workplace on 11 March 2012, he left a detailed portfolio of documents consisting of letters, emails, formal requests, audio and video recordings addressed to family members and several trade unions. He had been in conflict with two senior managers who he believed were trying to get rid of him. The portfolio contained written summaries of previous interviews with managers and two CDs, one with a video recording and one with an audio recording of earlier meetings where he sought to communicate his grievances. He also included an email addressed to the chief executive of La Poste, but never sent, in which he declared that his career was finished and that he had planned to kill himself twice over the previous six months (*Libération*, 14 March 2012). In a legal case taken by his wife against La Poste, the judge ruled in March 2016 that his suicide was a work-related accident for which the company was liable. In a different case, a 53-year-old shop manager who had worked for the discount department store Tati in Paris for 24 years, killed herself in January 2012, leaving three handwritten letters, one for the police, including cheques to pay her taxes and rent, one to her brother and one to her step-son. In the latter, she details over ten pages 'a year and a half of suffering and humiliation at work', giving precise dates and details of instances where she was bullied or intimidated by her managers. It emerged, in the enquiry into the suicide, that employees at the branch where she worked had made repeated complaints to trade unions, referring to intense pressure and miserable working conditions. In July 2018, the courts condemned her former boss to a one-year suspended prison sentence for moral harassment (*20 minutes*, 11 July 2018).

Some individuals seek to use their suicide to achieve a social purpose, by drawing attention to a perceived injustice or improving working conditions for others. Suicide is a deeply conflicted gesture that attempts to reconcile both a surrender and affirmation of personal agency and a rejection and rehabilitation of social ties (Parisot 2014). For Anthony Giddens, suicide is an attempt to assert power and impose change from a situation of utter powerlessness, and this is 'in an inverted way an attempt at *mastery*: an attempt to control and rectify an intolerable state of affairs' (1971 113). A 54-year-old France Télécom employee who threw himself under a train in July 2008 left a letter for his trade union in which he remarked: 'I only wish my gesture could serve some purpose [...] If you could talk to others or escalate this, so that others know and realise that this irresponsible lot are prepared to do anything to get people to leave' (quoted by Decèze 2008, 29). A manager at the health insurance company CPAM presents his suicide as a sacrificial act that will prevent others from suffering as he has: 'It is my duty to ensure that this can maybe help all those who might find themselves in my situation, to prevent them finishing up like me. This is the reason for this message' (*France Soir*, 1 March 2012). A postal worker who hanged himself at work stated in an email to his trade union: 'If you could try to make sure that this leads to something positive and constructive for the company and our colleagues' (*L'Humanité*, 13 March 2012). A postman who attempted suicide by hanging stated in a letter: 'I hope this gesture will serve some purpose and that my colleagues will be listened to' (*Libération*, 7 March 2013).

Alongside these broad social intentions, some individuals seek in their suicide letter to achieve an instrumental end by establishing the company's responsibility in their death and thereby helping to secure compensation for their family. Some letters are drafted in the form of formal documents that can serve as testimonial evidence in a court case. In the portfolio of documents left by a postal worker addressed to trade unions, he included a document entitled 'annex' in which he asks whether it might be possible to secure compensation for his family 'by ensuring that this desperate act is categorised as a work-related accident' (*Libération*, 14 March 2012). Similarly, in his suicide letter, a France Télécom technician who killed himself on the night of the 10 to 11 August 2009, remarks: 'France Télécom is largely responsible for what has happened to me. This must be categorised as a work-related accident and be sent to the industrial tribunal' (quoted by Catala 2010, 24).

Alongside written communications, work suicide is used as a symbolic act in which private suffering is forced into the open in a performance of violence that denounces working conditions and compels others to become witnesses. Some individuals choose to kill themselves in their place of work in order to inscribe their act of violence within the functional spaces of the office building, call centre or post office. Witnesses are forced to confront the act of suicide and a corporeal display of extreme suffering. Of the 12 suicides that took place at France Télécom in 2008, at least three, not to mention two further attempted suicides, took place in the workplace. At La Poste, a 42-year-old manager who had been on sick leave for four months took the decision to return to work on a Sunday in order to hang himself in the postal depot where he worked. In his suicide letter, he remarked: 'I wanted to do this in the workplace, because the managers are responsible' (*Ouest France*, 11 May 2016). In at least four cases of attempted suicide at France Télécom in 2009, employees tried to take their own lives in the offices where they worked and where they would be witnessed by others. On 17 March 2009, a technician who had worked for the company for 24 years and who was responsible for telecommunications networks was interrupted by colleagues whilst trying to break open window locks so that he could throw himself out. His response to his colleagues was: 'You will no longer hear from me tomorrow. I am doing it here, so that they can see. This must serve as an example' (Catala 2010, 51). On 26 May 2008, a 55-year-old public service employee and accountant attempted to throw himself out the window during a meeting with a manager and complained of unbearable pressure linked to constantly changing working methods. In an everyday workplace that negates signs of extremity under a veneer of ordered productivity, the corporeal agency of suicide pushes material suffering to the surface and forces others to confront it.

In his autobiographical account, *Ils m'ont détruit!* (They Destroyed Me!, 2009), Yonnel Dervin, a France Télécom technician who attempted suicide during a work meeting on 9 September 2009, describes the 'slow descent into hell' which led him to this act (2009, 9). The day before his suicide attempt, he had been informed by a manager that he was to be redeployed and move from his existing specialised job maintaining telephone networks to a low-skilled maintenance job repairing customers' phones. He describes how he did not want to disappear in a quiet or insignificant way, but intended to transform his suicide into a symbolic statement that would call France Télécom to account:

> Since I am reduced to nothing and to nobody, since they have slowly consumed me, I will kill myself later. But not by any means or in any place. If that seems presumptuous or naïve, it doesn't matter: I want my act to be symbolic, to explode before everyone's eyes like a terrible accusation. (ibid., 11)

He meticulously plans the details of the suicide, including the time, place and method, his clothing and the instrument he would use. He decides to kill himself during a meeting scheduled for the next day between managers and staff to discuss the ongoing restructuring process, and to use the work tool that permanently hung from his belt: 'Everyone will understand that it is the company and the company alone that has broken me after many years of dedication' (ibid., 18). During the meeting the next day, after his manager had spoken and confirmed that Dervin and a colleague were to be redeployed, Dervin stood up to express his disagreement with this decision and then plunged his work knife into his stomach. He was immediately hospitalised and subsequently recovered from his injuries.

Once a rare and extreme act associated with political protest or religious sacrifice, there has been a rise in cases of self-immolation motivated by socio-economic causes, and according to one study, there are 30 cases in France each year (*Le Monde*, 17 December 2013). Recent cases have taken place in public spaces, often in front of others, and are intended to make a dramatic social statement. The web documentary *Le Grand Incendie* (The Great Fire, 2013) examines the phenomenon of self-immolation focusing on six recent cases (four of which are work-related) in which individuals took their own life in a public place (a job centre, a hospital, a school playground, a France Télécom car park, a social housing block) to protest against working conditions, workplace bullying, benefit cuts or unemployment. The film frames the suicides explicitly as a desperate mode of communication by individuals experiencing intense social pressures who lack alternative means of expression and its subtitle reads: 'They set themselves alight to make themselves heard'. The documentary presents testimonies by suicidal individuals, family members or colleagues who recapitulate the circumstances leading to the suicide. In one testimony, the wife of a management controller who killed himself by self-immolation observes that his suicide was an extreme act of revolt and this was 'a visceral and communicative act of protest that speaks to others'. She notes that his suicide had succeeded in laying bare deplorable working conditions at France Télécom, but that in undertaking this act, he had paid the highest price imaginable.

Work suicide might be seen as a desperate attempt to reclaim voice in the face of a corporate language that strips employees of words and deprives them of subjective identity. In the contemporary workplace, alienation is no longer experienced solely as a worker's dispossession from the products he or she makes, but is characterised by an estrangement from language itself. Hence the term 'novlangue', or newspeak derived from Orwell's *1984* is used to refer to a corporate discourse which forces employees to communicate using entirely artificial and technical terms: 'The encroachment of work on life takes place within language itself which the company uses for instrumental ends' (Engélibert 2011, 52). Thierry Beinstingel's novel *Retour aux mots sauvages* (Return to Primitive Words, 2010) is closely based on the case of France Télécom, where the author himself worked for several years. It follows the narrator, Eric, an electrician who has been redeployed to the phones in a call centre when his own job is axed, against a background of rising suicides at the company. The novel depicts a world of work where the individual is forced to imbibe fake and instrumentalised words designed to persuade a client to buy a product or device. The script recited daily by Eric and his colleagues over the phone is experienced as a kind of dispossession that strips them of their sense of self: 'Sentences invented by others, recited by colleagues mechanically, the mouth a tool suspended at the microphone, the tranquil breath of learned, obvious, logical words, whispered so they never displease' (Beinstingel 2010, 32). The path towards resistance entails a recovery of self through a return to primitive words taking the form either of violence and the brutal statement of suicide or a life-affirming rehabilitation of language and of the self. Drawing on a recent suicide, construed in terms of a perverse recovery of language,

Eric observes: 'the implacable words of the person who claimed: I am killing myself because of my work. Because of. Origin, foundation, reason, motive. Brutal return to primitive words' (ibid., 105).

Blaming Work

Suicide letters are a mode of social sanction in which the act of self-destruction is used to signal a perceived injustice, designate those responsible and incite moral disapprobation. A key aspect of the suicide note is the 'negotiation of blame', as its author absolves some people of blame whilst rendering others blameworthy (McCelland et al. 2000). Maurice Halbwachs in *Les Causes du suicide* (The Causes of Suicide, 1930) argues that suicide has been used since Antiquity as a form of retribution against an enemy either within a community or belonging to an outside warring faction: 'Here, by curious inversion, the victim becomes the demon who will return after death to torment the living' (1978, 300). Although the suicidal victim is silenced, his/her enemy must answer to the causes of the former's death. What is striking in suicide letters is that they simultaneously blame work as the cause of their self-killing and express forgiveness and love towards family members. In one suicide case for which Renault was subsequently held liable, a 38-year-old technician hanged himself at home on 16 February 2007. He had been working on a new model of Laguna and was under pressure to produce the new design by a tight deadline. In a suicide letter addressed to his family, the victim made clear that work, rather than familial issues was to blame: 'This has nothing to do with you. I can't go on. This job is too much for me' (quoted by Moreira & Prolongeau 2009, 130). Similarly, a 28-year-old senior manager who killed himself by jumping from the top floor of the postal centre where he worked in Rennes on 29 December 2012, left a letter which clearly separated home from working life and blamed management for his actions: 'I should however have everything to be happy, a loving wife, an adorable daughter. However, all this professional anxiety has encroached on my private life and I can no longer experience joy like before' (*Le Nouvel Observateur*, 4 March 2012). In a related case, a 45-year-old production manager who worked for the steel manufacturing corporation Arcelor Mitall at a site in Belgium took his own life on 12 October 2013, two years after the company announced the closure of Belgian sites. In a letter addressed to his family, trade unions and the Belgian media, he denounced the chief executive of the company:

> I have been fighting for 31 years [...] Dear government, are you finally going to save jobs for thousands of families who are worth the effort? My wife and my daughter, I want you to know that I love you, but Mr Mittal has taken everything from me: my pride, civility and the courage to fight for my family.

Having started work in a factory at the age of 14, he had risen rapidly to the position of manager and was described as 'an exemplary and conscientious worker'. He requested that this letter be read at his funeral in order to raise awareness of the plight of workers at the company (*Le Monde*, 15 October 2013).

Some suicide notes engage in a 'pointing out of culprits', naming specific managers or bosses as responsible (Douglas 1971, 140). On 24 March 2009, a 56-year-old IT director at Deshoulières, a family-based porcelain factory in Chauvigny in the Poitou-Charentes region, took his own life by drowning himself in a pond. Following severe financial difficulties stemming from the rise of cheap imports from Asia, its owners sold the company to a Russian multinational. Two new bosses were recruited in 2008 in order to undertake a radical restructuring of the company. Immediately following their arrival, a nearby factory was closed down and 80 lay-offs were announced at the Chauvigny production site. In his suicide note, the IT director, who was also a trade union delegate, explicitly blamed the two new bosses for his actions, writing in capital letters: 'CYRILLE AND GERARD have killed me. The pressure and psychological bullying that they have subjected me to since 1 October 2008 have become unbearable' (*Libération*, 15 April 2009). According to the investigation into this death, the suicidal individual deplored the effects of the job losses on the local community and was divided in his role as company director and trade union representative.[4] In a different case, the suicide note of a Renault draughtsman who took his own life on 16 February 2007 names Renault's chief executive and his line manager as responsible

---

4   This suicide case inspired a theatre production by director Jean-Pierre Bodin, *Très nombreux, chacun seul*, which focuses on the atomisation of social relationships in the workplace and was staged at the Avignon Festival in summer 2012.

for his death: 'I wouldn't know how to make Gosn [*sic*] and Patrice H's shitty Top Series' (quoted by Moreira & Prolongeau 2009, 130). Because he had killed himself at home rather than in the workplace, his suicide note was critical in the successful legal case that was brought against Renault to establish its responsibility in the man's death. Suicide letters identify particular structural transformations or managerial practices in the contemporary workplace as the source of extreme subjective suffering.

Chaotic Restructuring

Company restructuring is often experienced as a profoundly destabilising process that disrupts the terms of working lives and imposes conditions of constant and meaningless change. Suicide letters often describe a workplace that has been plunged into chaos and disorder, that is subject to ceaseless change and arbitrary decisions and which has lost all sense of order, stability and ethical value. These letters give us a glimpse into economic processes at the systemic edge, revealing forms of suffering that are often obscured by rational economic processes. Saskia Sassen describes the systemic edge as 'the point where a condition takes on a format so extreme that it cannot be easily captured by the standard measures of governments and experts and thereby becomes conceptually and analytically invisible, ungraspable' (2016, 77). In May 2008, in the first wave of suicides at France Télécom, two suicides took place in close succession in north-eastern France, the first in Longwy (3 May) and the second in Strasbourg (17 May). Both employees were male technicians in their early fifties whose working lives had been rendered dysfunctional by restructuring, and both killed themselves using a gun. In the first case, the employee had recently been informed that his job was to be axed, and in the second case, the employee had been forced to endure daily changes to his schedule and was facing redeployment to a new site. He left a note stating: 'the causes of my act are my health, which is deteriorating every day, and changes to my schedule which are difficult to bear'. Both cases were presented in the criminal trial against France Télécom on 3 June 2019. Family witnesses and colleagues remarked that both employees had been happy and stable but that their lives had been flung into chaos by restructuring (*France Inter*, 3 June 2019).

This experience of restructuring as a destabilising of working life is given representation by Sophie Bruneau and Marc-Antoine Roudil in the documentary *Ils ne mouraient pas tous, mais tous étaient frappés* (They didn't all die, but they were all struck, 2005), which focuses on testimonies by four workers who have left their jobs following a physical or mental breakdown and who are filmed within the confined space of the doctor's office as they recount their experiences. Each of them describes a sudden rupture in their working life as a result of company restructuring or a takeover which transforms work and pushes them to breaking point. One of the narratives by Mme Alaoui, who has worked on an assembly line since the age of 17, describes a profound disjuncture in her working life following the takeover of her factory by an American company and the arrival of new managers. She refers to an old world of work characterised by friendship, conviviality, a sharing of food and tasks on the assembly line: 'Before it was like a family, now it has become a factory'. New management imposes productivity targets that require workers to move at accelerated speed and prohibit all forms of human interaction on the assembly line. It is through this pared-down, unmediated, visceral, yet unremarkable human experience that the film offers an indictment of the economic order.

Under the leitmotif of 'mobility', thousands of employees at France Télécom were forcibly redeployed into posts below their career level or were pushed into jobs in different cities. Hence, highly skilled engineers and technicians were forced to join the 'front line' of the company in sales roles and work as telephone operators in call centres. In one well-publicised case, a 53-year-old technician who had been redeployed to a call centre from his existing role monitoring satellite communications when the centre where he worked had been shut down, threw himself under a train on 2 July 2008. Prior to his suicide, he had sent a letter to his trade union representative that contained over a dozen documents outlining his repeated requests to management to change position. His suicide letter emphasises his frustration with his new role, for which he had no professional experience or training: 'You know, I could no longer bear to be in this hell, spending hours in front of a screen like a mechanical puppet faced with the determination of some people to let us die like dogs'. He criticises management tactics and asks his trade union to let others know what is going on: 'If you could speak about this or escalate it so that others know and realise what this reckless lot are prepared to do to get people to leave' (quoted by Decèze 2008, 29–30). On 26 April 2011, a 57-year-old management controller and father of four set fire to himself in the car park outside a France Télécom office building in Mérignac near Bordeaux upon arriving at work in the morning. A detailed open letter that he had written to company bosses in September 2009 was published in the French press after his suicide and is seen as a premonition of his later act. His letter is written in the context of the NExT restructuring plan that introduced massive job cuts through a policy of forced redeployment. The letter veers from the pragmatic – he observes that restructuring is necessary in order for France Télécom to survive – to a scathing attack on management practices that have rendered employees' lives intolerable. He describes how thousands of employees have been forced into jobs (often in call centres) for which they have no professional experience or training. He observes that employees who take their own lives have a similar profile to himself and are senior managers in their fifties who are deemed to be worthless, 'cadres dispossessed of their power'. Reflecting on his own situation, he remarks, 'I am part of this segment' and concludes 'suicide remains the solution' (*Le Parisien*, 27 June 2019). The destabilising effects of restructuring on the workplace are reaffirmed in another letter by a colleague of a France Télécom employee who killed himself on 17 May 2008. In this letter, published in the press, the colleague states: 'we live in a situation of permanent stress, pressure, restructuring and doubts about the future' (quoted by Decèze 2008, 30–1).

Work Intensification
According to recent studies, the majority of victims of work suicide in large French companies had no prior history of mental illness and were typically committed, conscientious and dedicated employees who tended to identify their own personal goals with those of the company (Dejours & Bègue 2009; Baudelot & Gollac 2015; Clot & Gollac 2017). In this respect, French suicides seems to bear similarities with the Japanese phenomenon of *karo-jisatsu* or suicide by overwork that is rooted in a highly pressurised corporate culture (Kawanishi 2008).[5] Linked partly to a workplace ethos which emphasises the values

---

5   In Japan, the phenomenon of *karo-jisatsu* (suicide by overwork) is considered an urgent public health concern on which the government has passed legislation to protect workers. One thousand of the estimated 30,000 suicides that take place in Japan each year are deemed to be work-related (*Red Pepper*, 16 September 2014). According to police sources, 1,978 people took their own lives in 2016

of dedication, sacrifice and duty and expects employees to devote themselves fully to the company, *karo-jisatsu* affects those exposed to extremely long hours, who are under enormous mental and emotional pressure to attain a goal or meet a target. They are typically 'corporate warriors', exemplary employees who demonstrate a work ethic and commitment that is highly valued by the company (Kawanishi 2014, 65). For suicide experts such as Edwin Shneidman, suicide is a desperate form of escape from something that enslaves the person and from which they can find no other means of release:

> The common *purpose* of suicide is to seek a *solution*. Suicide is not a random act. It is never done without purpose. It is a way out of a problem, a dilemma, a bind, a difficulty, a crisis, an unbearable situation [...] Suicide is best understood as moving toward the complete stopping of one's consciousness and unendurable pain, especially when cessation is seen by the suffering person as the solution – indeed the perfect solution – of life's painful and pressing problems. (Shneidman 1996, 130).

For victims of *karo-jisatsu*, suicide represents an exit from a working life that is experienced as relentless torment and from which no other escape seems possible. In the French context, it might be said that work suicides derive less from the impact of an enduring corporate culture than from more recent neoliberal transformations that have disrupted working conditions across large French companies.

In many recent suicide cases, an employee has taken his or her own life following a period of intense pressure linked to the exigencies of meeting company goals. In the French context, suicide by overwork is often attributed to the phenomenon of 'burn out' where an employee experiences a severe breakdown as a result of work pressures. Burn out occurs following a period of hyperactivity, when an otherwise zealous and conscientious employee works continuously to meet often unmanageable targets. In examining the phenomenon of burn out and investigating why work increasingly kills employees, Emmanuelle Anizon and Jacqueline Remy describe the phenomenon in the following terms:

because of exhaustion linked to overwork or workplace bullying (National Police Agency, Government of Japan, https://www.npa.go.jp/publications/statistics/index.html).

The net closes in on them as they wait for some form of recognition that never comes, as they are overwhelmed with demands that are impossible to meet and take on the burden of a vast workload. They discover that their managers are incompetent, cynical and unethical. They suddenly have the impression that they are going around in circles, that they are not good enough, that they are trying to reach the impossible. (2016, 12)

The successful legal cases taken by families against Renault rested on demonstrating that a suicidal individual's long working hours and vast workload was not a matter of personal choice, but rather a response to external structural pressures and, in particular, the constraints imposed on them by the company's strategic plan. At La Poste, suicides often involved postmen and women whose delivery rounds were vastly increased, as they were pushed to take on the rounds of other employees and accelerate their delivery times. At France Télécom, suicides were typically highly skilled employees who had been forcibly redeployed to call centres where they were subject to intense target-driven pressures, routine surveillance and mistreatment.

Suicide letters reveal the mental and emotional states that precede a suicide or attempted suicide that is linked to chronic overwork. In one testimonial account that was published in book form (*Quand le travail nous tue*, When Work Kills Us), former human resources manager Aude Selly describes the circumstances that led to her attempted suicide at the age of 30 whilst working in her 'ideal job' for a large retail company (Selly 2013). Having secured a desirable and well-paid position after a rigorous four-stage interview process, Selly was keen to prove her worth to her managers, particularly as the previous occupant of the post could not cope with the pressure and had walked out. She observes that there was no official job description for her role and she found herself accepting ever more tasks until her workload became completely unmanageable. She worked long hours, arriving at work before anyone else, leaving later and taking no breaks throughout the day. She began to reflect on her job obsessively, lying awake at night ruminating over unfinished tasks, so that she developed severe insomnia. What is striking in her account is that the psychological effects of the extreme pressure she experienced had physical symptoms and she developed a musculo-skeletal disorder, insomnia, heart palpitations and a digestive disorder. She opens the book by describing her journey to work one morning, when she broke down in tears on the train and was paralysed with anxiety. Having been taken to see a doctor, she was subsequently hospitalised, placed under the care of a psychiatrist and signed off work for over a year. She describes burn out as an experience that is distinctive from other forms of depression or exhaustion, in that the person experiences a complete emotional, physical and mental breakdown that requires hospitalisation and a prolonged period of sick leave.

At France Télécom, a technician who attempted suicide in December 2008 made a statement to a subsequent workplace enquiry in which he referred to the pressure of an ever-increasing number of targets and a stress that spills over from work into private life. He evoked experiencing 'constant pressure', to the extent that 'you end up exploding'. He observed that 'all that counts is the figures [...], there is no separation between work life and home life' (Catala 2010, 50–1). Another technician who attempted suicide on 6 January 2009 left a letter for his colleagues in which he complained of an unmanageable workload: 'I have so many clients [...] I'm unable to finish what I started' ibid., 48). He describes a feeling of being overwhelmed and crushed by work demands and points the finger at five managers he deems to be responsible for his distress. The ongoing case against La Poste for corporate manslaughter brought by the wife of a senior communications manager who took his own life on 25 February 2013, has linked his suicide to the 'excessive pressure' he experienced holding two separate jobs in the company (quoted by Cazes & Hacot 2015, 199).

Underwork
Paradoxically, suicides have been triggered both by the pressures of overwork and the psychological distress of underwork, when employees deliberately have work taken away from them against their will as a means to humiliate and isolate them. Many recent suicide cases involve employees who were victims of a 'mise au placard' (literally 'closeting'), an abusive management technique whereby an employee, typically over fifty years of age and on a high salary, is deliberately sidelined in order to get them to leave the company of their own accord. An employee of a health insurance service who hanged himself on 29 February 2012 sent an email to his managers, family members, colleagues and a member of parliament entitled 'Adieu': 'I wanted to

inform you that my act is the direct consequence of the psychological hell that I have endured over the past two years which I have tried to overcome with all my strength for my wife and children, but today I can no longer continue'. He describes his sense of pride in building a successful career and climbing the ranks from a modest file-keeping role to the status of manager. Following a merger between two sites, he was sidelined and had all his responsibilities removed: 'I have been professionally assassinated and psychologically destroyed'. He ends the letter poignantly by stating 'My name is … I would be 52 on 31 May 2012' (*Midi Libre*, 1 March 2012).

In some suicide testimonies, employees describe their self-killing as the material fulfilment of a slow violence initiated by management who were intent on excluding them. In a statement made at an enquiry into his attempted suicide on 5 November 2007, a 54-year-old France Télécom technician described how, because of his age and salary level, he was targeted by eliminatory management tactics and left without any work. He was employed in a Paris branch of the company that specialised in providing software packages to business, which had seen three suicide attempts by employees between 2007 and 2009. He describes how when a project was set up in the branch, he and other older workers were suddenly left with nothing to do:

> No progression, no training, I was abandoned […] I was left without work from the end of 2006 and throughout 2007 […] Suddenly I realised I had nothing to do […] You wait for work and nothing comes. A new division was being set up and there was to be a new distribution of work: work for the old employees of which I am one and a new project with plenty of work for the young employees. (Catala 2010, 46)

In a testimony that forms part of a case for gross negligence against France Télécom, a 54- year-old technician who attempted suicide in October 2009 described how from 2007 onwards, he was obliged to attend 'reorientation seminars' where he had to rewrite his CV and was offered a financial incentive to leave the company and set up as an estate agent. On 1 January 2008, his job was axed and all his work was taken away, but he was not formally notified and continued to work even though his job did not exist in contractual terms. He was only informed three months later in a meeting with a human resources manager when he was given the option of either accepting three alternative job offers or leaving the company. Meanwhile, his desk and belongings were moved and placed in a workspace for secretarial staff (*Nouvel Observateur*, 8 July 2016).

Management Bullying

In a context in which line managers are exhorted by companies to pressurise employees to increase their productivity or leave, bullying has become a routinised management strategy. Suicide letters denounce management practices based on harassment, bullying and intimidation that are designed to force them to act against their will, to push them out of their job or humiliate them. These letters have been used in a number of high-profile legal cases against large companies that are accused of using bullying as an institutionalised management strategy. The French labour code prohibits 'moral harassment' defined in terms of harm to the dignity, the physical or psychological health of the victim or his or her career' (Social modernisation law of 2002). Alongside the Labour Code, French criminal law allows for a criminal sanction against a perpetrator of moral harassment, who can be sentenced to up to two years of imprisonment and receive a large fine (article 222-33-2 of the French Criminal Code). On the night of the 10 to 11 August 2009, a France Télécom technician took his own life and left a letter for his family complaining of bullying by a series of managers whom he named. He had been redeployed to a customer-facing role seven months previously, which was a source of considerable distress. The year before his suicide, occupational doctors had issued a warning about rising mental health problems amongst employees at the branch where he worked. In his letter, he stated: 'My job is making me suffer [...] X is persecuting me [...] I can't bear this job and France Télécom doesn't give a damn [...] I have been criticised, insulted and humiliated [...] I am furious with this company' (Catala 2010, 24). In another case, a 51-year-old employee who worked at a call centre in Nancy killed himself in February 2011, four days after appearing before an industrial tribunal in relation to a claim of bullying that he had allegedly suffered at his workplace since 2008. A work inspector had confirmed in an earlier enquiry that he had been a victim of bullying by his manager. He left a letter blaming his employer, but its contents were not published (*Le Figaro*, 3 March 2011).

A Contested Space

A testimony is not a neutral affirmation of truth but a biased interpretation of events that is often confronted by competing narratives. Suicide letters are situated in a highly contested discursive space in which they are challenged by countervailing interpretations of the causes and meaning of suicide. According to Slavoj Žižek (2008b), a situation of profound crisis can open up opportunities for new narratives to be constructed which in turn reorder events, assign blame and impose new representations of the social world: 'When the normal run of things is traumatically interrupted, the field is open for a "discursive" ideological competition'. Indeed, he suggests that the consequences of a crisis are determined less by real events than by how these events are ideologically reconstructed and by which particular narratives come to prevail. The French suicide crisis was characterised by the emergence of two opposing narratives, each of which provided a very different interpretation of its meaning. The first narrative, articulated by suicidal individuals and their families, attributed the deaths to social and structural factors, such as working conditions, restructuring or tyrannical management practices. The second, put forward by business and political elites, sought to individualise the causes of suicide, linking them to flaws of character or mental imbalance and disconnecting them from any links to work.

Debates over the meaning and causes of suicide have prevailed in France since the nineteenth century, with a division between those who see suicide as an individual problem of a medical or biological nature and those who locate its causes in social forces external to the individual. Etienne Esquirol, who was the main proponent of a psychiatric theory of suicide in the first half of the nineteenth century, expressed a prevalent view that suicide was an expression of madness, as he wrote in 1838 that 'Man takes his own life only in delirium, and all suicides are insane' (quoted by Minois 1999, 320). This approach was challenged by the rise of sociological theories of suicide towards the end of the century and, in particular, through the work of Emile Durkheim. Anthony Giddens refers to 'the suicide problem in French sociology', whereby emerging sociological explanations of suicide oppose individualist psychological approaches which had dominated for much of the century (Giddens 1971). In the case of recent work suicides, these differing narratives have little to do with scholarly differences about the meaning of suicide, and instead express the vested concerns of two virulently opposed groups. Whilst families seek to attain justice, moral recognition and, in some cases, financial compensation, companies seek to thwart attempts at legal and financial litigation and to protect their corporate image and reputation.

A work-related suicide is not a *de facto* social category, but a reality that needs to be legally and discursively constructed after the event, through an analysis of documentary evidence including suicide letters, witness statements, medical reports and workplace enquiries. Suicide letters have been widely used as documentary evidence in judicial cases to establish suicide as a work-related accident, thereby rendering a company legally and financially liable. In French legislation, any suicide that takes place in the workplace is presumed to be work-related and the burden of proof is on the employer to establish that it is not connected to work. This presumption of causality is meant to protect the employee (in an attempted suicide) or his or her family and circumvent the need for them to engage in legal action in the aftermath of a traumatic event in order to prove that the employer is liable. Even in cases where a suicide takes place outside of work, it is still investigated as a work-related accident where the victim (in the case of attempted suicide) or the family can prove a causal link to work, based on the evidence of a suicide letter, a work uniform, a company car or work tool. In these cases, the suicide letter acts as a critical piece of evidence in mounting a prosecution case against a company (Lerouge 2014).

Company bosses tend to present a narrative that configures suicide as an isolated, sporadic or random phenomenon that is disconnected from any structural links to the workplace. Following the suicide of a technician on 2 July 2008 who left a letter explicitly blaming France Télécom, company bosses vehemently denied any connection between his death and working conditions and affirmed to the press that recent suicides are 'in general independent cases with multiple causes' (quoted by Du Roy 2009a, 16). Similarly Louis-Pierre Wenes, deputy director, declared that employee suicides were 'particular situations often linked to great personal difficulties' (Du Roy 2009b). Following the death of a 32-year-old France Télécom employee who killed herself at work in Paris, chief executive Didier Lombard callously referred to a suicide 'trend' ('cette mode du suicide') at the company, a remark that triggered his subsequent dismissal from the company (*Le Monde*, 16 September 2009). Despite the efforts of France Télécom to deny any link to the workplace, this particular suicide was recognised by the social security authorities as a work-related accident and the company was required to pay compensation to the family. Following two suicides at France Télécom in May 2008, one of whom left a letter blaming work, France Télécom's regional director made a statement claiming that there was no evident relationship between the two suicides and their work, and refused to recognise the suicide letter as legitimate because it was not dated (Rabatel 2010). When a 51-year-old employee who took his own life in July 2009 left a letter blaming France Télécom for his actions, management responded dismissively, saying 'there are always multiple causes of a suicide' (*La Croix*, 29 July 2009). During a meeting with trade unions on 18 September 2009, France Télécom managers insisted that the suicides were nothing to do with management and were 'individual dramas' with no connection to work (Rabatel 2011, 5). When he was placed under judicial investigation in 2012 on charges of working bullying, Lombard continued to dissociate the suicides from workplace factors and emphasised the pressures of external financial constraints and the need to save the company in the context of a competitive global market. In an interview published in *Le Monde*, he protested his innocence and affirmed, 'I forcefully reject the idea the [restructuring] plans, vital to the survival of the company, might have been the cause of these human tragedies' (*Le Monde*, 5 July 2012).

Similarly, when French political leaders intervened in the France Télécom suicides after a long period of silence, it was often to minimise their significance. The then Minister of Work, Xavier Darcos commented that suicide cases at France Télécom were unexceptional by national standards. In another statement, he trivialised the working conditions that drove individuals to suicide and remarked, 'there is something worse than stress at work and that is stress when out of work' (quoted by Diehl & Doublet 2010, 92). In his statements, Darcos tended to invoke vague and mysterious factors, referring either to global economic processes beyond human control or to the unfathomable human impulses that push someone to kill themself: 'a suicide at work is inevitably an emotional event, even if clearly one doesn't take one's own life simply because things are going badly at work' (quoted by Rabatel 2010, 44). Following the twenty-third suicide by an employee at the company, Claude Guéant, the general secretary at the Elysée asserted in a statement that 23 suicides could not simply be reduced to 'a problem of work organisation' (quoted by Rabatel 2011, 5). In a radio interview on 29 September 2009, Xavier Bertrand, then head of the ruling right-wing party the UMP, defended France Télécom's chief executive, arguing that he could not have foreseen the wave of suicides taking place and added that even the trade unions were in the dark about the impending crisis (ibid.).

This conflict between competing narratives was evident in the case of a 39-year-old engineer at Renault who jumped from a walkway on the fifth floor onto the lobby of the Technocentre where he worked outside of Paris on 20 October 2006. Like his colleagues, he had been placed under intense pressure since the introduction of the Contrat 2009 restructuring plan that had vastly increased the workload and production targets of all employees. In the face of what she described as the 'fortress' mentality of company bosses and their alleged efforts to tamper with evidence, his wife launched judicial proceedings against the company (Moreira & Prolongeau 2009, 48). In the initial enquiry that followed the suicide, management rebutted any suggestion that the suicide was work-related and intimated that the engineer was experiencing marital difficulties and that this was the source of his distress. In the court case to determine the cause of suicide, Renault drew on evidence from a 'psychological autopsy' based on interviews with family and friends conducted after the suicide in order to argue that he was psychologically vulnerable and suffering from 'a major anxiety-depressive syndrome' (*Le Monde*, 8 November 2009). However, the Versailles Court of Appeal ruled in favour of the wife and condemned Renault for gross negligence on 19 May 2011. The judge concluded that the engineer had been burdened with an unmanageable workload and that his physical signs of suffering and distress had been ignored.

In an interview with French writer Hervé Hamon, chief executive of La Poste Jean-Paul Bailly expresses a conventional view amongst business elites that work suicides are exceptional incidents which are at odds with an otherwise contented, fulfilled and secure workforce. In his view, suicides affected employees who were socially lacking or losers ('des gens un peu inadaptés') who were unable to cope with change, stuck in the past and often inclined towards depression: 'My diagnosis [...] is that there isn't a malaise at La Poste, but certain employees find themselves in difficulty when restructuring is combined with professional failings and personal vulnerabilities. The suicide rate in our company is lower than that of the general population' (Hamon 2013, 84, 83). For Bailly, trade unions had manipulated suicide cases, turning incidents of private tragedy into an instrument of political bargaining and had exaggerated and amplified their significance.

These contesting voices are represented in the interactive web documentary *Le Grand Incendie* (The Great Fire, 2013), which presents a diversity of testimonies linked to recent cases of suicide and attempted suicide by self-immolation. The film presents the testimonies on screen in the form of sonic waves, but the spectator can only listen to one voice at a time by clicking on a particular wave. At the top of the screen are official speeches and comments by politicians and company bosses and at the bottom are the personal testimonies of suicidal individuals and their families. The former enunciate economic arguments that emphasise the value of work, the pressures of global competition and the need for workers to adapt to necessary change. The personal testimonies, by contrast, focus on stories of immense suffering, describing the circumstances which led an individual to resort to suicide. For each case, the film uses a stationary camera to present a single unchanging scene, that of the spot where a suicide has taken place, whilst we listen to these different oral testimonies. The scenes present ordinary and functional spaces, and there is nothing to distract us from the dramatic intensity of the act that has been committed. We hear the case of a 43-year-old unemployed man who set himself alight outside an employment agency in Nantes on 13 February 2013 when his benefits were cut. The suicide letter that he wrote is read out and expresses the profound sense of injustice that motivated him when he exceeded the maximum number of working hours allowed and lost his benefits.[6] We hear the testimony of his wife, who describes her husband's deep sense of betrayal when, having lost his job, he was then refused the help that he needed. We also hear statements by government ministers who intone against an overin-dulgent and lavish benefits system, one that promotes dependency and

6   The man in question had been sanctioned by the employment agency for failing to declare a temporary job which he had held in August. He had worked throughout the month of December as a night maintenance worker in a transport company. He was required to refund 600 euros to the employment agency and his rights to benefits were cut, placing him on the 'allocation minimum' (*Libération*, 11 March 2013).

discourages individual responsibility. Suicide is presented in the form of a cacophony of discordant voices each of which is asserting a claim on the meaning of the suicide.

Conclusion

Jacques Derrida emphasises the importance of testimony and of bearing witness, as a form of 'surviving in dying' in which the witness speaks out on behalf of those who are no longer here (2005, 66). The horror of survival does not reside in confronting or recounting the experiences of dead victims, but in forgetting the dead or refusing to bear their weight on our shoulders. While suicide notes are intensely private documents written during moments of trauma, they are also turned outwards onto an external social world and seek to bear witness to the effects of external forces on lived experiences. In an economic order that hides the human suffering that brings products and services to us, suicide letters force suffering into the open in a violent act of enunciation. They act as a form of radical social accusation that subverts top-down economic discourses that present economic transformations as necessary, rational and inescapable. In their letters, suicidal individuals seek to apportion blame, challenge social injustice and improve conditions for others. Their suicide is not a silent retreat from the world, but a noisy and desperate act of communication that calls into question the values underpinning the economic order as a whole.

Drawing on testimony studies, *I situate suicide letters at a juncture between the everyday and the extreme that unsettles a veneer of normalised social reality in the contemporary workplace.* These letters are not confined to marginal spaces at the radical periphery, nor are they enclosed within a particular moment of history; instead they spill over into everyday life and into a continuous present. Some critics invoke a metaphor of extremity and the paradigm of the Holocaust to denote the violence of contemporary management practices and economic processes. They compare social relations in the neoliberal workplace to those of the concentration camp, where cruelty and violence towards others were a primitive means of survival. I have suggested here that the workplace is best understood in terms of everydayness and that this is a routine, ordered and functional space in which productive activity is harnessed into endless repetition. Analysing the everyday and localised spaces of the workplace can make visible a model of neoliberal and financialised capitalism in which the quest for profit takes precedence over human life and pushes some workers to extreme acts of self-destruction.

Chapter 3

Going Postal

The term 'going postal' denotes a state of becoming extremely and uncontrollably angry, often to the point of violence and usually in a workplace context. It entered American slang following a series of rage killings during the 1980s and 1990s, when workers, notably in several cases employed by the US Postal Service (USPS), went on killing sprees, shooting co-workers, managers and members of the public, before turning the gun on themselves.[1] In the media, these incidents were framed as the work of a lone and mentally deranged individual who had suddenly snapped with unforeseen and tragic consequences. The causes were to be found in the disturbed mind or psychopathic tendencies of the individual killer. Yet rage killings were not random acts of violence that came out of the blue, but rather the consequence of historically determined structural transformations that took place in the workplace at a specific moment in time. Mark Ames situates this phenomenon in economic transformations introduced under Reagan, when constant restructuring, downsizing, and lay-offs became the *modus operandi* for corporate America. The new corporate morality prioritised competition and shareholder value and dispensed with the

---

1   The first incident of workplace rage from which the term 'going postal' was coined took place on 20 August 1986 in Edmond, Oklahoma, when postman Patrick Sherrill shot and killed 14 employees and injured six others before killing himself with a shot to the forehead. A notorious recent example involved Stephen Craig Paddock, who was responsible for the 2017 Las Vegas shooting where he shot 58 people at a country music festival from his hotel room, before killing himself with his gun. Paddock was a former postman, having worked for USPS between 1976 and 1978. Thirty-five people have been killed in 11 US post office shootings since 1983 (*Insurance Journal*, 15 June 2019).

notion that companies should provide basic rights and security for their workforce. It was no coincidence that incidents of workplace violence were concentrated amongst postal workers. American postal services were the largest and earliest agency to undergo semi-privatisation and bore the brunt of Reagan-era economic transformations. Ames observes that the first year the federal government stopped subsidising USPS was the year the first postal shooting took place:

> Do people just snap when they go postal? Do they act 'without any cause or provocation' [...]? Or are they reacting to grievances both specific and institutional: grievances that we are barely able to see because we lack distance, grievances which seem as banal and part of the natural turn-of-the millennium landscape as strip malls and stress-palpitations, yet grievances which will be perceived as obviously unbearable twenty, thirty, fifty years from now? (2015, 67)

Rage killings, for Ames, were a systemic phenomenon that went beyond individual mental pathology and called into question the foundational values and structures underpinning the American economic model.

During the 2000s, France experienced its own home-grown version of the going postal phenomenon. Unlike the US, where workplace rage was directed against others in acts of murderous violence, in France, postal violence was usually internalised by the individual employee, giving rise to a series of suicides and attempted suicides by postal workers. In the French context, rage against working conditions triggered acts of self-inflicted violence that rarely implicated others, except in the guise of witnesses to the act of suicide. According to one account, 97 employees at La Poste took their own lives or attempted suicide between 2009 and 2013 (Burgi & Postier 2013). Other sources place this figure much higher. In a communiqué to government, the SUD trade union accused La Poste of bearing responsibility for over 200 suicides amongst its employees between 2008 and 2012 (*InfoSocial-RH*, 3 September 2013). According to another internal source at La Poste, there were 50 employee suicides in 2016 alone, a figure confirmed by two trade unions but challenged by management (*Le Point*, 16 December 2016). In 2016, La Poste was forced to suspend its restructuring plans temporarily following stark warnings from a range of occupational health experts who pointed to a mental health crisis that was endangering the lives of employees (*Le Figaro*, 14 October

2016). Press headlines evoked a 'suicide wave' at the company and drew comparisons with an earlier suicide crisis at its former affiliate, France Télécom. Newspapers published suicide notes by former postal workers and television news programmes interviewed employees who blamed organisational restructuring for creating unbearable pressures in their daily lives. Documentary films investigated the circumstances of suicide cases, often contrasting the extreme and singular act of violence with the dull and functional ordinariness of the post office space. Following the pattern established in the US, French postal suicides make visible historically specific working conditions and elucidate the impact of structural transformations on flesh and blood experiences of work. French suicides emerged at a particular juncture, following the liberalisation of La Poste, a giant, formerly state-owned company and as it was transforming itself from a *service public* into a commercial enterprise driven by a new logic of competitiveness and economic profit. Suicides coincided with the implementation of a vast restructuring programme that was designed to transform the terms of working life and define a new workplace culture in which commercial gain became the *sine qua non* of working activity.

This chapter investigates the series of suicides by French postal workers during the 2000s, situating them in the context of the company's liberalisation and subsequent restructuring. For many postal workers, restructuring was experienced not as a piecemeal economic reform or an incremental change, but as a 'cultural revolution' that disrupted the deeply held values and relationships by which they defined themselves and their place in the world (Teissier 1997, 14). Beyond its impact on external material conditions of work, restructuring was experienced by some as a kind of existential crisis that called into question modes of social belonging and collective identity. Economic reform came into conflict with a public service culture that gave meaning to individual work and constituted an inviolable ideological whole, so that the dismantling of this culture was experienced as a 'splintering of the self' (ibid., 85). La Poste's restructuring seems to correspond to what Emile Durkheim describes as a situation of profound social crisis or 'disturbances of the collective order' that undermine the values, meaning and identity by which individuals define themselves (Durkheim 1930, 271). Such moments of crisis, according to Durkheim, tend to generate 'anomie' or a moral and social disintegration that may trigger suicidal tendencies.

This chapter examines the new modes of surveillance that were introduced across the company during restructuring, which were intended to measure, control and prescribe working activity. I draw on Michel Foucault's (1991) conception of disciplinary surveillance to examine how these methods went beyond external changes and sought to transform workers themselves, in their ways of being, thinking and acting. Restructuring sought to achieve a conversion of the individual employee by eradicating internalised public-sector norms and inculcating mannerisms, values and behaviour that were honed towards commercial ends. In her ethnographic study of postal workers in a Parisian suburb, Fabienne Hanique (2014) observes that restructuring sought not only to modernise structures and practices, but to modernise workers' subjectivities and instil values that were attuned to the commercial goals of the company.

The chapter combines an analysis of critical scholarship on the French workplace, with a study of primary material, including internal company documents, worker testimonies and suicide letters. French postal services have been the focus of a number of fascinating ethnographic studies that provide valuable insight into everyday work and, in particular, the impact of structural transformations on lived experiences (Siblot 2006; Vezinat 2012; Hanique 2014). These studies bear witness to experiences of despair, trauma and disorientation amongst workers, as the company underwent a 'cultural modernisation' (Hanique 2014, 7). As for the other companies studied in this book, I draw on a corpus of suicide letters in which postal workers seek to explain the reasons why work has driven them to such desperate extremes. The chapter draws on a close analysis of 21 suicide cases at La Poste from 2005 onwards (18 suicides and three attempted suicides), 11 of which took place in the workplace. Of these 21 cases, ten left suicide letters in various forms, including letters, notes, emails, texts, formal documents and audio recordings. We will see that whilst liberalisation and restructuring were justified in terms of the company's survival in the face of competition, suicide letters explain why the pressures generated by these transformations pushed these workers towards self-killing.

Postal Myths

In the iconic post-war film *Jour de fête* (*The Big Day*, 1949), postman François, played by the film's director, Jacques Tati, is the soul of a rural community, roaming its country lanes and village square every day on a bicycle, delivering letters and thereby connecting this secluded rural place to the outside world. François is amiable, bumbling and clownish, and his daily delivery round always culminates in absurd comic exploits. More than a village eccentric, François is a metaphor for a certain vision of France, as a familiar, unchanging, yet vanishing world that is struggling to find its feet on the cusp of post-war modernisation. When the fair comes to town, François and a neighbour peek into the cinema tent set up in the village square, where they glimpse a newsreel about US postal services. They see an impressively modern, mechanised and highly efficient system that delivers vast volumes of mail speedily to the population. The American postman is portrayed as a daredevil, who takes to the skies by plane or jumps to earth in a parachute, defying danger to fulfil his postal mission. Unlike the clumsy François, he is brave, dutiful, sexy and unwaveringly efficient. When the villagers taunt François about his slow and backward delivery methods, he sets out to prove them wrong. He is determined to become more 'American', speeding up his movements, streamlining his gestures and pedalling harder around the village. When he has to deliver a broken telephone to headquarters in the front basket of his bicycle on a quiet country road, he passes an American jeep and pretends to be making an important call to Paris on the phone. The American soldiers in the jeep are so flabbergasted to discover such technology in backward rural France that they veer off the road into a field. Whilst alluding to the technological and cultural advances of the US, the film ultimately reasserts the authenticity and necessity of French rural life with its traditions, seasonal cycles and conviviality. The film expresses the triumph of a certain ideal of traditional France over the cold and efficient modernism of America and its inhuman pursuit of productivity (Bellos 1999).

Alongside a functional mandate to deliver mail, the postman or postwoman today continues to embody a certain ideal of France, rooted in notions of public service, community and cultural belonging. In the delivery round, the postman enacts an abstract notion of citizenship in the everyday, transforming it into a concrete human encounter that is repeated a million times over, across the French territory. The figure of the postman is cherished in French public life representing as he does 'the first sympathetic incarnation of the state and of public service' (Cazes & Hacot 2015, 27). According to opinion polls (TNS Sofres), the postman is the most appreciated occupation in France after the baker, and 92 per cent of those surveyed saw him as a figure of trust and reliability (RTL, 30 October 2012). The unique status of the postman reflects that of La Poste itself, as an institution steeped in tradition whose historical development mirrors that of the French nation itself. Hence, French postal services were critical to the construction of a modern, centralised nation state in the period that followed the French Revolution. Postal services, hitherto at the service of the king, were transformed into a public service that incarnated the values of the Republic and extended the influence of the state across the national territory. As a state administration, postal services were governed directly by a ministry in Paris which voted on its budget and nominated its chief executives. In 1793, postal employees were given the status of *fonctionnaires* (public service employees) and were entrusted with the mission of representing the state in civic life and safeguarding the general interest. By the end of the nineteenth century, the postal service, then known as PTT, had incorporated telegraph, telephone and banking services, and became a vast state-controlled network of communication and public service provision.

As a long-standing public service, La Poste belongs to the French national imaginary and is a 'major fragment of our national story' and a 'founding institution of the republican pact' underpinned by a 'legitimising myth' (Brillet 2004, 21). La Poste's familiar insignia, the yellow van, the bird in flight, the post box, are cultural signifiers that communicate a sense of cultural identity, community and belonging. Leading intellectuals such as Roland Barthes have contributed to this mythical image of La Poste. In a 1964 essay, Barthes observed that the postage stamp, beyond its economic function in gathering taxes, is a mirror held up to everyday French civilisation. It reflects concrete and material economic activity, that of building bridges or constructing monuments, but also represents an enduring cultural legacy and heritage. The stamp, according to Barthes, is a signifier of France's identity, telling the French who they are, how they think and how they live (Musée de la Poste 2015).

Beyond a transaction of wage labour, the postal worker participates in a moral and symbolic universe that gives meaning to everyday work and defines a mode of subjective identity and social belonging. Although La Poste stopped recruiting fonctionnaires in 2002 and new employees are hired mainly under private and short-term contracts (CDD), 41.8 per cent of the workforce are still fonctionnaires who are shaped by a particular workplace culture (*La Croix*, 27 August 2018). Recruited through open competition, where they had to demonstrate high levels of general culture and educational attainment in maths, French, history and geography, the postal worker held social status and prestige and wielded administrative power in the local area. In the words of a retired postal inspector: 'Postmen were lords. They made the laws, not the bosses' (Cazes & Hacot 2015, 121). The role of the fonctionnaire is bound up with a specific employment status that offered job security, career progression based on length of service, and social benefits. He or she was the guardian of the interests of the state and in return was guaranteed certain privileges and given protection from the vagaries of political power and the market. In his analysis of workplace culture in French postal services, Claude Teissier notes that a postman or woman's work combines external norms and overarching values with internal forms of subjective identification and individual engagement: the postal worker is embedded in 'a normative system that determines attitudes, behaviour and influences affect, resulting in a phenomenon of identification with a public service mission and to the principle of equality etc. that makes change very difficult. Because change inevitably requires a redefinition of forms of identification' (Teissier 1997, 281).

The myths associated with an idealised public service are also propagated by La Poste itself as part of its corporate marketing and branding. If public service is a mode of socio-cultural belonging for the worker, it is also a marketing tool deployed by the company to boost product sales. In its advertising, La Poste panders to a nostalgic image of the postman as a familiar and dutiful figure who embodies timeless civic virtues in a fast-changing world. In its glossy and nostalgic book *Facteurs en France* (Postmen in France, 2006), La Poste celebrates the postman as a symbol of everyday conviviality and duty whose daily round preserves a precious cultural legacy in a world of constant change and upheaval. Presenting the lives of 51 postmen and women, the book juxtaposes scenic photos of the delivery round with personal testimonies that recount passion, conviction and an unflinching commitment to the job. The postman or woman appears almost always on a bicycle and often engaged in unhurried conversation at a farmhouse door, at the local butchers or the garden fence. The backdrop is invariably a sun-drenched rural scene or a quiet medieval village. The postman is portrayed as an essential link in the social fabric of the nation who rebuilds civic and neighbourly connections in the everyday: 'with small discrete gestures, he mends the tears [in the social fabric]. This is why the postman is irreplaceable. If he didn't exist, we would have to invent him' (La Poste 2006, 11). In one testimony, a postman describes how he is immersed in people's daily lives and has become a trusted friend and confidante: 'we enter into people's lives: I know where and when they are going on holidays, if they are splitting up or if a company is going under [...] This affection cannot be explained. It belongs to the collective unconscious. The postman is witness to joy and sorrow and is also a source of advice' (ibid., 211). In this mythical imaginary, the postman or woman is no longer a corporeal being subject to the daily constraints of his or her labour but becomes a paragon of virtue, duty and courage. The material realities of work, with its intense pressures, precariousness and mounting workload are magically whisked away by the ideal of an everyday hero who 'incarnates every morning the values of La Poste and of public service' (ibid., 13).

For La Poste, this idealisation of the postman serves specific economic ends and is a strategic means to expand its commercial interests. The daily encounter between postal worker and citizen, forged within a public service tradition, offered a unique business model that opened up vast new economic opportunities. We will see that La Poste followed a particular model of liberalisation that sought to preserve a public service identity, while turning it into a source of profit. Rather than abandoning its public service image in favour of a global corporate brand, as its affiliate France Télécom had done, La Poste decided to reorientate its public service towards lucrative commercial ends. In projecting its corporate image, La Poste tends to combine a nostalgic appeal to the past with modernist references to economic dynamism and innovation. In one marketing brochure, in the form of a sketch with interactive web links, La Poste presents the postman as someone who combines public service familiarity and trustworthiness with slick commercial efficiency. He is presented as an amiable figure wearing the postman's familiar cap, satchel and sturdy boots, but, by clicking on the interactive links, the customer can discover a range of cutting-edge services, from reading electricity meters on a smartphone, to delivering shopping or visiting the elderly. In these examples, the notion of public service has been repackaged as a branding tool and a corporate slogan.

Following restructuring, La Poste reconfigured the identity of the postal worker, turning him or her into a public service figure who could also offer reliable commercial services for a price. Hence the 'Bonjour facteur' service that was introduced in 2011 sought to expand the traditional role of the postman to provide a whole range of paid-for services including the delivery of medication, meter readings, shopping delivery and recycling household waste. In some regions, such as the Dordogne, a new service was introduced whereby the postman would search for lost dogs for an itemised fee (Cazes & Hacot 2015). La Poste has also sought to capitalise on the 'silver economy', turning the routine exchange between the postal worker and elderly citizen into a commercial service. For instance, the 'veiller sur mes parents' (watch over my parents) service allows customers to pay a postal worker to visit their elderly relatives, check up on them and report back to members of their family. Equipped with an official set of questions, spontaneous conversation is substituted by a scripted exchange that must cover a checklist of issues. Although company executives view this as a smart business move, trade unions have criticised what they see as a cynical manipulation of a public service tradition for economic gain. Such commercial services are a perversion of La Poste's public service mission, according to the unions, as they generate inequality: only those who can afford to pay, benefit from the postman's time, whilst others are relegated to a second-rate service, subject to the pressures of the time clock (*Le Monde*, 24 May 2017).

Different critics have sought to capture the impact of structural reform on lived experiences of work at La Poste, describing this variously in terms of an existential crisis, a cultural rupture or a psychological trauma (Teissier 1997; Fontenelle 2013; Hanique 2014). At stake were transformations that transcended external working activity and structures and encroached on the intimate and subjective realms of the person. Teissier portrays La Poste's reform as a 'cultural revolution' that brought into conflict two diametrically opposed universes, the first defined by public service, a notion of the general interest and a protected social status, and the other by a commercial logic that reduces work to measurable and quantifiable results and reconfigures the public servant as a salesperson (Teissier 1997, 14). While La Poste's new commercial logic undermined the established values underpinning work, it did not offer any alternative forms of cultural or social belonging with which the worker could identify: 'it is experienced as a social and psychological void that shatters the bonds of routine, certainty and a vision of the future' (ibid., 86). For Maurizio Lazzarato, contemporary capitalism is characterised by a crisis of subjectivity, as capital destroys the social relations and cultural meanings that define identity, whilst failing to construct new forms of subjective identification: 'Today, the weakness of capitalism lies in the production of subjectivity. As a consequence, systemic crisis and the crisis in the production of subjectivity are strictly interlinked. It is impossible to separate economic, political, and social processes from the processes of subjectivation occurring within them' (2014, 8). With a dismantling of public service ideals, post office workers were obliged to renegotiate what Fabienne Hanique (2014) defines as the 'meaning of work' in the everyday and to search for new cultural and ideological references to orientate their working lives. For Sebastien Fontenelle (2013), restructuring transformed La Poste into a site of 'social suffering' in which overarching structural reforms driven by economic imperatives were transposed onto lived experience in terms of intense trauma, despair and psychological distress.

Freedom Narratives

French postal suicides have a specific history, reflecting the impact of overarching structural transformations on lived experiences of work, within the fixed and localised spaces of the post office. This section reconstitutes this history by examining structural transformations which radically transformed working conditions and disrupted a deeply rooted workplace culture. More specifically, it examines the transformations linked to La Poste's liberalisation and restructuring during the 2000s and their often catastrophic corporeal effects. La Poste's liberalisation was framed as a great emancipatory project that would reinvigorate a moribund state-owned company, remove regulatory constraints, deepen economic freedoms and strip away deadening bureaucracy. Economic transformations were grounded in a rallying call for freedom as a supreme and incontrovertible principle and a human right (Crouch 2011). We will see that although the company was gradually freed of controls, individual workers were subject to a tightening of surveillance and control over all aspects of their working lives. The freeing of economic power at the top of the organisation was accompanied by an extension of control over daily working life. The aim was to eradicate internalised public-sector values and reorientate the employee towards commercial values that were in tune with the strategic goals of the company. We will see that when capitalist rationality extends beyond working activity and encroaches on the complex, intimate and vulnerable dimensions of the person, this can have deleterious human consequences.

La Poste's liberalisation has its origins in a neoliberal shift in the European Union from the mid-1990s onwards, when ideas that had been propagated a decade earlier by Margaret Thatcher in the UK and Ronald Reagan in the US were integrated into official EU policy. This 'neoliberal counterrevolution' was characterised by an ideological and theoretical agenda to restructure European capitalist economies and do away with an existing national model based on public ownership, economic planning and a welfare state (Hermann 2007, 63). Liberalisation was a political project that sought to transform the relationship between state and market and redefine the role of the public sector within society. La Poste is therefore a microcosm of a broader European experiment with neoliberalism, and French postal workers' experiences mirror those of workers in other national settings, including Germany (privatisation of Deutsche Post in 2000), the Netherlands (PostNL privatised in 1989), Belgium (Bpost part-privatised in 2006) and the UK (privatisation of Royal Mail in 2014). Liberalisation appealed to classical ideals of freedom and autonomy to legitimise a radical transformation of the public sector across Europe. In *Le Nouvel Esprit du capitalisme* ('The New Spirit of Capitalism', 1999) Luc Boltanksi and Eve Chiapello suggest that whereas during the rise of industrial capitalism in the nineteenth century, the freedom narrative centred on liberating the individual from the oppressive and rigid structures of traditional society, contemporary neoliberal discourse promised instead to free the individual from the rigidities of capitalism itself, allowing them to become autonomous, flexible and self-fulfilled.

Liberalisation was driven by a series of directives that acted as a powerful market-making machinery, transforming abstract liberal ideas into economic policy and underpinning a hegemonic project to privatise public services. The first postal services directive was passed in 1997 and was subsequently amended by directives in 2002 and 2008. These directives champion abstract ideals of free trade, free capital mobility, fair competition, equal access and consumer rights. The 1997 directive sets out a regulatory framework for the creation of an internal market in postal services that will reinforce and extend the EU's founding principles and create 'a level playing field' in which conditions of unfair advantage are removed and all entrepreneurs have equal access to the market (Hermann 2007, 73). The 2002 directive reaffirms a value-laden vision of liberalisation and reiterates the importance of 'services of general economic interest in the shared values of the union' and of promoting economic and social cohesion (Directive 2002/39/CE article 3). The directive predicts that postal services have 'substantial growth prospects' and will foster economic dynamism and job creation (article 19). According to article 13, 'Market-opening will help to expand the overall size of the postal markets, and any reductions in staff levels […] are likely to be offset by the resulting growth in employment among private operators and new market entrants'. The 2008 directive reinforces the economic case for liberalisation, arguing that it will improve labour conditions and 'foster growth and create more and better jobs' (Directive 2008/6/EC, article 8).

In this reordered ideological framework, the traditional relationship between state and market that characterised European national economies is reversed. Under neoliberalism, state ownership of public services is no longer perceived as a means to deliver essential and equitable services and ensure democratic control over how public taxes are spent. The state is instead portrayed as a site of vested and particularist interest that is at best obstructionist, inefficient and monolithic and at worst, a threat to democratic rights and freedoms (Crouch 2011). A key imperative behind liberalisation is the need to eliminate monopolistic firms whose dominance distorts market pricing and prevents fair and open market conditions. The state is now portrayed as a threat to economic freedoms, whilst the market removes barriers to rights and freedoms and ensures better services for all citizens. Rather than envisaging a need to regulate the market, it is the state which needs to be monitored and controlled to ensure that it does not abuse its market power. Hence, states must adhere to 'principles of transparency, non-discrimination and proportionality' in providing financial support to postal services (Directive 2008/6/EC, article 29). However, as Christoph Hermann notes, liberalisation did not succeed in removing oligopolistic cartels and creating free and fair competition. In contrast to the rhetoric of 'free competition' in public services, liberalisation was characterised by the rise of large transnational service suppliers which dominate the supply of former public utilities including electricity, gas, water and postal services. The publicly owned monopolies that existed prior to liberalisation have been replaced by 'politically created multinational private oligopolies' (Hall quoted by Hermann 2007, 76).

European directives provided the framework for a profound transformation of La Poste, as successive French governments put in place legislation to dismantle its historical relationship with the state and deregulate its public service status. Law 90-568 of July 1990 prepared under the Socialist government separated postal services from telecommunications within the existing PTT and redefined La Poste as a 'public establishment of an industrial and commercial character' (Legifrance 1990). Alongside its mission to deliver a public service, according to a notion of universal mission, postal services were required to fulfil a commercial role and generate profit through an expansion of financial activities. This law overturned La Poste's tradition of employing only public service employees or *fonctionnaires* by allowing the company to recruit new employees on short-term contracts who no longer had the social or legal protection of the traditional fonctionnaire. In one testimonial account, Thomas Barba, a former postman and trade unionist, describes how when he began work as a postman in 1983, the low pay and physical hardship of work were mitigated by the sheer joy of his daily encounter with villagers in the tiny rural community of Lisle-sur-Tarn, in the south of France. He describes his visits to isolated farmhouses where the owner had chosen not to install a letter box, so that he could personally greet the postman each morning. He was frequently invited to share meals with a family and at Christmas, when he sold La Poste's calendars, he was able to double his monthly salary. For Barba, liberalisation destroyed a notion of public service that had defined the parameters of a daily engagement with the citizen and stripped postal workers of the status and prestige linked to their role as fonctionnaires (Barba 2013). Such testimonial accounts must be treated with caution, however, as they represent a nostalgic vision of La Poste's public sector past that is used by the left to challenge liberalisation as a political and ideological project. In 2010, La Poste changed status again, becoming a 'société anonyme' (limited shares company). Although the state remains the principal shareholder, this statutory change allows La Poste to pursue private-sector funding, by placing shares on financial markets. For some critics, this statutory change has fundamentally transformed La Poste, from a state-owned company underpinned by public-service ideals, to a private enterprise, driven by shareholder value (Brun 2013; Fontenelle 2013).

Liberalisation provided the backdrop for a restructuring of La Poste as chief executive Jean-Paul Bailly (2002–13) and, subsequently, Pierre Wahl (2013–), put in place economic strategies designed to modernise postal services, expand commercial activities and cut staffing costs. The 'Cap, Qualité, Courrier' plan, introduced in 2003 by Bailly under the leitmotif of 'modernisation', set out a strategy for a major reorganisation of La Poste designed to modernise its structures via the launch of a new commercial strategy. Modernisation was driven by a sense of urgency and necessity: in the face of impending market competition and the rise of the internet, La Poste had either to modernise or disappear. La Poste's bosses secured an investment of 3.4 billion euros from the state to support a large-scale modernisation programme that was intended to transform territorial structures that had remained unchanged since the Napoleonic era. As 66 per cent of the state's investment had to be repaid from La Poste's own resources, the need to generate profits became paramount. A report presented to the Senate in June 2003, prior to Bailly's plan, sets the tone for modernisation, invoking metaphors of La Poste's imminent demise: this is an organisation that is 'lacking oxygen', gasping for breath and suffocating under the weight of its own bureaucracy (Larcher 2003, 1). La Poste is configured as a great dying mammoth languishing under the weight of its own immobilism and facing imminent extinction. Its moribund condition is evoked using pathological terms including 'necrosis', 'atrophy' and 'asphyxiation'. Here, the public service role is no longer envisaged as a positive social good and a symbol of the general interest, but instead as synonymous with economic decline and backwardness. In contrast, the market is presented as a life-affirming force (an 'essential oxygen supply'), a source of vigour and vitality that will reinvigorate La Poste and unleash its entrepreneurial potential (ibid., 2). The report describes the two overriding objectives for La Poste's reform: firstly, a deep-seated modernisation of its operations and territorial networks; and secondly, an aggressive commercial strategy that would increase its profit margins. Market-driven reform is construed as an inescapable necessity, a matter of life and death that will determine the future survival of the company and shape the economic fate of the nation.

Pierre Wahl's 2014 strategic plan 'La Poste 2020: conquérir l'avenir' (La Poste 2020: conquering the future) is framed in a language of conquest, dynamism and innovation. In a rhetoric not dissimilar to that of a venture capitalist group, Wahl's ambition was to 'conquer new territories', 'change models' and 'stimulate innovation' (Groupe de La Poste 2014, 2, 3). His strategic priorities are to expand La Poste's profit-making activities, such as banking and commercial services, develop new technologies in online services and modernise public services by cutting costs. As part of this strategy, banking is identified as a core economic activity, with plans to raise profits from 547 million euros in 2012 to over a billion in 2020. The plan sets out a vision for a multitasking postman ('un facteur multi-tâche') who can deliver a wide range of services to his 'clients' for payment, and Wahl even suggests that in rural areas, postmen could help deliver shopping. However, Wahl's inspiring vision of economic innovation is counterposed against a brutal cost-cutting strategy for employees: 'no job replacements, put everyone under pressure for six months to a year and see what happens' (Cazes & Hacot 2015, 49). Though restructuring expanded financial and commercial activities, this did not represent a sudden rupture with the past: La Poste was France's main banking institution in post-war France until the 1970s, when mainstream banks took over this role (Vezinat 2012).[2]

Despite promises of greater efficiency, job creation and improved services, France's experience of liberalisation over the past 20 years has, according to critics, been overwhelmingly negative (Brun 2013; Fontenelle 2013; Cazes & Hacot 2015). Whilst promising to open up competition and create a more dynamic market, La Poste remains the only major operator in France and still controls over 90 per cent of the mail delivered to letter boxes. Although approximately 15 private companies now offer postal services, these are confined to parcel

2　La Poste had been assigned a role in financial activities since the late nineteenth century. In 1918, the first *chèques postaux* were introduced. In 1953, La Poste began providing private loans to households and was the main institution for banking in France until the 1970s (Vezinat 2012).

delivery and operate only in specific regions and localities. Conditions of access to postal services have been damaged by the widespread closure of post offices across the national territory: one third were shut down between 2002 and 2010, with some communal offices disappearing and others transformed into branches within supermarkets or other commercial entities that offer only minimal services (Cazes & Hacot 2015). Christian Tran's documentary *Poste restante*[3] (2005) was filmed in the Ardèche in south-eastern France, which was one of the first departments to undergo a restructuring of postal services. It investigates the human consequences of post office closures in a handful of remote rural villages and eloquently conveys how distant rationalist choices, underpinned by a drive to cut costs and increase profits, can have devastating consequences on rural communities. For La Poste's management, rural post offices are uneconomic and stagnant, but for villagers they are a focal point of community life and a place to meet, exchange views and converse, in the same way as church or the *boulangerie*. We follow the local residents and mayors in different villages as they campaign to keep their post office open, arguing the case for the human and civic interests of their community, against the company's drive to shut down unprofitable post offices. Paradoxically, the villagers demonstrate how closures, justified in the name of market competition, make poor economic sense, as there are no other companies willing to deliver to these remote areas, and local businesses tend to move away because of declining communication networks.

Yet it is with regard to working conditions that liberalisation arguably exerted its most damaging effects. Despite the claim that liberalisation would create jobs, there has been a sharp decline in employment in postal services across the vast majority of European countries. Between 2005 and 2015, postal sector employment decreased by 26 per cent in France, 30 per cent in Belgium, 23 per cent in Spain and 18 per cent in the UK (Netposte 2018). Privatised postal services in Germany created over 16,000 jobs, but Deutsche Post cut 38,000 jobs. In the Netherlands, there was a net loss of 12,000 jobs (Barber 2018). In France, there have been mass job cuts across the company, mainly through the

---

3   The term 'poste restante' translates as 'general delivery', meaning that post can be delivered and collected from a designated site other than a post office, but it also might be translated literally as 'remaining post office' denoting the gradual disappearance of post offices from the French countryside.

non-replacement of employees who leave. Whilst announcing, under Jean-Paul Bailly's leadership, that jobs and working conditions would be protected, La Poste cut one third of its jobs (84,000 posts in ten years) through the aforementioned non-replacement of fonctionnaires and shifted recruitment increasingly into precarious short-term private contracts. Meanwhile, working conditions at La Poste have deteriorated sharply with lower wages, work intensification, insecure work and a widespread use of surveillance technology. Workplace accidents have increased by 33 per cent and levels of absenteeism are on the rise and are significantly higher than the national average. Occupational doctors, trade unions and work inspectors have criticised poor and dangerous working conditions and pointed to a physical and psychological exhaustion of the workforce (CHCST 2014). For Christoph Hermann, one of the perverse economic successes of liberalisation has been to reduce labour costs for postal companies with a consequent deterioration in working conditions for employees themselves:

> In most regards, the liberalization of postal services did not bring about the results promised by the EU and the privatizers: postal services declined for citizens, while privatized business service delivery expanded. The European postal service privatization process has been, however, very successful in reducing labour costs and in turning what used to be a reservoir of stable and decent jobs, especially for low-skilled workers, into an area of precarious and low-waged work. (2014, 3)

Surveillance Mechanisms

While liberalisation was driven by an emancipatory rhetoric that freed the company of regulatory constraints, it was accompanied by an intensification of control over the individual employee. A freeing of economic power at the top of the organisation was matched by a tightening of control over everyday individual work at the grassroots. La Poste's restructuring was marked by an extension of regulatory control across every aspect of working life, from delivering letters to selling stamps or allocating benefits. No dimension of the everyday exchange between the post office worker and citizen was to escape the new forms of regulation. The new control methods seem to correspond to what

Michel Foucault described as a mode of disciplinary surveillance that aims to monitor, regulate and prescribe forms of human behaviour. For Foucault, the rise of modern disciplinary societies was characterised by an extension of surveillance across all facets of everyday life, so that the prison becomes the template for the whole of society. The shift to disciplinary societies is marked by 'the penetration of regulation into even the smallest details of everyday life' and an extension of control, so that 'the slightest movements are supervised' (Foucault 1991, 198, 197). He uses the metaphor of the Panopticon or watchtower, from which the prison inspector can observe all of the inmates simultaneously, or not at all, without them knowing when or if they are being watched. The individual is observed through a pervasive, all-seeing, yet invisible gaze ('thousands of eyes posted everywhere') that subjects them to constant scrutiny (ibid., 214). The purpose of surveillance, Foucault suggests, is not simply to observe and watch over but to dictate ways of being, so that the human being is better adapted to the designs of the system and enmeshed in a new power relationship. The aim is not only to monitor external gestures and visible activity but to achieve 'the ultimate determination of the individual, of what characterizes him, of what belongs to him, of what happens to him' (ibid., 197). For Foucault, surveillance is an instrument for producing 'docile subjects' who will obey, conform and execute what is required of them:

> The human body was entering a machinery of power that explores it, breaks it down and rearranges it [...] it defined how one may have a hold over others' bodies, not only so that they may do what one wishes, but so that they may operate as one wishes, with all the techniques, the speed and the efficiency that one determines. This discipline produces subjected and practised bodies, 'docile' bodies. (ibid., 138)

Some critics suggest that Foucault's model of the Panopticon, which describes the rise of disciplinary societies in the nineteenth and twentieth centuries, has lost its pertinence in our contemporary societies in which control takes on more fluid and less institution-alised forms (Deleuze 1990; Lyons 2006). Instead of a central and objective gaze projected outwards from a watchtower, contemporary capitalism exerts more diffuse, individualised and technological forms of control that may lack structure or objective form. Some critics argue that we need to 'go beyond Foucault' and develop new and alternative theories to describe the changing forms of surveillance that mark the twenty-first century (Manokha 2018, 221). Yet, as other critics point out, Foucault's writings pre-empt many of the features of digital surveillance and self-discipline that characterise contemporary capitalism. Foucault's Panopticon envisages a model of power in which relationships of domination are invisible to the individual, who therefore internalises forms of self-control and becomes his or her own overseer. In his *History of Sexuality* (1977), Foucault suggests that in the contemporary period we need to look not for a central locus of power, but for a microphysics of power that transcends any one institution or structure and pervades the whole of society. Individuals are controlled not only as objects of discipline, he suggests, but also as self-controlling subjects that impose their own forms of regimentation. Foucault's more recent work takes this argument further, and describes the forms of power that individuals exert over themselves, referring to 'technologies of the self':

> there is another type of [...] technique which permits individuals to effect, by their own means, a certain number of operations on their own bodies, their own souls, their own thoughts, their own conduct, and this is a manner so as to transform themselves, modify themselves [...] Let's call these techniques technologies of the self. (1985, 367)

In his analysis of the rise of self-imposed, differentiated and all-pervasive forms of surveillance, Foucault's work provides a rich lens with which to analyse the control mechanisms deployed within the contemporary setting of French postal services.

At La Poste, restructuring was characterised by the introduction of a barrage of new surveillance mechanisms that sought to measure, codify and prescribe working activity. Surveillance was intended to transform a public service exchange that took place in conditions of everyday, enclosed and 'ordinary intimacy' into a commercial transaction capable of generating profit (Hanique 2014, 187). Measurement mechanisms reached into the most routine transactions, in a 'supervision of the smallest fragment of life' that sought to extricate profit from diverse, everyday and previously autonomous forms of human interaction (Foucault 1991, 140). New software technology was introduced to quantify the number of products sold, their commercial value and the speed of individual transactions. Hence, in post offices, employees were connected to a programme, Morg@ne, that divided work into a series of tasks, each of which is given an 'efficiency ratio' and measured according to the number of sales achieved (CHSCT 2014). Meanwhile, in banking services, the Sept G sales method allocated a strict time limit to every banking transaction with a member of the public, from opening an account to transferring money (Vezinat 2012). Performance was evaluated not according to the quality of service provided, but the number of products sold, and each employee was graded according the quantity and value of sales achieved. In order to instil new commercial skills, new initiatives were introduced including 'challenges', whereby post office branches would compete against one another to achieve the highest product sales, or 'sprints', where a specific product had to be sold within a specified period of time.

Fabienne Hanique describes how the new sales culture, imposed through regulatory methods, was a source of anguish and division for many employees. Some would cheat the system in order to avoid having to push sales onto members of the public. One male post office worker in his forties found himself unable to adapt to the new sales culture: 'Jacky n'est pas un vendeur' (Jacky is not a salesman). And in order to meet his monthly sales target, he would buy pre-stamped envelopes in bulk and pass them on to his wife who then sold them to the stationary department in the accountancy firm where she worked (Hanique 2014, 122). This allowed Jacky to gain his monthly bonus, whilst preserving his sense of professional integrity and his public service values: 'to get a bonus without getting your hands dirty' (ibid., 127). For others, the drive to commercialise a public-service relationship was a source of immense psychological distress, requiring employees to assume a personal disposition that was at odds with their ethical values and sense of identity: 'It is this intimate engagement with values that everyone confronts in a sales situation that makes this new dimension of post office activity difficult from a subjective perspective, if not costly from a psychological point of view' (ibid., 128). Another ethnographic study focused on postal workers based in a tough Parisian suburb (*zone urbaine sensible*) reveals the resentment, frustration and anger generated by the introduction of enforced sales techniques. Postal workers often refused to follow instructions to push commercial sales onto socially disadvantaged customers and were angry that La Poste was manipulating a public-service reputation to achieve economic profits. These employees were sanctioned for poor performance according to new evaluation criteria that measured the quality of work according to sales figures alone (Siblot 2006). Such experiences are not limited to La Poste but reflect changed work practices across the French economy. In his study of call centres, Duarte Rolo (2015) shows how workers are forced to lie to customers in order to sell products and achieve prescribed targets, and that this practice of 'lying at work' causes many workers to experience immense ethical suffering resulting in identity fragmentation and dissonance.

At La Poste, surveillance was also a mechanism for improving efficiency by pushing the employee to work harder, increase his or her productivity and speed up working activity. The aim of modern surveillance, according to Foucault, is to convert time itself into productive value and to eliminate any activity that is deemed to be unproductive:

> It is a question of extracting, from time, ever more available moments, and from each moment, ever more useful forces. This means that one must seek to intensify the use of the slightest moment, as if time, in its very fragmentation, were inexhaustible or as if, at least by an ever more detailed internal arrangement, one could tend towards an ideal point at which one maintained maximum speed and maximum efficiency. (1991, 154)

Just like François in *Jour de fête*, who tries to pedal harder, increase his speed and become more American, each postal worker had to speed up daily activity, become more efficient and cut out wasteful time. For instance, the 'Facteur d'avenir' (Postman of the future) strategy introduced in 2007 was intended to measure, quantify and monitor the delivery rounds of the postman in order to attain a maximum speed and efficiency. Whereas delivery rounds had traditionally been monitored by a postal inspector who would take into account human variables such as the age of the postman, whether the terrain was hilly or flat, whether it was rural or urban and weather contingencies, the new mechanisms relied on software ('corrective technology') which often ignored the human realities of the delivery round (Foucault 1991, 224). The Metod software calculated optimal time slots to speed up delivery rounds that used arbitrary criteria disconnected from the human activity involved. Trade unions criticised what they saw as a policing of work that removed individual autonomy and exerted intense pressure on the individual (Siblot 2006).

This new regime subjected workers to intense and, in some cases, unbearable pressure in daily working life. The television documentary *Une tournée dans la neige* (A Delivery Round in the Snow, 2016) by Hélène Marini portrays the human consequences of a postal service which imposes ever-increasing pressure on the worker in the interests of greater profits. Contrary to the traditional image of the postman or woman as a friendly figure who is immersed in a local community, the documentary presents a postal service staffed by a succession of low-paid employees on short-term contracts who move on before they can form any meaningful bond with the community they serve. The documentary focuses on the real-life case of a 21-year-old postwoman, Pauline, who after completing an arduous delivery round in the snow in a remote rural area in the Haute-Loire, goes home and hangs herself on 15 February 2013. When locals on her delivery round are interviewed in the documentary, few of them know her name or know what she looked like. She is a nameless and anonymous figure fulfilling a temporary role, soon to be replaced by another employee on a short-term contract. The film portrays the pressures of a postal service in which workers are obliged constantly to speed up their delivery times (39 seconds allotted for delivering a parcel) and to take on ever-increasing delivery rounds. It emerges that Pauline had just taken on a third delivery round in six months and had to assume the work of a postman who had left on sick leave two days earlier. Unable to cope with the backlog of three days' mail, she was exhausted, and the snowy conditions aggravated her difficulties, making it impossible for her to finish the round, despite completing an 11-hour shift. In a report on her suicide, the trade union organisation, the Observatory of Workplace Stress, reported that during the preceding year, 2012, there had been 30 suicides or attempted suicides at La Poste, ten taking place in the workplace.[4]

For Foucault, the purpose of surveillance is to observe and control, but also to function as a kind of laboratory that can be used to carry out experiments, to alter behaviour or correct individuals: 'an architecture that would operate to transform individuals: to act on those it shelters, to provide a hold on their conduct, to carry the effects of power right to them, to make it possible to know them, to alter them' (1991, 172).

---

4   See 'Peut-on arrêter les suicides en série à La Poste?', L'Observatoire du Stress Entreprises, https://ods-entreprises.fr/peut-on-arreter-les-suicides-en-serie-a-la-poste/.

At La Poste, restructuring aimed at a conversion of the individual employee in order to eradicate the internalised norms of a public-service culture and harness the employee towards commercial forms of behaviour and disposition. Surveillance operated on workers and their subjective resources, including their values, mannerisms and behaviour. Hanique notes that although La Poste had undergone a succession of organisational reforms since the 1960s, these were limited to external working activities and did not call into question an underlying public-service mission or encroach on the individual's values or identity: 'a change in ways of doing without undermining ways of being' (Hanique 2014, 19). The new phase of neoliberal reforms, by contrast, was focused on a modernisation of workers themselves: 'it is no longer solely a case of changing ways of doing things, what is required is to change ways of being' (ibid., 20). One set of measures introduced prescriptive norms that were designed to control forms of individual expression and sociability used by the post office worker in his or her daily exchange with the citizen. The aim was to achieve a 'Taylorisation du sourire' (Taylorisation of the smile) by instrumentalising the most intimate and subjective dimensions of the human personality in the interests of capitalist rationality (Ariès 2014). An early example of this was the BRASMA technique (*Bonjour, regard, attention, sourire, merci, au revoir*), introduced in 1996, which instructed the postal worker when to smile, how to maintain eye contact and greet the customer politely. Management set as its goal to ensure that 100 per cent of employees were 'en état de Brasma' ('Brasma compliant') (Oblet & Villechaise 2005, 350). Post offices were regularly inspected by a 'client mystère', an inspector posing as a customer who would evaluate the post office worker, adding or deducting points according the quality of their greeting and whether a product sale was achieved. Hanique (2014) describes how, in the aftermath of such an inspection, employees were chastised for failing to comply with prescriptive norms and the inspector reported that their commercial reflexes were poor. As a result, all employees were sent on a workshop to provide 'corrective training' where they had to rehearse their prescribed lines and learn how to better satisfy customers (Foucault, 1991 170). For some critics, these techniques are designed to condition, infantilise and control employees in order to construct a type of employee whose every impulse, thought and emotion was attuned to the economic interests of the company (Balbastre 2002).

Suicide Notes

On 13 October 2016, occupational experts from eight independent agencies wrote an open letter to the chief executive of La Poste and the French government that was published widely in the press and warned of a rapid deterioration in working conditions that was endangering the health and lives of employees. They had decided to sound the alarm, in this public way, they stated, in order to force company executives to respond to an escalating crisis, made evident through rising suicides and individual cases of extreme psychological distress, depression and chronic stress. They accused La Poste's management of destabilising working life through sweeping structural reforms, while exploiting their employees' deep-seated commitment to public service. La Poste, they stated, continued to capitalise on 'the trust with which postal workers are held within the general population, whilst destroying the conditions that make this possible' (RTL, 14 October 2016). Instead of acting to protect the health and safety of their employees, the letter argued, La Poste had obstructed investigations into working conditions, blocked workplace enquiries in the courts, destroyed official documents and refused to engage in dialogue with workers' representatives.

The letter followed the suicide of a 53-year-old postman who hanged himself at his home on 17 July 2016, having worked at La Poste for 34 years. He left two letters, one addressed to his wife and two children and one for his employer. In this second letter, he made his motivations clear: 'In recent years, La Poste has slowly destroyed its employees, the true ones, those who are in contact with the people. In my case they have totally destroyed me'. He presents himself as a lone defender of public-service values against an organisation that is bent on destroying them: 'Let's move with La Poste and die because of La Poste' (RTL, 27 August 2016). According to his son, he had reached a state of exhaustion in the face of continuous pressure to take on a heavier workload and speed up his delivery times: 'La Poste pushed him to the edge of the precipice: pressure, profit, money. That's all that matters nowadays' (ibid). In seeking to convert the individual worker into a salesman, La Poste's restructuring seemed to disrupt the complex and intimate values by which many employees defined their working activity and also their subjective selves.

La Poste's management strenuously denied any connections between rising suicides and workplace conditions and attributed acts of self-killing either to personal or family difficulties or to broad economic processes outside of human control. Following the suicide of a 54-year-old postman in Aurillac in the Auvergne region, who hanged himself at home during his lunch break on 3 May 2010 and who had recently been informed that his delivery round was to be axed, La Poste issued a statement to the press calling for 'caution regarding possible interpretations; it is dangerous to draw a causal link between the professional situation of this employee who, besides, had health issues, and this suicidal act. This act was the result of a choice, a personal decision and, moreover, it took place at his home' (*L'Humanité*, 3 June 2010). In the aftermath of the suicide of a senior executive in 2013, the company's chief executive Jean-Paul Bailly stated that suicides were 'personal and familial dramas in which the work dimension is non-existent or marginal' (*Libération*, 7 March 2013).

Yet such individualising narratives have been countered by suicidal individuals themselves, who in their mode of self-killing often make the connection to work manifestly clear. Of the 21 suicide cases analysed in this chapter, 11 took place in the person's place of work. These include the case of a postal worker on sick leave who took the decision to return to the postal depot where he worked on a Sunday to hang himself on 11 March 2012. Following lengthy legal proceedings brought by the deceased's wife, a tribunal in Rennes ruled that his suicide was a work-related accident for which La Poste was liable. The judge noted in his statement that the employee had been in conflict with management following a forced redeployment and made clear that he had 'made the symbolic choice to take his own life in the workplace' (Tribunal administratif de Rennes 2016, 3). Another case involves a postal worker who hanged himself in the post office where he worked during his lunch break on 31 October 2012 after sending an email to management entitled 'Adieu'. Judged by his manager to be too slow and meticulous in his work, he had recently been placed under disciplinary review. In his email, the employee pointed to a lack of recognition by managers for the work he had done: 'I waited until the last moment to receive a real message of hope that would show a little, just a little recognition for all the work I had done at La Fère, but no, nothing at all' (*L'Express*, 2 November 2012). Other suicides carried out in the workplace include a postman who attempted to kill himself by hanging at a postal sorting centre on 4 March 2013, a 34-year-old postwoman who attempted suicide in the post office where she worked in Montpellier by swallowing pills on 18 October 2016, and a manager and father of three who killed himself in the sorting centre where he worked near Alençon on 13 June 2017 (*20 minutes*, 12 September 2019).

In other cases, postal workers have chosen to kill themselves in a public place, often by spectacular means, so that their actions are witnessed by others. On 29 February 2012, a 28-year-old manager threw himself out of the window of the central post office where he worked in Rennes, onto the busy street below where he died instantly. He left two letters, one at work and a second for his wife in which he complained of 'permanent anxiety', an oppressive working environment and of constant and humiliating criticism from his managers: 'This life has become unbearable to me. The work I carry out every day is not appreciated. I am constantly criticised for everything I do [...] I prefer not to continue living in this oppressive environment' (*Le Point*, 12 March 2012). Described as ambitious, he had risen quickly through the ranks from the position of postman to that of senior manager, but he had been destabilised by frequent redeployments and had been assigned to a new role below his career level three weeks earlier. According to his wife's testimony, he was a consummate professional and 'He thought only about work. He no longer slept'. His suicide letter was publicised by his wife, who read extracts at a press conference in order to draw attention to working conditions at La Poste. His was one of four suicide cases at La Poste in 2012 in which a work-related cause was established. In an earlier case of suicide by defenestration on 15 September 2011, a 52-year-old female employee who worked at La Poste's financial centre in Paris threw herself from a window on the fourth floor of her office block. She had restarted work that morning following an accident and had previously been on extended leave for depression. The work inspector who investigated her suicide filed charges of manslaughter against La Poste (*Nouvel Observateur*, 1 March 2012).

Alongside the symbolic connections of the location or mode of suicide, the motivations for suicide are also set out explicitly in written form in the letters, emails, texts, dossiers and audio recordings that have been left behind. In nearly half of the 21 suicides examined here, a suicide note was left addressed to family members, bosses or union representatives. What is striking in these letters is that they consistently blame work as the cause of their actions. A 35-year-old female postal worker who stopped her car in a wood on her way to work and killed herself on 24 March 2007 left a note for her family that stated, 'work, which was my reason for living, has become my reason for dying'. She had been the victim of an armed robbery at the post office where she worked several months previously and had experienced difficulties at work ever since. A few days before her suicide, she had been notified that her contracted hours were to be reduced because she was deemed to be 'medically unfit' (Fontenelle 2013, 98). In the legal case that followed, it emerged that she had complained of excessive work pressures on several occasions and had written a letter to her manager a month before, that set out her difficulties. When an investigation was launched into whether her suicide was work-related, La Poste's regional management attempted to block the investigation and stated in the tribunal: 'the difficulties that she experienced in the workplace are not of a nature that would explain her action and it seems likely that she had long-standing personal problems outside work' (ibid., 100). A 49-year-old senior manager who killed himself on 15 January 2008 left a letter for La Poste's chief executive in which he stated, 'I am informing you that my suicide is due entirely to La Poste' and complained that he had been unable to take a single day's holiday in two years. On 4 March 2013, a postman who attempted to hang himself in the sorting centre where he worked left a letter entitled 'La Poste m'a tué' (La Poste killed me) (*Libération*, 7 March 2013).

Some letters evoke the suffering caused by relentless pressure, ever increasing workloads, tight surveillance and continuous restructuring. Some workers find themselves in a state of physical and mental exhaustion and see their death as a desperate form of escape from this daily grind. In December 2005, a 45-year-old senior manager at a post office in the medieval town of Albi in southern France took his own life, leaving a letter for his family: 'Not seeing any way out of a situation that is getting worse every day, I decided to take my own life. My professional role is the primary cause; it has crushed and suffocated me to the point where I can see no escape'. Entrusted with managing a restructuring project, he was under immense pressure and had begun to work continuously, not stopping during the evenings or at weekends. According to one account, 'the company's demands had crept into every millimetre of his personal life' (Barba 2013,

7). He had confided to a friend that his working life had become unmanageable and that he was being pressurised constantly by his boss. When the case brought by his family against La Poste was dismissed by the courts, one of his daughters in turn took her own life (ibid.). In a subsequent case, a 51-year-old director of communications who worked at La Poste's head office in Paris hanged himself at home on 25 February 2013. He had allegedly been coping over several months with an impossible workload, as he was covering three jobs, two of which had not been filled because of job cuts, alongside his already demanding role managing internal communication. Pushed to physical and mental exhaustion, he had been on sick leave for burnout in the three weeks prior to his death. The suicide has been recognised by the courts as a work-related accident and his wife is pursuing further charges of gross negligence against the company. She claims that during the period of sick leave prior to his suicide, her husband was hounded constantly by phone calls and emails from work, and on the day of his suicide, he had been sent over 50 work emails (*Paris Normandie*, 25 October 2016).

Alongside the daily hardship of work, some letters describe their writers' experience in terms of an assault on values and on a whole moral universe through which they defined themselves. A postman who hanged himself in the depot where he worked on 11 March 2012 left a letter in which he accuses La Poste of destroying his beliefs: 'I consider La Poste to be responsible for my loss of bearings and for calling into question the profound values on which I had built my life'. He refers again to the 'values I made my own and on which I based by life and that of my family'. In a letter entitled 'My demands' he requests that no manager be present at his burial and no words be presented on behalf of the company (*Ouest France*, 11 May 2016). In a subsequent case on 4 March 2013, a postman attempted suicide by hanging himself in the sorting centre where he worked in Bayonne in the Basque country.[5] In a letter, he laid the blame unequivocally on work, accusing La Poste of destroying his life. As part of its efficiency drive, his delivery round had been expanded to include 500 additional letter boxes, placing him and his colleagues under increased pressure. His letter refers to a

5   His case attracted considerable public attention, because alongside his job as a postman, he was also a well-known stand-up comedian who had performed to audiences in theatres across France (*Libération*, 7 March 2013).

denigration of working values which had driven him to despair. He points to a perverse management system in which 'the general interest and human respect had given way to toxic careerism and systematic contempt'. As in other cases, he envisions himself as a lone defender of values in the face of a profit-driven and morally bankrupt organisation. He ends his letter by referring to a sense of moral exhaustion that made it impossible for him to continue: 'I realise that I am too exhausted to believe in it any more and I don't have the strength to continue' (*Libération*, 7 March 2013).

Suicides are an extreme manifestation of a more generalised suffering across the workforce which has been made evident by rising absenteeism, chronic stress, burnout and depression. La Poste has been identified as a site of social suffering where overarching transformations in working conditions have triggered a crisis in the mental health of the workforce (Kaspar 2012). In recent years, occupational doctors, work inspectors, health and safety committees and independent agencies have repeatedly warned La Poste's management about the dire state of working conditions at the company. One study by the independent agency Stimulus found that a third of employees at La Poste were experiencing 'hyperstress'. A letter addressed to La Poste's management and the French government warned of suicides that had reached unprecedented levels and of a workforce characterised by 'physical and psychological exhaustion' (*L'Humanité*, 4 June 2010). In 2012, two suicides by postal employees in close succession, both in the workplace, prompted La Poste's boss, Jean-Paul Bailly, to launch a full-scale enquiry into working conditions that led to the publication of a detailed report and set of recommendations (Kaspar 2012). This report presents a contradictory picture of La Poste's liberalisation and subsequent restructuring in which economic successes, according to a wide range of indicators, are contrasted with evidence of a workforce experiencing unprecedented levels of pressure and psychological distress. La Poste's restructuring had been 'crowned with success' with an increase in net profits (+23%), improvements in service quality and in formal workplace conditions, with a steady rise in salary levels and an extension of permanent contracts (ibid., 18). Yet employees themselves were experiencing a severe deterioration in the quality of their working lives with rising job dissatisfaction. The report highlights the contradiction between a liberalisation that removed centralised bureaucratic controls and transferred greater freedom and autonomy to local agencies and the realities of a workplace where these newly acquired freedoms were subject to strict production targets, prescriptive norms and digital surveillance.

A report published in June 2014 summarised the findings of nearly 60 enquiries by occupational experts into working conditions in post offices across France. It described a workplace at breaking point: 'The organisation is under pressure, on the edge of implosion: employees are working in worsening conditions and experience considerable suffering both physical and mental' (CHCST 2014, 20). It points to the damaging psychological effects of a prescribed model of work that is disconnected from the realities of everyday work and that creates a 'gap between what is prescribed and what is real' (ibid., 32). Post office employees are forced to comply with behaviouralist norms that reduce work to a set of standardised and robotic gestures and that dehumanise a public-service relationship. Rather than improving the quality and efficiency of work, this prescribed model forces employees to betray deeply held professional values and deliver a service of poor quality or one that is inappropriate or abusive. As a consequence, La Poste's workers are subject to 'polymorphous suffering' generated by a profound sense of alienation, intensified pressure and psychological distress (ibid., 16).

Despite the large-scale enquiry into working conditions that culminated in the Kaspar report, suicides at La Poste have continued, with five cases in 2013, the year after the report was published (four suicides and one attempted suicide). There was one suicide documented in 2017, which took place in the workplace. In October 2018, two female postal workers, both based in the Dordogne in south-western France, killed themselves within two weeks of each other. The first case involved a 44-year-old postwoman who hanged herself at home. On the morning of her death, she sent text messages to a number of colleagues in which she complained of bullying at work. She had been on sick leave for work-related depression in the period prior to her death. The post office where she worked was undergoing restructuring to cut costs and increase workloads, and her own job was apparently due to be axed. Whilst management warned against jumping to conclusions, a representative from the CGT union commented that her suicide 'is not a surprise'. In the second case, a 52-year-old female postal worker and mother of three who had been on long-term sick leave hanged herself in her parents' house. A few hours before her death, she had spoken to a trade union representative and complained of her experiences of suffering at work: 'for three hours, all she talked about was La Poste'. Interviewed by the press, the trade union representative claimed that the two suicides were a product of 'restructuring and managerial pressure' (*Le Figaro*, 8 November 2018).

Conclusion

Liberalisation and restructuring were framed, in European and French texts, as an urgent and inescapable necessity, a matter of life and death and a question of La Poste's survival in the face of market competition. Sweeping structural reforms were needed to keep the company alive, to restore its oxygen supply and avert the imminent demise of an ageing public service. Yet, tragically, reforms executed in order to breathe life into this company were won at the expense of the mental health and lives of many employees. La Poste's suicide crisis has its origins in structural transformations in the workplace that took place at a specific historical juncture that followed the company's liberalisation. Like the 'going postal' phenomenon in the US, suicide was rooted in systemic causes that transcended the individual and which determined the social conditions of work. Although La Poste had experienced successive reforms throughout the post-war era, the new phase of restructuring went beyond external material changes and targeted the whole person. The individual worker was required not only to change their working practices but to change their very selves. Although liberalisation freed the company of regulatory constraints, it was accompanied by an intensification of surveillance over all aspects of individual working activity and subjective personality. For Michel Foucault, the key feature of a disciplinary regime is that it goes beyond observation and seeks to determine the person, alter behaviour and states of being. Whereas Foucault's model of disciplinary surveillance was drawn from the template of the prison, this chapter shows how surveillance is used routinely in the workplace in the pursuit of strategic economic goals. At La Poste, employees were under pressure to instrumentalise a public service relationship and turn it into a cold cash transaction by placing their own personality and beliefs at the disposal of the company.

La Poste's management framed suicides as a consequence of personal problems stemming from either the mental health or private life of the individual. Yet, in their mode of self-killing and its subsequent narration, suicidal individuals provide compelling testimonial evidence to the contrary. In their letters, emails, official documents and audio recordings, they explicitly attribute the causes of their self-inflicted violence to work and conditions of work. Their letters bear witness to a rapid deterioration of working conditions that accompanied the company's liberalisation and subsequent restructuring and its devastating human effects. Transformations justified in the name of economic rationality and a call for freedom were experienced by many workers in terms of unbearable pressure, chronic stress and severe distress. Suicide letters were written by workers who had been pushed to the very limits and who envisaged self-killing as a desperate mode of escape. A striking aspect of suicide letters is that beyond the material conditions of work, they also appeal to values and to a more deeply rooted and inviolable sense of self. Their work is experienced not solely as external material activity but as an essential part of themselves and as a core referent of cultural identity and social belonging. Suicides may reflect the rise of a model of 'sacrificial labour' that combines personal sacrifice and identity work with conditions of profound structural insecurity. Sacrificial labour is a mechanism whereby workers align their identities to the needs of organisations through self-sacrifice, whilst foreclosing the possibility of building stable and meaningful futures (Monahan & Fisher 2019).

Chapter 4

Orange on the Inside

Introduction

When the former state-owned telecoms company France Télécom rebranded as Orange in 2013, it sought to transform its image and reinvent itself as a global player in innovative digital technologies. In the corporate world, where brand image matters, the Orange label helped to modernise, simplify and aestheticise the company's image. It evoked warmth and vibrancy, conjuring up the ideal of a bright and innocent future, as expressed by the company's slogan, 'The future is Orange'.[1] As part of the company's restructuring, employees were urged to become 'Orange on the inside' and to embrace this corporate strategic vision by making it part of themselves (Diehl & Doublet 2010, 85). The ideal employee was to be bold, flexible and audacious, striving to achieve the company's ambitions in a fast-changing world. Rebranding would reach beyond external productive activities and harness the employee's intimate thoughts, dreams and desires towards strategic economic goals. The company's new brand identity gestured towards the future, pointing to an exciting new age of global

---

1 Orange was first created as the name for a UK mobile operator owned by Hong Kong's Hutchison in the early 1990s, before it was acquired by France Télécom from Vodafone in 2000. The advertising slogan 'The future is bright, the future is Orange' was created in 1994 by the UK operator and was used to define the company's brand identity until recently. In 2015, Orange launched a new brand plan, 'Essentials 2020', which appeals to a sense of fun, playfulness and connectivity, summed up by the slogan 'Nous sommes ici pour vous connecter à ce qui est fun pour vous' (We are here to connect you to what is fun for you) (TeleGeography, 17 March 2015).

connectivity and playful digital gadgets. Yet it also acted on the past and was a means to wipe the slate clean and start again as a company without an infelicitous history. Rebranding was intended to erase the reputational damage caused by recent violent events and in particular a wave of suicides among the company's employees. There were 69 suicides at France Télécom between February 2008 and October 2011 and a further 41 employees attempted suicide, according to trade union sources (Chabrak, Craig & Daidj 2016). Twelve suicides were recorded in 2008, 19 in 2009, 27 in 2010 and 11 in 2011. In March 2014, the company was placed under 'serious alert' following ten suicides since the beginning of the year (Waters 2014a). The Orange brand was intended to sanitise these messy, brutal and visceral events. It was best to forget that the transition to a privatised finance-driven enterprise had been won at the expense of the suffering and, ultimately, the lives of employees.

The France Télécom suicides have a specific history and are situated within broad structural transformations in the economy, in particular the shift to a finance-driven order, and the impact of these transformations on everyday working conditions. I draw on scholarship on financialisation and, in particular, the rise of shareholder value, examining its impact on the changing status and conditions of labour (Froud et al. 2000; Lazonick & O'Sullivan 2000; Lapavitsas 2013). Most critics agree that shareholder restructuring has had wholly negative consequences for labour, generating job insecurity, work intensification, management abuses and mass job cuts (Peters 2011; Cushen 2013; Mazzucato 2018). Some link the rise of finance to expulsionary dynamics that extract value from workers until they are no longer profitable and then expel them as an obstacle to further growth (Sassen 2017; Haskaj 2018; Christiaens 2018). Following its privatisation, France Télécom was transformed from a public service company underpinned by a logic of the general interest and technological excellence, to a finance-driven entity orientated towards generating shareholder value and characterised by an 'obsessive search for financial returns' (Chabrak, Craig & Daidj 2016, 514). The existing value of work rooted in qualitative criteria of professional skill, knowledge and technological expertise was increasingly replaced by a quantitative model that used accounting metrics, financial algorithms and performance targets to measure value. The shift to a shareholder model tends to diminish the value of skilled knowledge work in a system of capital accumulation and this is treated as 'secondary to the appeasement of financial actors' (Cushen 2013, 329). For France Télécom's vast workforce, the company had been transformed from a champion of technological innovation and public service into a 'crushing machine' that set itself against its employees in a mode of institutionalised violence (Decèze 2008). In the newly restructured company, the individual worker was no longer viewed solely as a source of productive value, but was reconfigured as a factor of adjustment and a surplus cost to be removed in the interests of improved financial performance. At Foxconn in China, which experienced a similar suicide wave in 2010, the deaths were linked to a 'deep-rooted corporate ideology [whose] purpose [was] to maximize shareholders' value rather than pursue other objectives, such as the well-being of its employees' (Xu & Li 2013, quoted by Chabrak, Craig & Daidj 2016, 509).

France Télécom constitutes an 'emblematic crisis' symbolising the excesses of finance capitalism and its catastrophic consequences for the workforce at one of France's largest companies (*Mediapart*, 20 October 2009). This chapter contextualises the suicide crisis, situating it in the company's privatisation and subsequent financialisation and the rise of a new management model underpinned by expulsionary techniques. The chapter goes on to examine a dossier of suicide cases that were presented to public prosecutors as part of a legal case brought against France Télécom by a work inspector in February 2010.[2] This dossier includes a corpus of testimonial material, including suicide letters and witness statements, that allows us to reconstruct the links between the individual act of suicide and external structural transformations within the company. Because of its broad social and cultural resonance, the suicide crisis at France Télécom has attracted considerable interest from cultural producers and become a motif for France's painful transition to a neoliberal economy.

Alongside testimonial material, the chapter draws on a rich corpus of novels, films and documentaries that help to elucidate specific

---

2 Sylvie Catala, Rapport de l'inspectrice du travail au procureur de la République du 4 février 2010 (Référence SC no. 22). Sections of this report were made publicly available and published in the press following its release. For instance, Elsa Fayner analyses extracts in an article published in March 2010. This legal case initiated the subsequent criminal trial against executives at the company, which began in May 2019.

dimensions of this crisis. Some fictional accounts have been written by former France Télécom employees who draw on their own lived experiences of work at the company. These writers occupy a unique position as external observers of an objective social world and as insiders who are deeply implicated in the events they describe (Beinstingel 2018). The novels by Marin Ledun (2010), Thierry Beinstingel (2010) and Cathy Raynal (2010) draw on their years of experience working at France Télécom in order to portray a dehumanising and violent world of work. The fictional films *Corporate* (2016) and *Carole Matthieu* (2016) are closely based on events at France Télécom and give representation to the management methods that were used at the company and which triggered the suicides. Employees themselves have participated in this cultural production and the play *Les Impactés* (The Impacted, 2007), which dramatised the crisis at France Télécom, was commissioned by employee representatives at the company. Meanwhile, former employees such as Yonnel Dervin, who attempted suicide in September 2009, have written testimonial accounts of their experiences (Dervin 2009).

A Beacon of Privatisation

Analysing the France Télécom suicides requires a retracing of the causal connections that link the extreme subjective act of suicide with objective and overarching structural transformations that changed the status of labour within the company. Suicides took place when the company was integrating a new finance-driven logic orientated towards the creation of short-term financial returns and shareholder value. Financialisation is widely accepted to be a historic change, a 'systemic transformation of capitalism' that has profoundly transformed the nature and value of economic activity (Lapavitsas 2013, 792). Financialisation is marked by a pattern of accumulation in which profits accrue from speculative activities – transactions and flows of money on financial markets, including mergers, acquisitions, share buy-backs – rather than trade, services or productive activity. This is a model of capitalism in which profits are generated from flows of finance that may operate outside of the realm of productive activity (Lapavitsas 2013). Some situate finance capitalism in opposition to the real and productive economy as a predatory force that destroys and extracts wealth from the latter. Indeed, the concept of financialisation emerged within Marxist political economy in an effort to relate booming finance to shrinking production (Lapavitsas 2011).

For some, finance is destructive of the real economy because it seeks to convert productive activity into abstract financial value, in a process of dematerialisation: 'In the sphere of the financial economy, the acceleration of financial circulation and valorization implies an elimination of the real world. The more you destroy physical things, physical resources, and the body, the more you can accelerate the circulation of financial flows' (Berardi 2012, 105). Saskia Sassen suggests that finance is a type of predatory formation that extracts value and destroys the fabric of productive and social life (2017). Yet, as economists such as Costas Lapavitsas show, finance does not operate in a disconnected or nebulous sphere, but is embedded within the productive economy, to the extent that companies themselves have been financialised and operate according to a changed economic logic: 'Finance is a well-defined field of capitalist economic activity, not a nebulous realm into which capital seeks to escape when, and if, profitability is low in production' (Lapavitsas 2013, 298–9). Financialisation is marked by 'the intrusion of finance and the capital market into the boardroom' as companies acquire financial capacities and increasingly behave like banks (Froud et al. 2000, 774). The purpose of many large companies is to use production or services not as a source of value in themselves, but as a lever to generate financial gains and increase shareholder value. Companies are less inclined to invest in production, technological innovation or human capital skills in an economic order driven by value extraction rather than by value creation (Mazzucato 2018).

Financialisation is not simply an economic process, as it also restructures social relationships, creating a 'deeply unequal regime' that has exacerbated profound structural inequalities (Lapavitsas et al. 2014, 177). Some point to the rise of a new class of rentiers made up of powerful elites and owners of capital ('a parasitical economic entity') that extracts wealth without producing (Lapavitsas 2011, 615). In the workplace, finance has generated new forms of social stratification and has reasserted the power of capital over labour (Peters 2011). Most critics agree that the rise of finance and shareholder value has been wholly negative for labour in terms of its status and conditions (Lazonick & O'Sullivan 2000; Thomson 2003; Peters

2011; Cushen 2013). The shift to shareholder value has led many companies to restructure and change their employment practices and consequently they are more likely to downsize, outsource, intensify work and integrate low-cost labour (Peters 2011). This has led to a generalised deterioration of working conditions: 'financialization in addition to creating employment insecurity and work intensification, can also prompt role insecurity, suppression of voice' and 'prompt distress and anger' (Cushen 2013, 329, 314). Some studies of the impact of shareholder restructuring suggest that there are winners and losers and that core elite workers benefit at the expense of insecure or unemployed workers. 'Survivors' of company downsizing can benefit from a new regime as employees and shareholders reap the gains of improved financial status (Froud et al. 2000). Yet in the case of France Télécom, there were few winners as the workforce as a whole was subject to intense and unbearable pressure designed to improve the company's financial position.

Along with other critics, I interpret the suicide crisis at France Télécom as a consequence of 'a management imperative to maximise shareholder value' in the aftermath of the company's privatisation (Chabrak, Craig & Daidj 2016, 501). The French government envisioned France Télécom as a beacon of privatisation ('un laboratoire pour le privé') that would blaze a trail towards economic autonomy and showcase the methods that could be used to privatise other companies stifled by the yoke of state ownership (Decèze 2008, 25). This was France's largest and most extensive privatisation and would transfer billions of euros worth of shares from the state to financial markets. Through France Télécom, the state would redefine its economic role and identity, moving from a *dirigiste* and protectionist role as guarantor of the general interest to a facilitator of economic innovation and global openness in a fast-changing world. Debates in the Senate presented France Télécom's privatisation (although this term was conspicuously avoided in favour of *sociétisation* or 'corporatisation') as an opportunity not to be missed and a means to affirm French economic power on the international stage. Without autonomy from the state, France Télécom would remain 'anchored in the port', unable to release its entrepreneurial energies or achieve its technological potential, while its competitors reaped the rewards of global economic competition (Sénat 1996). As France Télécom was, at the time, a profitable and successful company, proponents of privatisation needed to instil a sense of urgency, by evoking future market threats that might reverse the company's fortunes at any time. The Senate report compares France Télécom's existing position in the global economy as a state-controlled entity to that of a horse pulling a carriage in a race where all the other international competitors are running freely. Privatisation is presented as a necessary, natural and inevitable course of action without which the company would be consigned to the economic scrapheap and relegated to a secondary ranking on the world stage.

Beyond a shift in the source of France Télécom's capital, from the state to financial markets, privatisation would involve a profound transformation in the culture of an organisation that was steeped in a public service tradition. With its origins in the creation of a Ministry of Posts and Telegraphs in 1878, France Télécom was part of a national project to modernise France's infrastructure, connect each citizen to the state and consolidate national values of citizenship and public service. Its purpose was to serve the collective interest and to incarnate the enduring values of citizenship and social justice by which the Republic defined itself. Alongside its public service identity, France Télécom also prided itself on being a pioneer of technological innovation, defining France's place in the world as a modern and economically advanced nation. Despite its centralised and bureaucratic structures, the Ministry of Posts and Telegraphs employed brilliant and inventive engineers who were at the vanguard of technological progress. Soon after the Second World War, France pioneered the world's first experiment with long-distance automatic dialling. In 1978, it opened a data transmission network based on the Transpac packet-switching system developed by French industry. Over a decade before the internet became ubiquitous, France Télécom had invented the Minitel, a digital communications network provided free to anyone with a telephone. Under the tutelage of the state, France Télécom had become a world leader in telecommunications, not only in terms of its technological progress, but in the practical applications of these inventions in daily life (Ardagh 1990). At France Télécom, as in many other large French companies, financialisation profoundly destabilised the established workplace culture, collective identities, shared values and social relationships that were associated with a public service tradition (Palpacuer & Seignour 2019).

Following European directives on the privatisation of telecommunications, France Télécom changed its status in 1990, acquiring formal autonomy from the state as a 'public law entity'. Prior to this, the company was run directly by a government ministry and its budget was approved each year by a vote in the National Assembly. In 1996, it changed status again, becoming a public limited company (*société anonyme*) and opened up its capital to financial markets, whilst the state remained a majority shareholder. The plural Left government (1997–2002) pushed privatisation further than any preceding government, and on 6 October 1997, 20 per cent of France Télécom shares were listed on the financial markets. Every year, a greater proportion of shares was transferred onto financial markets. Ivan du Roy observes that the company's 165,200 employees were prepared to accept this partial privatisation on the grounds that they could retain their status as public servants or fonctionnaires and therefore continue to benefit from the job security and guaranteed income that came with this status. They were also given the opportunity to buy their own shares, in a bid to gain their support for privatisation. Yet this protected status would soon prove to be counterproductive and used by management as a weapon against them: 'this protection will work against them. Those who remain find themselves trapped in an infernal spiral' (Du Roy 2009a, 71).

At the outset, the sale of France Télécom shares proved to be extremely lucrative, bringing over 12 billion euros into the French government's coffers. A new law introduced by the right-wing government in July 2003 allowed the state to reduce its proportion of shares to below 50 per cent, thereby relinquishing its status as a majority shareholder within the company. The transfer of shares to financial markets meant that France Télécom's fate was increasingly determined by external financial variables and it was obliged to comply with performance indicators put in place by financial analysts to measure the company's share value on international markets. This new financial logic meant that value was no longer measured solely by the products and services that the company provided, nor by the skills and expertise of its workforce, but more crudely, by the price of its shares: 'The ultimate goal of management is henceforth to create share value. Not to lead an industrial project, nor to support employees in the development and production of telecommunication services. All that matters now is to increase the share price' (Diehl & Doublet 2010, 52).

France Télécom executives embraced privatisation, seeking to transform the company from a national service provider into a leading multinational corporation and a key player in the vast planetary network of telecommunications (Du Roy 2009a). Following privatisation, chief executive Michel Bon (1995–2002) engaged in a frenzied series of mergers and acquisitions, seeking to capture an increasing share of the global market in telecommunications. His 'spending spree' included mobile phone operator Orange, the struggling German operator Mobilcom, data carrier Equant and internet service provider Freeserve, as well as new mobile phone licences. By the end of 2000, France Télécom had become an international leader in telecommunications and had operations across 75 countries. These acquisitions were made through vast borrowing and, like other company executives, Bon was driven by an unshakeable belief in the rising value of international share prices and the certainty that he would be able to repay his debt. Like other European telecoms firms, France Télécom was caught up in the tech stock boom of 1999 and 2000 and the subsequent bust. Bon's reckless spending led the company into massive debt. By the time he stepped down in 2002, the company's share price had fallen by 70 per cent, while its debts ballooned to 60 billion euros. France Télécom now had the dubious honour of being the most indebted company in the world, and Moody's downgraded its shares to the status of junk bonds (Decèze 2008; Du Roy 2009a; Diehl & Doublet 2010). Bon was fined 10,000 euros by the Court of Budgetary and Financial Discipline and only avoided a charge of financial misconduct because the government, which was still the company's main shareholder, had done little to prevent his disastrous spending (*Challenges*, 25 July 2008).

During Bon's period of leadership, half of the company's executive board was still composed of state representatives. Interviewed by a parliamentary commission on the company's investment errors, Bon blamed external market forces beyond his control and claimed that the fault lay with 'the collapse of shares which completely derailed our refinancing plans' (quoted by Du Roy 2009a, 88). Meanwhile, trade union representatives on the company's executive board denounced privatisation as a national disaster and called for the company to be renationalised. Having benefitted from the sale of company shares through privatisation, the French government under Prime Minister Jean-Pierre Raffarin was obliged to recapitalise France Télécom to the tune of 15 billion euros. This meant that, henceforth, the company had one overarching strategy: to reduce its debts and recoup profits by whatever means necessary.

Scholarship on financialisation shows how the shift to a shareholder model in large companies tends to reorientate management strategy towards meeting the interests of financial investors on whose capital they increasingly depend. Management increasingly tends to favour short-term strategies to boost immediate returns, including taking on debt, limiting internal investment and cutting jobs (Froud et al. 2000; Peters 2011). In order to redress France Télécom's massive debt burden, consecutive bosses prioritised a reduction of costs as the single most important imperative driving the company. As a large proportion of company costs were linked to salary payments, the workforce was to become the adjustment mechanism needed to fulfil this economic strategy. Thierry Breton, celebrated as a 'turnaround whizz' by the *Wall Street Journal* and appointed chief executive in 2002, set as his mission to shake up the company and set it on a path towards profitability (*Wall Street Journal*, 18 December 2002). As part of his 'Ambition France Télécom', he set a target of 15 billion euros in 'cost killing' to come largely from an elimination of jobs. His deputy, Louis-Pierre Wenes, was hired from management consultancy firm AT Kearney, who were 'cost killing' specialists. Yet these cost-reduction efforts were impeded by a legal agreement reached on 31 December 2003 that guaranteed that France Télécom's public service employees could retain their status regardless of future changes in company ownership (Chabrak, Craig & Daidj 2016). Prior to the transfer of further shares in September 2004, a trade union official warned of the impact of further privatisation on working conditions: 'For the workers, the situation is already difficult: worsened working conditions, stress, sickness, despair, even suicides, because of the massive elimination of jobs, the incessant restructurings, the forced mobility. Total privatization will only aggravate this situation' (quoted by Jones 2012, 5). When Didier Lombard became chief executive in 2005, he put in place a new strategic plan, NExT, whose central objective was to shed 22,000 jobs in the space of three years and to redeploy a further 10,000 employees. In a speech at a board meeting that was subsequently leaked to the press, Lombard set the tone for the new strategy: 'We must shed our image as a mother hen [...] I will achieve [job cuts] by whatever means possible, by pushing people through the window or the door' (*Libération*, 7 May 2013). His director of human resources also expressed his unwavering commitment to achieving job cuts: 'I will have failed personally if we don't achieve 22,000 departures. For the company, this represents a cash flow of 7 billion euros'.[3]

France Télécom's privatisation and its human costs have been given representation in various documentary accounts. Some have been written by former employees and give an inside view of events, observing the gradual rise of a pernicious and brutal model of management under successive bosses. In one testimonial account, *Orange: le déchirement* (Orange: The Rupture), written by two management consultants, one of whom had worked at France Télécom for 20 years, the authors situate suicides within a transformation of power relationships at the company. They argue that mounting financial pressures triggered an autocratic drift and the rise of a form of hyper power that exerted itself with violence against the workforce. They locate a moment of rupture within the company between a humane management model directed towards developing human resources and an autocratic management regime that sought to eliminate those same human resources:

> The causes of this rupture are to be found in the spheres of power: in an autocratic drift, imposed over several years by the company's management and their partners, to which can be added a degeneration of the conception of management that is reduced to a technique that protects the interests of shareholders. (Diehl & Doublet 2010, 9)

Another testimonial account, *Pendant qu'ils comptent les morts* (While They Count the Dead, 2010), consists of a detailed interview between former employee Marin Ledun and an occupational psychiatrist, Brigitte Font Le Bret. Ledun writes both as witness and victim of the workplace suffering he describes as, following his own mental breakdown, he became a patient of the psychiatrist he now interviews in the book. As the book's title suggests, Ledun's aim was to challenge a statistical approach to suicides which consists of counting dead bodies and to turn his attention instead to the complex human stories that lie behind these figures. The psychiatrist describes individual cases of patients

---

3 It is noteworthy that France Télécom was successful in achieving its targets. By the end of 2008, 22,450 employees had left the company, and 14,000 had been assigned to new (generally inferior) positions in the company. Between 2001 and 2008, 44,700 jobs were cut, of which 94 per cent were fonctionnaires (Desriaux & Magnaudeix 2009).

who came to see her, retracing the links between their bodily disorders and the structural transformations taking place at the company. She observes that workplace suffering is distinct from other forms of mental disorder, as it has an external chronology and a structural context and can be traced to specific workplace transformations that have occurred at a precise place and time. Workplace suffering does not express an ongoing pathological condition, but reflects a sudden rupture in working life in which external social conditions generate a temporary state of subjective trauma (Ledun & Font Le Bret 2010).

Time to Move

In a financialised economy, corporations pursue differential management practices that seek both to produce entrepreneurial subjects and to expel surplus populations whose existence is deemed to threaten the vitality and productivity of the whole (Sassen 2014 and 2017; Christiaens 2018; Haskaj 2018). Financialisation transforms the way corporations operate by making them 'dependent on the approval of financial agents to attract capital, which incentivizes the expulsion of groups that trouble statistics' (Christiaens 2018, 17). Following its privatisation and shift to a shareholder model, France Télécom's overarching human resources strategy was one of financial expulsion, as it sought to eliminate labour's salaries from the balance sheets. Between 2003 and 2008, when France Télécom's overarching priority was to maximise shareholder value, revenues increased by 16 per cent and employee numbers dropped by 14.8 per cent (Chabrak, Craig & Daidj 2016). Management sought not simply to abandon workers or relegate them to obsolete roles, but to actively remove them from the workplace in order to generate positive financial value (Haskaj 2018; Christiaens 2019). In a bid to transform Orange into 'a brand without employees', bosses engaged in an orchestrated campaign of psychological violence against the workforce (*Mediapart*, 20 October 2009). Management strategies were characterised by a form of 'savage sorting' that segregates and reconfigures workers as either productive or unproductive and seeks to eliminate the latter category as quickly and efficiently as possible (Sassen 2014, 4). The company's human resources director described the new management strategies in terms of a 'systematic identification and compulsory registration of people' (quoted by Palpacuer

& Seignour 2019, 6). According to state prosecutors, senior managers were responsible, through their use of these tactics, for 'endangering the lives of others' (*Le Parisien*, 7 May 2013).

On 28 September 2009, a 51-year-old technician and father of two who had been redeployed to a France Télécom call centre in Annecy a few weeks previously threw himself off a bridge on his way to work in the morning and died instantly. In a letter left in the passenger seat of his car, he alluded to relentless pressures at work and his difficulty adapting to his new role. He had been targeted by the company's new HR strategy of 'mobility', which pushed employees out of their existing jobs into the 'front line' of the company selling products in call centres. His suicide was the focus of a television documentary, *Orange amère* (Bitter Orange, 2011) directed by Patricia Bodet and Debord Bernard, that investigates the circumstances of his self-killing, the twenty-eighth suicide at the company in a period of under two years. The investigation into his suicide found that the branch where he worked had been shut down earlier in the year and the jobs of all of the employees had been axed. Along with others, the technician was given the choice of either keeping his existing post but moving to a new city, and therefore being separated from his family, or switching to a sales role in a call centre and staying in Annecy. Having initially chosen to move to Lyon to avoid demotion, he changed his mind and decided to take a job in a call centre in order to stay close to his family. This latest case was 'un suicide de trop' (one suicide too many) for France Télécom and precipitated a dramatic change in stance by the company's bosses, who had previously refused to accept any responsibility for the suicides. Chief executive Didier Lombard, together with his deputy and head of human resources, went immediately to Annecy in order to talk to workers and trade union representatives at the branch where the technician had worked. At the end of the meeting, Lombard announced to the press that the policy of systematic redeployment of all managers every three years would come to an end. The company would change its management approach in order to put the 'human being at the centre' (*La Croix*, 29 September 2009).

In its drive to fulfil an overarching goal of reducing debt and increasing shareholder value, France Télécom had put in place a management strategy based on 'financial expulsion' that was designed to push as many workers as possible to leave the company (Christiaens 2018, 3). Euphemistically branded 'Time to Move' by HR executives, this strategy was presented in the company's internal communication as an exciting entrepreneurial opportunity and a career enhancement, and was articulated in a language of adventure and boundless possibilities: 'Our energy is constructive and turned towards the future. We rely on our strength to push back our limits. Our enthusiasm and optimism are communicative'. Behind this management jargon lay a 'brutal conception of management that savagely reduced workers to simple variables of economic adjustment' (Diehl & Doublet 2010, 84, 11). This was to be achieved by putting the entire company into a phase of continuous restructuring or 'perpetual movement' that was intended to break the fixed and stable relationship between the employee and his or her job and to destabilise working life to such an extent that workers would choose to leave the company of their own accord (Du Roy 2009a, 152). This strategy was characterised by 'incessant and absurd reorganisations' that followed no coherent logic or rationale other than to destabilise workers and push them to leave (Diehl & Doublet 2010, 88). Some were encouraged to leave the company and find work elsewhere. Alternative career possibilities endorsed by the company included opening a creperie, a pizzeria, a rural guest house, a bowling alley, a florists or a bookshop, with the possibility of returning to France Télécom after a two-year period. In his testimonial account, Marin Ledun recalls a 'surreal' meeting with a manager who tried to convince a group of workers to leave France Télécom and become florists. The manager outlined the practical steps required to open a flower shop and presented this as a romantic ideal and a chance for the employee to fulfil his or her dreams (Ledun & Font Le Bret 2010). Between 2006 and 2011, France Télécom reduced its workforce by 24,421 employees on permanent contracts (Chabrak, Craig & Daidj 2016).

The experimental play *Les Impactés* (The Impacted, 2007) portrays the human story behind France Télécom's corporate restructuring and draws on real-life cases gathered through extensive interviews with employees.[4] Produced in close collaboration with employees and trade unionists, the play depicts the organised and strategic nature of

4   The play was produced by the experimental leftist theatre group Naje (Nous n'abandonnerons jamais l'espoir, 'We will never give up hope') in 2007. The production of the play was later the subject of a documentary film by Thibault Dufour, also called *Les Impactés*, which includes scenes from the play, interviews with its producers, actors, trade unionists and employees at France Télécom.

the management methods put in place at the company. It opens with the new chief executive talking to her deputy about the absurdity of her situation as the head of a company composed entirely of fonction-naires and therefore resistant to change. Her deputy hints at ways of overcoming this bureaucratic obstacle and suggests that the strategy to be followed is comparable to that of constantly moving a full glass of water backwards and forwards: 'By the tenth time it is moved, only half its contents will be left'. In a speech to employees, the chief executive presents the company's restructuring plans as an exciting adventure and a leap into the unknown:

> A new era opens before us that is risky but equally filled with excitement. We are leaving the protected shores of the public sphere and taking to the high seas, where we will brave the storms unleashed by the stock market and enter into combat with the pirates of high finance.

In the play, audience members, consisting of real France Télécom employees, are invited to come on stage and participate in a form of role-play where they confront a manager and speak out in defence of their interests and those of their colleagues. The play has a political function, encouraging workers to perceive their own situation as part of a broader power struggle between workers and employers. It aims to counter the individualising strategies put in place by management, by opening up a space in which shared strategies, collective consciousness and resistance might be formed.

A key aspect of the NExT strategy was forced redeployment intended to unsettle long-serving employees (90 per cent of employees were over 40 years of age and had been at the company for two decades or more) and increase company profits by transferring employees into commercial roles where they would boost product sales. Employees were exhorted to accept the logic of mobility as a guiding principle and were appraised not on the basis of their professional skills or experience, but on their capacity to adapt continuously to new roles and situations. Management promoted mobility as a virtue in itself, irrespective of the suitability of an employee for a new position. In interviews with managers, employees were asked if they were ready to embrace change, 'Etes-vous prêt à la mobilité? ('Are you ready for mobility?'), and those who refused to move were urged to overcome their psychological barriers and reject immobilism (Du Roy 2009a, 152). In most cases, employees were redeployed from highly skilled roles as engineers or technicians into low-skilled sales positions in call centres or mobile phone shops. They moved from a professional situation where they exercised considerable autonomy and professional expertise to a situation in which they had to recite scripted lines and ask permission to go to the toilet. Many call centre workers experienced a widespread sense of disorientation, humiliation and anguish and felt terrorised and controlled by their supervisors (Rolo 2015). Photographs and personal items were prohibited at workstations, where managers instead posted incentives to achieve greater sales. Calls had to be restricted to just over three minutes and operators had to recite a prewritten script. It is no coincidence that a majority of suicides at France Télécom had a similar profile: most were male technicians in their fifties who had worked at France Télécom for over 30 years and had been pressurised to join the front line and work in call centres.

The sense of abasement and humiliation experienced by many workers is given representation in recent novels inspired by events at France Télécom and set in fictional call centres (Ledun 2010; Beinstingel 2010; Raynal 2010). In *Les travailleuses sans visage* (The Faceless Workers, 2010) Cathy Raynal, who worked at France Télécom for 30 years, portrays a world of work in which human exchanges are reduced to faceless, anonymous and simulated commercial transactions. Her novel gives a satirical and humorous slant to work through the stories of a group of women employed at the same call centre. These women lead full, chaotic and engaged lives which contrast with the dull, regimented and repetitive regime in the call centre. We learn that they have five minutes to complete each call, five seconds between each call and a ten-minute break at the end of their morning shift. Jennifer, in her twenties, balances the tedium of work with a social life of clubbing and romance. In a fantastical scene, she describes a dream where the world and its entire population have been wiped out by some unknown catastrophe. The call centre is the only building left standing and its occupants, the last survivors. In these extreme circumstances, they talk to each other for the first time, make practical arrangements and share common interests, building a solidarity that was never possible when the call centre was fully operational. Claire is a trade union representative who plays in an African percussion group in her spare time and decides to take part in a demonstration against the invasion of Iraq, where she plays music to the crowds. With its miserly drive for ever-increasing profits, the world of the call centre seems petty, mundane and meaningless by comparison. Sylvie has been demoted to the call centre after being forced out of her previous job as a manager where she was sidelined by her boss. In the call centre, she is constantly criticised for being too compassionate, for taking time to listen to customers who are either lonely or broke, rather than trying to push products on them. Under relentless pressure, she cracks and attacks a colleague with a pair of scissors. The novel represents these women in their struggle for humanity and friendship in the deadening and stultifying world of the call centre.

In *Retour aux mots sauvages* (Return to Primitive Words, 2010), Thierry Beinstingel represents the sense of humiliation and existential crisis experienced by the narrator Eric as he is demoted from a skilled manual job as an electrician to a role as a call centre operator. He describes this experience in terms of a shift from a world of work in which he used his hands, honing his dexterity and expertise, to a world in which his mouth has become his sole working instrument, deployed in a purely robotic and unthinking way:

> fingers which knew exactly what pressure to apply to the tool, eyes which focused, gauging distance out of habit, four metres to the connection box, a brain which calculated how long the job would take, two hours for a complete rewiring of the electrical board. And now his job was to read, speak, listen, reformulate and note everything down on the computer. It wasn't easier, it had become more repetitive and immobile. He had lost the capacity to judge time and distances. Thousands of gestures that he had accomplished since technical college had been brutally erased from his memory. His work had become abstract and reduced to the simple movement of a plastic mouse. (Beinstingel 2010, 72–73)

Throughout the novel, Eric regularly examines his hands, noting how they have become soft, fleshy and redundant. This softening of his hands is a motif for a deeper existential crisis and loss of professional skill and masculine identity.

Another dimension of the new management strategy was to force staff to relocate frequently to branches in new cities or towns. Such relocations were often chaotic and unplanned and served no other purpose than to unsettle the workers involved. In many documented cases, workers were pushed to move to a new branch in a new town, only to have this branch close down, requiring them to move elsewhere. Whilst forced redeployment is a widely used management technique to achieve staff cuts, this was the first time the technique was used on a systematic basis to slash thousands of jobs on a national scale. In his book *La Machine à broyer* (The Crushing Machine), Dominique Decèze provides detailed testimonies of France Télécom employees who were forced to accept continuous relocations. One reported having to move to five different branches in six years; another spoke of having to change jobs every six months. For workers with families, this was often disruptive and a source of considerable distress. One of these employees wrote an open letter to former president Nicolas Sarkozy in 2007, expressing his frustration at being forced to leave his family and move to a new city when he was approaching retirement age: 'Having nearly reached retirement age (in eight years), they want me to go off and finish my career in large towns such as Montpellier, Toulouse, Nantes and Lyon. It's impossible and too late. My life, my home, my children are here. I don't wish to start over again' (Decèze 2008, 99). Forced redeployment meant that family life was no longer protected from the economic pressures of work and instead became an adjustment mechanism to be manipulated by the company. In another testimonial published in *Le Monde*, one employee described how he was forced, with five days' notice, to accept a new job in Lille, 500 kilometres from his home, and he was obliged either to accept or resign (Diehl & Doublet 2010).

The new management model was characterised by the use of psychological tactics as a routine management tool and a means of achieving strategic economic objectives. Several cases of suicide at France Télécom have been explicitly linked to the effects of bullying by managers in the context of the NExT strategy. Such management brutality has been given representation in recent films. Louis–Julien Petit's film *Carole Matthieu*, adapted from a novel by Marin Ledun, presents the management methods the latter experienced when working at France Télécom between 2000 and 2007 and which triggered his nervous breakdown. The eponymous lead character, played by Isabelle Adjani, is an occupational doctor who bears witness to the catastrophic effects on her patients of the daily psychological torment inflicted by managers. We witness an opening scene in the call centre where managers begin the day's shift of phone calls by hurling insults and abuse at employees in order to push them to meet their targets: 'Vous êtes des putains des fucking vendeurs' ('You are motherfucking salesmen'). We see that their most intimate speech processes, gestures and thoughts are subject to constant surveillance, as supervisors listen in to their conversations, time their calls and monitor their breaks. This is a world in which the drive to achieve economic results reduces human relations to a primitive fight for survival. Matthieu struggles in vain to bring the endemic suffering of employees to the attention of the company's bosses, but this is either dismissed or normalised in a context of global economic pressures. We observe how Matthieu herself becomes a victim to the spiral of violence that she witnesses, slipping into mental disorder and self-medication with painkillers. Only a further act of deadly violence perpetrated by Matthieu herself will make visible a form of psychological suffering that is hidden, denied and occluded by the corporation.

States of Denial

When confronted with events that are deeply unsettling, disturbing or traumatic, societies tend to enter 'states of denial' that disavow the reality of events or push them to one side. This can lead to 'an unspoken collusion to ignore (or pretend to ignore?) the whole subject' (Cohen 2001: xi). The phenomenon of work suicides whereby individuals, in the face of extreme pressures at work, choose to take their own lives, often within the ordinary and mundane setting of the workplace, brings to the fore experiences of suffering that are difficult to contemplate or imagine. Yet, beyond a collective instinct towards denial which tends to push this issue to one side, work suicide is also subject to specific modes of repression that seek to keep it hidden from public view. Work suicide is subject to a 'negationist tendency' that disavows the connections between the suicidal act and working conditions (Dejours, 2014).[5] For some critics, a 'collective denial' prevails on the question of work suicide and keeps its social and structural causes concealed (Alemanno & Cabdedoche 2011, 30). Such 'states of denial' serve the vested interests of business and political elites, whose reputation

---

5   Christophe Dejours, interview with the author, 4 November 2014.

and financial interests might be damaged by the media exposure of suicides. In the global telecoms industry, where gadgets such as the mobile phone are presented as slick, carefree and aesthetic commodities disconnected from messy corporeal realities, suicide constitutes a brutal intrusion of flesh and blood. Work suicide gives material embodiment to often hidden relations of production in the form of unspeakable pain, trauma and distress. Because of the high political and economic stakes involved, suicides are subject to repressive tactics, including discourses that aim to deny, individualise or rationalise them and that either blame the individual for his or her own death or rationalise it in relation to higher and ineluctable economic forces. Elites also use modes of repression that seek to control information on the suicides, impede their investigation or censor the media.[6] Recognising work suicides and the forms of repression that seek to conceal them is crucial if we are to take account of the profound human and social consequences of neoliberal restructuring and shareholder-driven management tactics in the workplace.

Suicides threaten political elites whose policies of economic liberalisation and labour market reform have defined conditions in the 'restructured new workplaces' in which suicides take place (Danford, Richardson & Upchurch 2003, 26). As critics have shown, the shift to neoliberalism was driven by 'a politically transformed state' whose role was no longer to protect social rights in the face of market forces, but to act as the 'defender of global corporate interests' (Webster, Lambert & Bezuidenhout 2008, 25). The French government removed regulations that constrained corporations, facilitating the rise of multinationals with unparalleled power and reach. At the same time, it restricted labour rights in terms of wages, social benefits, contractual rights and collective bargaining. The shift to economic liberalisation was legitimised in the public sphere by appealing to the general interest

---

6   In China, the state responded to the wave of employee suicides at Foxconn at a Shenzhen production site in 2010 by censoring the media in order to contain the damage to Foxconn's corporate reputation. On 28 May 2010, following an attempted suicide by a 25-year-old employee the previous day, the Chinese government imposed a media blackout prohibiting any reporting on Foxconn, apart from the state's official news agency (Xinhua News) and Foxconn's own public statements. Rather than investigating and taking action to protect and improve working conditions, state efforts focused on suppressing negative media reporting of the suicides (Pun et al. 2014).

and to universal social benefits such as increased jobs, investment, competitiveness and growth. In their political speeches, leaders invoked 'the globalisation myth' that promised that the short-term pain of economic restructuring would lead to long-term social rewards for all (Danford, Richardson & Upchurch 2003, 7). The reality of restructured workplaces in which some workers are placed under such intense economic pressures that they choose to take their own lives interferes with such positivistic rhetoric about the public good. It places the economic choices of governments under public scrutiny and raises questions about the social and moral ends of state-driven economic liberalisation.

The French state was implicated in the suicide crisis at France Télécom, as it partially owned the company and defined the employment status of the public service employees who took their own lives. France Télécom was cherished by governments as an economic champion ('a national monument') and its privatisation was driven by state-led concerns with reasserting French economic interests on the international stage (*Le Monde*, 11 May 2009). According to critics, the French state knew about the devastating effects on the workforce of management policy following privatisation, but chose to do nothing about it. Journalist Ivan du Roy suggests that the government assumed a voluntary 'blindness', preferring to stick its head in the sand rather than confront the reality of the crisis (2009a, 175). In 2002, Senator Gérard Larcher presented a detailed report on France Télécom's privatisation in which he invoked the suffering of the workforce, referring to 'a world of work that has been completely disrupted'. In his report, he cites a trade union leader who describes a 'deterioration of working and living conditions' since privatisation.[7] Similarly, Senator Marie-Claude Beaudeau took a close interest in France Télécom and intervened regularly in parliament to signal the changed conditions affecting the company's workforce. In a speech on 3 February 2004, she declared that 'workplace suffering has been rising at an alarming scale in recent years [...] Physical and mental exhaustion is increasing, as is despair and depression. Stress is commonplace' (quoted by Decèze 2008, 239). At the height of the suicide crisis, the state was still the company's largest shareholder, holding 27 per cent of its shares (in 2009), and government was represented directly

7 Rapport no. 274, 'Le bilan de la loi no. 96-660 relative à l'entreprise nationale France-Télécom', 26 March 2002.

in the company's decision-making, having a number of seats on the company's executive board. According to one trade union representative (CGT), 'The state threw its weight behind management policy until the suicides took place. Its three representatives on the administrative council never criticised company policy, unlike employee represent-atives on the committee' (De Gastines 2016, 9).

In a nation in which political and business elites are closely intertwined, the majority of France Télécom bosses came directly from government ministries or joined government after their period at France Télécom. For instance, France Télécom's chief executive since 2010, Stéphane Richard, who was appointed by government in response to the suicide crisis, ran two ministerial cabinets before joining the company and worked for the French Minister of Finance, Christine Lagarde. Another chief executive, Thierry Breton, left France Télécom to become Minister of the Economy in 2005. In 2007, at a time when suicides were beginning to rise, Didier Lombard was awarded the Légion d'honneur by the French state, France's highest decoration (Breton and Richard have also been awarded this accolade). Far from being an innocent bystander to economic events beyond its control, the state was implicated in defining the structural conditions in which the suicides took place. For Gildas Renou, the suicides should not be treated as an epidemic that has pathological causes but as the outcome of political decisions 'orchestrated deliberately and knowingly from the top to the bottom of the company hierarchy' (2009, 1).

France Télécom's bosses have been accused of ignoring repeated warnings about the devastating effects of the company's restructuring policies on employees' mental health. When privatisation was initiated in 1997, occupational health doctors began to sound the alarm about rising stress levels, and investigations into workplace stress were carried out at France Télécom sites in Paris, Lyon, Marseille, Grenoble, La Rochelle and Voiron. Yet, faced with mounting evidence from a range of occupa-tional specialists, management 'went into denial' (Du Roy 2009a, 176, 182). The ongoing prosecution case against France Télécom's executives claims that the company received repeated warnings between 2005 and 2009 from health and safety committees, trade unions and medical doctors, but either ignored these warnings or refused to respond to them (Catala 2010). In their annual reports, many occupational doctors reported an alarming rise in psychiatric disorders, chronic stress and depressive illnesses in the context of the company's restructuring.

The documentary *Orange amère* (Bitter Orange, 2011) includes an interview with an occupational doctor, Monique Fraysse, who displays a letter that she sent to France Télécom's bosses in 2008, signed by seven doctors, warning of the deleterious effects of the company's strategies on employees' mental health: 'We alerted France Télécom's bosses to a growing malaise that we were aware of, but it went unheeded. When they say that they didn't know what was going on, it isn't true. They knew what was happening but chose to overlook it because the priority was to cut 22,000 jobs'. Occupational health doctors were also subjected to pressure and forced in some cases to modify their findings or to remain silent about them. A number of doctors who resigned from France Télécom criticised management for preventing them from working properly and compromising their impartiality. When two occupational health doctors were invited by trade unions to speak at a training event on workplace stress in December 2007, France Télécom's management prohibited them from doing so, arguing that they had a duty to respect 'confidentiality' and 'impartiality' (Du Roy 2009a, 179). The union representing occupational doctors (National Union of Occupational Health Professionals) wrote to the chief executive of France Télécom in 2007 to denounce attacks on medical practice and on the independence of doctors.

In 2007, trade unionists from the leftist SUD and the managers' union CFE-CGC set up a new syndicalist structure, the Observatory of Stress and Forced Mobility (L'Observatoire du stress et des mobilités forcées) to examine the impact of management policies and, in particular, policies of forced redeployment on the workforce. One of their first initiatives was to launch an online questionnaire for all France Télécom employees that was intended to gauge levels of stress in the workplace. Patrick Ackermann, one of the founders of the Observatory, described what happened next:

> I called the Director of Human Resources to let him know what we were doing and to ask for his support. Within an hour of this call, the link to the questionnaire on the company's website was shut down. We then asked employees to complete the questionnaire privately using their own computers at home [...] The results were astonishing and gave evidence of dangerous levels of stress amongst employees at France Télécom. Two out of three employees suffered from work-related stress and one out

of two wished to leave the company. Of course, management rejected this evidence, arguing that the results were unscientific and they referred us to an earlier staff questionnaire that they had conducted themselves, even though its results were never made publicly available. (Waters 2014b)

In a radio interview in November 2007, which was intended to counter mounting criticism of the company, the head of human resources, Olivier Barberot, criticised the results of the questionnaire and suggested that morale was good across the workforce. A joint declaration made by all six trade unions at France Télécom on 30 June 2008, included as evidence in the case for the prosecution, stated:

How many suicides have to take place before management decides to confront this problem and respond to it? Your systematic refusal to face this question makes sense to the extent that it confirms fears about the management methods called into question. These acts are partly linked to the impact of incessant restructuring and unbearable pressure exerted by management against the workforce. (quoted by Catala 2010, 64)

In 2009, SUD lodged a formal complaint with public prosecutors that accused France Télécom of psychological bullying (*harcèlement moral*) against its workforce.

Company bosses also used specific modes of repression in order to prevent enquires into workplace stress from taking place. Between 2005 and 2009, the company went to court to block a third of the 64 requests for workplace investigations into serious health risks made by health and safety committees in different branches across France (De Gastines 2016). Hence, in the Limousin in 2005 and in Auvergne in 2006, France Télécom went to court to prevent investigations into the health effects of workplace restructuring. Following the suicide of a 37-year-old computer technician in Paris on 16 September 2008, France Télécom went to court to block an investigation into workplace stress in the branch where he had worked. Similarly, following the attempted suicide on 6 January 2009 of a technician who had left a letter complaining of humiliation and harassment by his superiors, France Télécom management sought to hinder an enquiry by an external agency and ordered its staff not to speak to the consultants involved. It was only as a result of direct intervention by the

French government that Didier Lombard took the decision to suspend temporarily the policy of forced redeployment and it was shelved when Stéphane Richard took over as company CEO in 2010.

The company's official response to the suicides consisted of individualised forms of support including a counselling service and an emergency hotline. Such approaches tended to treat suicide and the workplace trauma that gave rise to it as a matter of individual psychology, rather than as a question that concerned structural conditions of work. While putting in place provisions for individual therapy, the company's restructuring process continued unabated even when workplace suicides were at their peak. In fact, a communiqué published by France Télécom's human resources department on 26 August 2009 emphasised the urgency of pressing ahead with restructuring, referring to 'the necessity for the company to pursue its transformation in a context of rapid evolution and strong competitive pressure' (Du Roy 2009b: 5). It was only after 28 suicides and in the face of intense pressure from the media that company executives finally reacted publicly, acknowledging the links between the suicides and company management strategies.

France Télécom on Trial

Suicide letters have been used as documentary evidence in litigation before the courts and in the pursuit of justice by families of those who have taken their own lives and by suicide survivors themselves. A suicide letter establishes a verifiable connection between the individual act of self-killing and the workplace and can be used alongside other evidence to prove a company's responsibility in a suicide.[8] France Télécom is the only company in France to have faced a criminal trial in relation to its systematic mistreatment of employees, with three former bosses found guilty. The legal process began when the work inspector responsible for investigating suicides at France Télécom

---

8   Where a suicide takes place outside of the workplace and a connection to work needs to be proven, a suicide letter holds particular legal weight. A France Télécom technician who killed himself at home on 10–11 August 2009, left a letter blaming work for his actions and requested that it be used to launch legal action against the company: 'You must declare this as a work-related accident and send them to the industrial tribunal' (Catala 2010).

brought a case before public prosecutors in February 2010, accusing the company of pathogenic management practices and of endangering the lives of its employees (Catala 2010). Invoking article 40 of the penal code, which obliges any public-sector employee to alert public prosecutors where he or she suspects a crime has been committed, the case was intended to signal to the courts a serious violation of the public good. Drawing on extensive testimonial material including suicide letters, emails, workplace investigations, occupational safety reports, HR documents and employee testimonies, this legal dossier was the point of departure for an eight-year judicial investigation into the suicides which culminated in a criminal trial in May 2019. In this section, I closely examine the documentary evidence presented in this legal dossier, investigating the causal links it establishes between individual suicide cases, the minutiae of their personal and professional lives and external working conditions at a specific moment in time. The 82-page legal dossier draws on 13 suicide cases (seven attempted and six completed) over a two-year period (from November 2007 to September 2009). It includes as evidence five suicide letters and four testimonies by survivors of failed suicide attempts.

The legal dossier reconstructs the chronology of individual suicide cases, situating them in the context of external company transformations that triggered a reaction of profound trauma in the individual employee. In six cases, the act of suicide immediately followed a notification that the person was to change jobs as part of the company's policy of forced redeployment. The dossier presents the case of a female product manager who had worked at France Télécom for 30 years and who tried to take her own life on 6 August 2009 by swallowing pills in a meeting room at her office in Le Havre. She was described as a highly skilled and conscientious professional who was devoted to her job, achieved excellent results and was held in esteem by her colleagues and managers. She had been informed by her manager the day before her suicide attempt that she was to be redeployed to a commercial job in a different sector, moving to a post that bore little relation to her professional experience and expertise. In a letter to her regional manager written two weeks after the suicide attempt that explains her motivations, she evokes the climate of fear and uncertainty that prevailed in her workplace over the preceding months, as managers sought to push employees out of their jobs against their will. Employees lived in dread of the arbitrary power exerted by managers and of seeing their name appear on the list of those to be redeployed. She communicates a sense of profound humiliation at being forced out of a job despite her exemplary record and her dedication to the company:

> They have treated me like a piece of shit. They have thrown me down the toilet and flushed it. Over the last few months everyone hoped that their name would not appear on the list. Since the previous day, I felt that I had been rejected, despite all my dedication. In my mind, I'd simply become a pawn that was being moved. When I opened my drawer, I saw the pills. I said to myself that since I was disappearing from my sector, I might as well disappear altogether. (ibid., 31)

Other cases in the dossier also establish a direct connection between forced redeployment and the decision to die. On 2 July 2008, a 54-year-old technician who had been redeployed to a call centre, threw himself under a train. He had allegedly made repeated requests to management to change jobs to no avail. Both his trade union representative and occupational doctor had alerted management to his difficulties with his new job, but they hadn't received a response. On 2 April 2009, a 42-year-old engineer who worked in an insurance branch in Paris took her own life at home. She had been forced out of her job a year earlier and was effectively left without any work other than that of searching for alternative jobs outside of France Télécom. An occupational doctor had stated several months before her death that she was suffering from a 'severe medical pathology' because of the instability of her professional situation and that she was a suicide risk (ibid., 45).

As the legal dossier shows, some employees experienced the policy of continuous restructuring as a profoundly unsettling process that disrupted their sense of professional identity, social belonging and stability. In five cases, suicide was a consequence of the chaotic reorganisation of a branch and the instability that this generated in everyday working life. A 54-year-old technician who managed business accounts in a Paris office attempted suicide at home on 5 November 2007. He had been subject to considerable pressure following the introduction of a new software system for which he was allegedly given no training or managerial support. In the face of his apparent difficulties in adapting to the new system, his manager ostracised him, pressurised him to leave and left him with no work. In an interview given as part of the enquiry into his attempted suicide, he described being left entirely on his own to cope with the new software system: 'No development, no training. I was abandoned'. Referring to an interview with his manager who remarked that he was too old to adapt to the new technology, he observed: 'I was shocked to learn that I was no longer good for anything' (ibid., 46–7). The legal dossier notes that there were three attempted suicides by employees at the branch where he worked between 2007 and 2009.

On 26 May 2008, a 55-year-old accountant who worked for an agency in Rouen attempted to jump out of a window during a meeting with his manager. He was under considerable pressure following the introduction of a new software system for managing bills which was not functioning properly and resulted in a rapid escalation in his workload. An enquiry into the attempted suicide pointed to mounting tensions at the branch, as a result of three successive phases of reorganisation which generated 'incessant changes in working methods' with deleterious effects on employees' mental health (ibid., 39). In another case, a technician responsible for mobile phone networks in Marseille whose working life had been rendered dysfunctional by constant restructuring, took his own life in July 2009. He left a letter that described a world of work that had been flung into chaos though constant restructuring, incessant change and relentless pressure. The investigation into his suicide established that the site where he worked had been merged with another and that 65 employees had been redeployed, with the remaining staff, including the employee who took his own life, left in a state of uncertainty regarding impending job cuts.

Some employees point to a routine use of intimidation, bullying and humiliation from managers to push them to leave the company. In a number of cases, the individual frames his or her own suicide in terms of a perverse fulfilment of the company's strategy to cut jobs at all costs. In taking their own life, employees are removing a cost burden and therefore helping the company to achieve its overarching economic goals. For instance, on 2 July 2008, a 54-year-old former production and maintenance technician who had been redeployed to a call centre a few years previously threw himself under a train, explaining in a suicide letter: 'At least you will be able to sleep peacefully. I've got rid of the problem. Wasn't that your aim? Seeing as there was apparently nothing else for me [...] All means are possible to meet fixed targets and at least you all agree on that'. In a second letter to a colleague, he remarks: 'Better to let employees die (unfortunately I am not the only one) at least, it is one less, which is good for the targets' (ibid., 18). Through the act of self-killing, the employee who has been pressurised to leave the company takes control of their own departure, simultaneously subverting and fulfilling the company's strategic objectives. In a situation of forced redeployment where the individual is denied autonomy or control over the terms of their working life, suicide is envisioned as a desperate form of agency and empowerment.

This legal dossier triggered a large-scale investigation into France Télécom during which hundreds of documents were seized and executives were summoned before investigating magistrates. In July 2012, Didier Lombard (former chief executive), Olivier Barberot (former head of HR) and Louis-Pierre Wenes (deputy chief executive) were placed under investigation for *harcèlement moral* and for undermining employees' mental and physical health. In 2013, they were accused of endangering the lives of others. In 2016, Paris prosecutors recommended that the bosses be put on trial for bullying. They also recommended that four other executives, two of whom still worked at the company, be put on trial for complicity in bullying. At stake in the prosecution case was the claim that France Télécom used methods that transcended the parameters of professional life and manipulated the intimate resources of individual employees for strategic economic ends. The prosecution also argued that France Télécom knowingly deployed these techniques despite being aware that they would damage workers and endanger their lives. The prosecution's case draws on an HR file consisting of PowerPoint slides that were used at an official training seminar to instruct 4,000 managers in techniques that would push employees to their limits. According to the prosecuting lawyer, 'It is a question of a deliberate and organised crime with a massive number of victims' (quoted by De Gastines 2016, 6). Thus managers were trained in psychological techniques and were taught how to identify the different psychological and emotional states experienced by an employee who had been targeted for redeployment. The techniques were inspired by the 'grieving curve' model, which was originally formulated by American psychologists in order to help terminally ill patients cope with the news of their imminent death, and has since been incorporated into business practices in order to help employees adapt to organisational change. Managers were instructed to wait until employees had reached the final stage of their grieving curve, that is 'acceptance', before proposing a plan for redeployment or voluntary redundancy. According to the prosecution, HR managers knew that some employees would not survive the restructuring process and the training material states, in a matter of fact way, that not everyone would make it to the end.

In June 2018, the Paris prosecutors leading the judicial investigation announced on the basis of all the material evidence that France Télécom and seven of its executives would face a criminal trial. In a landmark case, France Télécom itself, as a 'moral entity', was also on trial on charges of institutional bullying. This was the first time that a large French company had been tried before the courts. Under article 222-33-2 of the penal code, each executive faced two years in prison and a 30,000 euros fine if convicted. The executives and their lawyers denied the charges and claimed that the projected figures for job cuts were 'indications' rather than 'goals', and that they were trying to save the company and therefore were acting in the interests of the collective good. They remarked that France Télécom should not become the scapegoat for a problem that touched all of French society. Some trade unions sought to pursue litigation further and bring charges of corporate manslaughter against the company and its former bosses. In May 2019, the criminal trial against France Télécom opened and the prosecution presented 39 cases before the courts, consisting of 19 suicides, 12 attempted suicides and eight cases of severe depressive or related illnesses in the period from 2008 onwards (*Le Monde*, 6 May 2019).

Conclusion

Scholarship on financialisation demonstrates some of the damaging effects of the shift to a shareholder model on the status and conditions of labour within large multinational companies. Financialisation has been linked to a profound deterioration in working conditions by generating job insecurity, work intensification, organisational instability or social disintegration (Peters 2011; Cushen 2013). In many large companies, financialisation redefined management strategies and employment practices, so that the priority was no longer to invest in human capital, develop technological skills, enhance professional expertise, but to push out as many workers as possible. This reflects the broader dynamics of finance capitalism, which has been marked by a shift from a logic of incorporation to one of expulsion that seeks to eject consumers and workers from the core spaces of economic and social life (Sassen 2014, 2017). At France Télécom, an ideology of maximising shareholder value at all costs led company bosses to resort to 'insane heights of managerial violence' in order to remove workers (Palpacuer & Seignour 2019, 8). It was not simply a question of abandoning labour or relegating workers to obsolete roles, but of actively eliminating them in order to improve the company's financial performance. Suicides were the tragic outcome of 'normalised violence' and expulsionary strategies authorised by executives at the very top of the company (Evans & Giroux 2015, 4). At France Télécom, labour was segregrated, classified and reconfigured as either productive or unproductive, with the latter category ejected from the workplace as quickly and efficiently as possible. Cost-cutting techniques that removed workers were rewarded financially in terms of an increase in the company's share price, liquidity and credit rating. Despite the suicides, the company was still classified on financial listings as an ethical company and a model of social responsibility (Marcelo 2011). In their testimonial accounts, some suicidal employees perceived their self-killing as a perverse means to fulfil and subvert the company's strategic goals by taking control of the terms of their own departure.

Chapter 5

Fast Cars and Vital Exhaustion[1]

Introduction

In June 2013, a French court of appeals found car manufacturer Renault guilty of gross negligence for a third time in the case of a suicide by one of its employees. This case reflects a wider pattern of suicides in France's highly pressurised and globalised car industry, as there were ten employee suicides and six attempted suicides at Renault between 2013 and 2017, with further cases at rival car company Peugeot-Citroën.[2] What generated widespread shock at Renault was that the suicides involved elite knowledge workers, highly skilled professionals who held ostensibly desirable and well-paid jobs in which they were responsible for designing cutting-edge cars for global markets. They worked for France's foremost carmaker, a company steeped in national history that continues to project its economic prowess to the outside world. Renault is recognised as a 'cathedral of industry' that encapsulates a distinctive part of France's industrial past and is bound up with ideals of economic power, national pride and social progress (*Independent*, 15 July 2004).

Since its creation by three brothers in the late nineteenth century, the company had constructed an image for itself as a vanguard of social

---

1   The term 'fast cars' echoes the title of Kristin Ross's seminal book, *Fast Cars, Clean Bodies: Decolonization and the Reordering of French Culture* (1996), which includes a chapter on French car history.
2   There were seven suicides at PSA Peugeot-Citroën in 2007–2008, five occurring within a single factory at Mulhouse in eastern France, near the Swiss and German borders (*Le Parisien*, 1 April 2008).

progress that was helping the nation to forge a path towards modernity. While a minister of the Third Republic, Maurice Bokanowski, famously remarked about Renault's Billancourt factory in Paris, 'Quand Billancourt éternue, la France s'enrhume' (When Billancourt sneezes, France catches a cold), Renault claimed for itself the advertising slogan 'France avance, Renault accélère' (France advances, Renault accelerates) (Costa-Lascoux & Temime 2004). From the outset, suicides therefore transcended the realm of personal tragedy and raised profound questions about France's economic model, its social and cultural values and the costs of its transition to a neoliberal and globalised economic order. Some wondered whether the company's recent rise to become the leading car manufacturer in the world, following its merger with Japanese company Mitsubishi, had been won at the expense of the lives, mental health and future of its employees.

The Renault suicides took place not in the emblematic spaces of the factory, where the first people's car, the 2CV was mass-produced, but in the company's research centre, the Technocentre, where new models of car were invented, conceptualised and designed. Located at Guyancourt, 30 km to the west of Paris, the Technocentre, France's largest research and development centre, was designed as an ambitious architectural project that would mark a rupture with the past and with an outmoded model of mass production. Just as Billancourt had symbolised a post-war model of uniform and standardised assembly line production, the Technocentre encapsulated a research-driven model in which creativity and expertise were channelled towards making innovative and bespoke consumer objects. The shift from factory to research centre was both symbolic and material: Renault devoted increasing resources (both financial and human) to research and design activities in France, whilst outsourcing manual production work to countries where labour was cheaper.[3] Unlike the *métallos* or car workers at Renault's post-war Billancourt factory,

---

3   Car assembly and production activities (principally car motors) are concentrated at ten production sites (and two subsidiaries) in France, compared with 22 Renault factories located elsewhere in countries including Spain, Romania, Slovenia, Morocco, Algeria, Brazil, the Soviet Union and China. The Technocentre employs 12,000 workers, but production sites in France employ far fewer workers, the largest factory, at Cléon, employing 3,345 employees and the smallest, at Villeurbanne, employing 215. See https://group.renault.com/en/our-company/locations/our-industrial-locations/.

the new research centre employed cognitive workers who used their intelligence, expertise and creativity to design cars both as functional and aesthetic commodities. Of the 12,000 workers employed by the Technocentre in 2006, 4,202 were technicians, 4,353 engineers and only 129 were categorised as workers or *ouvriers* engaged in various forms of manual labour (Goussard 2016). Employees worked in bright, airy, majestic open spaces designed to allow creative ideas to flow freely, unimpeded by any external obstacle. Here, there was no hulking machinery, stopwatch or authoritarian foremen to dictate the pace and cadence of work. The series of suicides seemed to disrupt assumptions about the social and material progress linked to the closing of the factory and the transition to a knowledge economy that was seemingly free of physical drudgery and disciplinary regimentation. Suicides undermined Renault's self-representation as a force of modernity, an image which it had carefully constructed over the decades through its own film production service (Hatzfeld, Rot & Michel 2006). In the context of its slick corporate identity, suicides were a brutal transgression that exposed the extreme, yet often hidden suffering of workers at France's best-loved and most revered company.

This chapter situates the Renault suicides in the economic transformations that mark the transition to a knowledge economy in which the mind rather than the body has become the critical economic resource. The shift to a knowledge economy was underpinned by a utopian vision that conceived the human mind as source of ceaseless innovation and tireless productivity that broke free of the material and physical restrictions of manual labour. Unlike the body of the industrial worker, which was limited by fatigue and a depletion of productive energies, the mind was envisioned as an inexhaustible resource that could replenish itself endlessly through networked collaboration and exchange. Such idealistic discourses underpinned a model of management that sought to capture the internal resources of the mind and push them to achieve vastly expanded levels of productivity. The Renault suicides occurred at a particular historical juncture, following the introduction of a new strategic plan, Contrat 2009 (Contract 2009), which set unprecedented and ambitious productivity targets for the workforce. At the Technocentre, the company's nerve centre, employees were required to plan, design and produce new models of car at accelerated speed and in vastly expanded volumes. They were exhorted to redouble their efforts, give fully of themselves and identify their own personal goals with the goals of the company. The Technocentre was characterised by a culture of 'surengagement' or overinvestment and employees were typically dedicated professionals who pushed themselves to work long hours in order to meet the objectives set by the company (Technologia 2008). This chapter conceptualises the Renault suicides as a form of vital exhaustion that extends beyond the physical resources of the body and engulfs the whole person, depleting the intimate, subjective and complex resources of the self. The suicides were a consequence of a management model that reified the mind as a source of productivity and refused to recognise its external limits, its finite capacities and its corporeality.

The chapter examines the Renault suicides and explores their wider social, economic and cultural significance. It draws on a corpus of primary material linked to the legal cases that followed three suicides, each of which resulted in a ruling of gross negligence against the company. This documentation, consisting of family and worker testimonies, medical reports, workplace enquiries and legal summaries, provides a rich and valuable insight into an employee's life and his or her relationship to the workplace in the period preceding a suicide. It provides a means to retrace the causal connections between the extreme individual act of suicide and the objective and structural conditions of work which seemed to precipitate it. The chapter frames this primary documentation within theoretical perspectives that draw on scholarship on cognitive capitalism and fatigue in order to elucidate some of the complex and changing conditions of work that mark the transition to a knowledge economy. The chapter aims to look beneath the celebratory discourses that underpin the rise of a knowledge economy by drawing on a broad historical perspective that compares the different models of labour that mark the transition from industrial society to cognitive capitalism. Billancourt and the Technocentre each encapsulate a specific spatiality of labour, different forms of exhaustion and provide differing possibilities for exit from the constraints of work.

End Point

This chapter begins at an end point, in the act of work-related suicide and then moves in reverse chronological order to reconstruct the complex chain of events that culminated in this final act. In *Notes on*

Suicide (2015), Simon Critchley observes that suicide creates a peculiar inversion of biography whereby we read a person's life backwards from the perspective of their final act. Suicide is a singular prism through which the meaning of a person's entire life is reinterpreted though the lens of their violent end. In the case of a suicide allegedly caused by work, it is a question of looking beyond the personal realm and examining external working conditions and the particular pressures or demands that they imposed on the individual. This section focuses on an analysis of three suicide cases at the Renault Technocentre in 2006 and 2007, which all resulted in a verdict of gross negligence against the company. Each of the cases generated a vast corpus of documentary material consisting of family and worker testimonies, correspondence by the employee (diary entries, letters and email exchanges), official documents including work inspection reports, medical reports and legal summaries.[4] This material was used by the prosecution to establish a line of causality between the suicidal act and the workplace, and to demonstrate that the suicide was precipitated not by personal circumstances but by external working conditions. These three legal cases were preceded by two others that were not subject to legal proceedings, but where employees used similar methods, killing themselves in a visible manner in the workplace, during office hours, where they were witnessed by others.

In September 2004, an employee working for a subcontractor at the Technocentre attempted suicide by jumping from a suspended walkway onto the busy concourse below, in the Technocentre's main building, La Ruche (the Beehive). In July 2005, an employee working in the sales division took his own life in the same location, using the same means, by jumping to his death from the suspended walkway. The Renault suicides have been marked by a visible and spectacular dimension in which self-killing becomes a means to apportion blame through a desperate 'act of accusation' (Dejours & Bègue 2009, 4). Other suicides have also taken place since these legal cases, without giving rise to litigation. On 24 February 2008, an employee working for a subcontractor at the Technocentre who was

---

4   In the case of the first suicide of October 2006, I had access to the legal files used in the case for the prosecution. In the second and third cases, I draw on legal rulings published online, newspaper sources and published accounts (Moreira & Prolongeau 2009).

reportedly 'overworked' took his own life at home; on 8 October 2009, a 51-year-old engineer killed himself at home without leaving a note; a 31-year-old female engineer who worked at the Technocentre threw herself under a train in the United States on 4 November 2013; in February 2014, a female employee attempted suicide in the car park at the Technocentre. In a more recent case, on 23 March 2018, a maintenance technician working for a subcontractor attempted suicide by jumping from the roof of La Ruche. In total, there have been seven suicides and three attempted suicides by employees at the Technocentre since 2004, four involving jumping from a walkway or the roof of the same building.[5]

The three legal cases examined here share common features. The victims were what Christophe Dejours describes as ideal employees, hard-working and conscientious professionals who identified their own personal goals with those of the company and who were devoted to Renault's success (Dejours & Bègue 2009). They had stable social lives, secure jobs, financial security and had previously been happy in their work. In only one case was there a prior history of mental illness and depression. Before their deaths these employees each experienced a period of prolonged and intense pressure linked to Contrat 2009, which imposed vastly increased productivity targets on Renault's entire workforce. It was at the Technocentre that the new models of car which formed the centrepiece of Renault's strategic plan were to be conceived, designed and tested, and this was considered to be the nerve centre of the company's corporate operations. Employees were put under pressure to work harder, show unwavering commitment and internalise the notion that the future of the company rested on their shoulders. In the litigation that followed the suicides, the meaning of the act of suicide was subject to fiercely opposing interpretations, with the company attributing the causes to individual circumstances, pointing controversially at marital difficulties, mental instability or frustrated career ambitions, whilst family members pointed to a toxic work environment, unsustainable pressures and the company's failure to protect the health and safety of its employees. We will see that these

5   In a separate case, at a Renault production site in Sandouville near Le Havre, an assembly line worker attempted suicide by hanging himself in his workplace in April 2017, wearing a placard around his neck that named his managers and stated, 'They have killed me' (*Ouest France*, 6 April 2017).

cases marked a breakthrough in judicial law, as for the first time a ruling of gross negligence was made against a company, not as a result of the actions of an individual manager or boss, but because of social conditions affecting the workforce as a whole.

The first case to give rise to a ruling of gross negligence involved a 39-year-old engineer who killed himself by jumping off a suspended walkway on the fifth floor of the Technocentre's main building, La Ruche, in October 2006. The son of an immigrant worker (his father had worked on the assembly line at Citroën), he had excelled at maths in school and went on to graduate from a prestigious *grande école*, joining Renault in 1992 as an engineer. The legal enquiry described the employee as 'anxious, perfectionist, even obstinate, constantly questioning himself', and as someone who 'worried about the quality of his work'.[6] The case established that he had a stable and happy social life with no evidence of personal or financial difficulties. He was married with an 11-year-old son, and his wife was also an engineer. He allegedly had no prior history of mental illness or depression and had never visited the occupational doctor at the Technocentre before his recent difficulties. He was proud of working for Renault, where he was responsible for calculating measurements on the vehicle body of the Logan car.

A budget family car, the Logan was identified as a strategic priority in the Contrat 2009 plan and was perceived by the company as an essential means to expand sales of budget cars outside France and, particularly, in emerging economies. As a consequence of the new strategic plan, employees were set accelerated design and production schedules, so that prototypes of the new designs could be ready for production as quickly and in as great a number as possible. His managers were satisfied with his performance and confirmed that his work was meticulous, rigorous and of high quality. His line manager stated in the initial enquiry: 'I never had cause to question his professional role, either in private or public'. Diary entries used in the prosecution case portray him as a self-disciplined professional who set himself high standards to manage his work and orientate his relations with others. In one diary entry used as evidence by the prosecution, he exhorted himself to 'be cautious', 'be lucid', 'be patient', 'be autonomous' in his dealings with managers.[7]

6   Tribunal des Affaires de Sécurité Sociale des Hauts de Seine. Jugement du 17 décembre 2009. Dossier 08-01023/N.
7   This material is taken from the legal case for the prosecution against Renault.

The employee had taken on a significant additional workload alongside his already pressurised job, and he had been assigned the task of writing and translating into Portuguese a detailed instruction manual for workers at the Brazilian production site. He had been given a three-month deadline to complete the task. Fluent in Portuguese, he had made several visits to Brazil in 2006 and was due to travel there the day after his suicide to help introduce the instruction manual and train local managers in the new assembly line processes. The Brazilian operation was identified as a strategic priority for Renault's chief executive because production at the plant was inefficient and costly compared with other sites. Another source of pressure was that the employee had recently been asked by senior managers to relocate to Renault's production site in Romania for a period of 18 months in 2007 in order to help launch a new model of car on the assembly line. He felt pressured to accept this request and therefore leave his young family for a long stretch of time (Renault only allowed one trip home per month). According to his wife, 'He didn't dare refuse, but he was distressed about having to leave us' (*Le Monde*, 17 March 2007). The Romanian plant had a reputation for its brutal working conditions, with local workers under intense pressure to work long hours for extremely low wages and tensions in the factory running high. As a result, many French employees dreaded going there.[8]

According to the prosecution, he was obliged to work on the instruction manual in the evenings, often getting up during the night to continue working in order to meet the tight deadline. His wife reported that prior to his suicide, he had begun to work obsessively, not stopping to eat, sleep or talk: 'Towards the end, he was only sleeping two hours a night and would often get up to start working. He had lost a lot of weight. He was sick, physically sick' (quoted by Moreira & Prolongeau 2009, 63). He submitted the completed manual a few days before he took his own life. On the morning of his suicide, he had a meeting with his line manager concerning a disagreement about the length of his stay in Brazil (he had requested a period of three weeks, but his line manager had refused on budgetary grounds, limiting the

8   At Renault's Romanian plant, poor conditions and, in particular, low salaries (between 200 and 280 euros a month) triggered a strike in 2008 in which 80 per cent of the workforce took part. The strike was successful and workers gained a 40 per cent increase in their salary (Moreira & Prolongeau 2009).

stay to one week). The email exchanges between the victim and his managers regarding this disagreement were included in the case for the prosecution. His wife reported that on the morning of the meeting, her husband was so exhausted he could barely stand and was trembling, anxious and disorientated.

In their initial response to the suicides, Renault tried to blame personal problems and suggested to the press that the employee was experiencing marital difficulties and that this was the cause of the suicide. The company subsequently argued in the courts that the suicide was a result of mental fragility and frustrated career ambitions, arguing that 'this desperate act was visibly caused by a series of factors inherent within the person, his psychological state, and was not caused by working conditions or methods put in place by his managers'.[9] This defence drew controversially on a 'psychological autopsy' consisting of interviews with family members and colleagues conducted in the aftermath of the suicide to argue that he was suffering from a depressive illness 'an anxiety-depressive syndrome', which was the cause of his suicide. The company alleged that the employee's working conditions were 'completely normal and did not require him to work at home or in the evenings'. Renault also denied that he had been asked to translate the manual, claiming he had taken it on voluntarily in order to demonstrate his value to the company. Management also insisted that the company was not forcing him to go to Romania and he had the right to refuse. In the words of the Technocentre's director, 'At Renault, you can always say no' (quoted by Moreira & Prolongeau 2009, 59). Meanwhile, the victim's wife criticised what she described as the company's fortress mentality and their refusal to cooperate with the initial enquiry or to speak to her afterwards. She was only contacted three hours after her husband's death, not by a company representative, but by a policeman who was present. She was refused access to her husband's office to recover his personal belongings and when an electronic agenda was returned to her, its contents had allegedly been erased.

The initial enquiry failed to establish that the suicide was work-related, but the investigator did not interview the victim's wife, who only found out about this decision by reading about it in a newspaper (it appeared in *Le Monde* on 2 February 2007). A second

9   Cour d'appel de Versailles, 5ème chambre, 19 mai 2011 no. 10/00954.

enquiry established that the suicide was work-related. The employee's wife subsequently launched litigation proceedings against the company for gross negligence. She claimed in the court case that her husband exhibited physical signs of extreme distress prior to his suicide which were ignored by the company, including severe weight loss, emotional outbursts, difficulty sleeping and eating. On 19 May 2011, Versailles Court of Appeal ruled that Renault was guilty of gross negligence, stating that 'the employer was aware of or should have been aware of the danger to which the employee was exposed and didn't take the appropriate measures to protect him'. The prosecutor confirmed that the employee had been subject to extraordinary pressure and an unmanageable workload and that the company had failed to assess the 'psychosocial risks' inherent in the Contrat 2009 strategic plan.[10]

In January 2007, the body of a 45-year-old technician was recovered from an artificial pond in the grounds of the Technocentre, where he had drowned himself two days earlier. He had worked for Renault his whole career, moving up from a low-skilled role in assembly line maintenance to a position as a computer technician responsible for developing the company's information technology systems. He was described in the legal enquiry that followed the suicide as a consummate professional who was devoted to Renault, identified strongly with his job and was valued for the 'rigour of his work'.[11] Following Carlos Ghosn's arrival as chief executive and a restructuring process, he was redeployed to a different site and was obliged to reapply for a position in order to stay at the Technocentre. His new role at the Technocentre involved checking the technical specifications of car parts on the assembly line, a highly specialised role for which he had no previous training or professional experience and where he felt completely out of his depth. The legal case drew on evidence of his repeated emails to managers appealing for training and support, with one email evoking an 'urgent need of help' in which he states, 'today I am still not in a position to check the specifications independently. I still have not undertaken the basic training' (quoted by Moreira & Prolongeau 2009, 97). These multiple emails were allegedly ignored or dismissed. In response to what the court identified as his 'extreme professional conscientiousness', his manager

---

10   Cour d'appel de Versailles (see note 9).
11   Cour d'appel de Versailles, 5ème chambre, 10 mai 2012 no. 10/05488.

responded to him by email, urging him to stop sending repeated requests for help. In January 2006, he sent yet another email requesting help regarding the specifications required for a new model of the Twingo car. The prosecution case drew on emails sent to his brother and written notes in which his state of mental distress was evident. In one email to his brother, he remarked of Renault's new boss that 'he has put in place methods that were tested at Nissan in order to reassure shareholders' which have generated 'increased workload' and 'management by stress' (quoted by Moreira & Prolongeau 2009, 102). Because the sector where he worked was under intense pressure, none of his colleagues was able to offer support or training in relation to his new role. The stress of working in a job in which he felt ill-qualified and overwhelmed triggered a depression, and he was hospitalised for two weeks in May 2006. On his return to work, an occupational doctor recommended assigning him to a less stressful post, but the employee continued to experience difficulties in his new role, with an unmanageable workload and long hours.

At a performance review meeting three days before his suicide, according to the prosecution, he was criticised for making too many requests for help, for not being competent and for not meeting his objectives. The police enquiry into the suicide established that he had been working excessive hours, an average of ten to twelve hours a day. During the judicial case, the company's management which emphasised the mental vulnerability of the employee and his previous history of depression, was brought into conflict with the family (his father, brothers and sister), who pointed to evidence of a heavy workload and a failure to respond to continuous appeals for help. The tribunal initially dismissed a case for gross negligence, pointing to the company's efforts to reassign him to a new post following his breakdown, but the family launched an appeal against the decision. On 12 May 2012, the Versailles appeals court condemned Renault for gross negligence, arguing that the suicide reflected 'the intensity of suffering he had endured for which death seemed the only escape' and pointed to an unmanageable workload, a negligence in regulating working hours and a failure to take the necessary precautions to protect the health and safety of its employees. Renault was also accused of failing to put in place measures following the earlier suicides at the Technocentre. As in the previous case, the suicide was interpreted as an extreme manifestation of dangerous working conditions and '[the victim's] gesture is an individual manifestation of pressures and intolerable stress to which all of the Technocentre's employees were exposed in 2006 and 2007'.[12]

Three weeks later, on 16 February 2007, a 38-year-old draughtsman working at the Technocentre took his own life at home, leaving a scribbled note that pointed the finger at Renault's chief executive and his line manager: 'I can't take it any more, this job is too much for me, they are going to fire me and I'm finished. I wouldn't know how to make their shitty Top Series' (*L'Humanité*, 10 March 2010). He had been working on calculations for the chassis of a new model of Laguna, which was identified as a strategic priority in the Contrat 2009 plan and was 'a symbol of resurrection' in the face of the company's declining profits (Moreira & Prolongeau 2009, 111). The Laguna project was one of the most pressurised sectors at the Technocentre and the prototype of the new car had to be ready to put on the assembly line by April 2007. In the words of one trade union representative:

> The pressure was at its most intense on the Laguna project. We had to produce a prototype of the highest quality. But we didn't have the capacity to do so in terms of staff numbers. There were no new employees recruited [...] Everyone gave of themselves. They didn't take shortcuts. Nights without sleep. Constant availability. (quoted by Moreira & Prolongeau 2009, 147)

Alongside his highly demanding job, the employee was also following evening classes as part of the rigorous preparation for promotion to the position of manager. This *mise en situation* or preparatory training required an employee to take on considerable additional tasks in order to demonstrate their value to the company and their ability to cope with high levels of pressure. When his manager suggested that he take over the job of a structural engineer who had resigned at the Sandouville factory near Le Havre, he agreed to take this on as part of his training for promotion. Under pressure with two highly demanding jobs at two different sites at considerable distance from each other and undergoing increased surveillance as part of the auditing measures introduced under the Contrat 2009 plan, he began to work with 'obsessive and disproportionate meticulousness' (ibid., 118). In her testimony, his wife reported that towards the end, he was working constantly, no longer

12   Cour d'appel de Versailles (see note 11).

eating or sleeping and getting up at night to work at his computer. She pointed to the contradictions of a workplace where the employee is supposedly autonomous and self-organised, yet is subject to relentless external pressure: 'Of course officially, no one obliged him to keep up this pace. That's the real horror of the system that gives the impression that everyone is free to manage their own time, when the implicit pressure is so intense, there are no other choices, but to play the game' (quoted by Moreira & Prolongeau 2009, 123–4). Because he had killed himself at home rather than at work, the initial enquiry dismissed any connections between the suicide and working conditions. However, on 27 June 2013, a tribunal at Versailles condemned Renault for gross negligence, requiring the company to pay compensation to his wife and son and noting that he had been subjected to an 'overload of work which had become difficult to bear physically' (*Infodroits*, 29 June 2013).

Renault was criticised for its response to the suicides, which tended to favour measures of individual psychological support rather than to address structural conditions of work or management strategies. Hence in the aftermath of the suicides, the Technocentre set up a telephone hotline for those experiencing severe stress and provided employees access to free psychiatric services (albeit at 30 km from the Technocentre) (Goussard 2016). Meanwhile, it sought to remove physical opportunities for suicide, by closing off access to three suspended walkways and installing safety barriers on others. As at France Télécom, the workplace enquiry that followed the suicides did not lead to any substantive organisational or strategic changes at Renault. The work inspector who visited the Technocentre in August 2007 described a workforce that was cracking under the pressure of productivity demands. She argued forcefully that the suicides were a consequence of these working conditions and that individual psychological measures failed to address this collective threat:

> Moral harassment was evident in the workplace organisation itself as a result of a breakdown in social relationships, an individualisation of working relations, with the introduction of individual performance evaluation, limited opportunities for the employee to organise their own work, contradictory and confusing prescriptive norms [...] Renault as a company is responsible because it refused to put in place the necessary measures to protect the health of workers and refused to

undertake essential action to identify and evaluate the psycho-social risks in their collective dimension.[13]

This notion of *harcèlement moral* or psychological bullying exerted by the company as a whole would constitute the key element in the subsequent rulings of gross negligence against Renault. These cases marked a breakthrough in French judicial law because culpability for the suicides was attributed not to an individual or group of individuals, but to a collective workplace organisation that had imposed an unmanageable workload and failed to protect the mental health of its employees.

The Cognitariat

Suicides can be situated in the transformations that mark the shift in France from a model of industrial production to a knowledge-based economy in which the mind rather than the body has become the critical economic resource. Some scholars point to the rise of a 'knowledge economy' in which the human brain, rather than muscle power, has become the engine of economic growth (Bell 1973; Castells 1996). Others refer to a new era of 'informational capitalism' in which information drives the economy and also constitutes a new mode of production (Castells 1996; Castells 2000; Hardt & Negri 2000). For Manuel Castells, the human brain has become the most important source of economic profit, productivity and wealth: 'the human mind has always been, but more than ever now, the source of wealth, power and control over everything [...] ideas and talents are ultimately the source of productivity and competitiveness' (Castells 2000, 304). Others point to a new era of immaterial labour that has replaced manual labour as the hegemonic class and thereby redefined the relationship between labour and capital: 'the contemporary scene of labour and production [...] is being transformed under the hegemony of immaterial labor, that is labor that produces immaterial products, such as information, knowledge, ideas, images, relationships and affects' (Hardt & Negri 2005, 65). In an era of immaterial labour, workers offer much more than physical resources, but invest their

13   Inspection du Travail Ref. DB/MG no. 1216, 20 August 2007.

whole person in an economic system that requires 'subjectivities that are rich in knowledge' (Lazzarato 1996, 1). Meanwhile, autonomist Marxists pointed to a new era of 'cognitive capitalism' in which brain power combined with networked computers have unlocked vast new economic potential (Virno 2004; Moulier Boutang 2011). The shift to a new knowledge economy has reconfigured social relationships with the rise of a new 'creative class' that invests its intellectual skills and creativity in forms of economic growth (Florida 2012). A new category of 'knowledge workers' has transformed their own expertise into a tool of economic innovation (McKercher & Mosco 2007). Some point to the 'cognitariat', who are not a new proletariat but a knowledge class which possesses its own source of capital and therefore has the capacity to liberate itself from capitalism. This section situates suicides in the context of the shift towards a knowledge economy that leaves few traces on the physical body, yet exerts intense and unprecedented pressure on the human mind. In the knowledge economy, the mind is treated as an inexhaustible economic resource and a force of tireless productivity that can be pushed to achieve limitless economic goals.

The rise of a knowledge economy was widely celebrated as a utopian phase of capitalism that seemed to liberate both capital and labour from the material constraints of industrialism and to open up new economic and emancipatory possibilities. For Franco Berardi, the knowledge economy was built on an alliance between a resurgent capitalism and cognitive labour and was driven by an irrational belief in the productive possibilities of the mind that involved an erasing or forgetting of the physical body:

> The integration of cognitive work and recombinant capital has produced a kind of euphoria, of hyper-excitation and has produced a demotion, an erasing, a forgetting of the physical, the erotic and the social body of the cognitive worker. We have been taken in by this kind of irrational exuberance and we have forgotten that we have a body – that we are a body. So the cognitive worker in this kind of hyper-excitation completely or partially has been forgetting the relationship to the society and the relationship to the physical body. (2003, 1)

A core assumption is that the mind is not exhausted in the same way as the body through manual labour and can 'expand itself without limits' (ibid., 1). Cognitive labour operates through networks and semiotic flows that exist outside of the physical world and constitute a new productive model characterised by 'the radical autonomy of its productive synergies' (Lazzarato 1996, 10). Unlike manual labour, whose energy is depleted in daily work and consumed during the production process, cognitive labour escapes capitalism's efforts to expropriate its resources and has a capacity to replenish itself continuously according to a principle of 'indefinite reproducibility' (Moulier Boutang 2001, 5). Like solar energy or wind power, cognitive capital is considered a natural, vital and renewable source of energy that can never be fully captured: 'It is elemental like air, fire, earth and water' (Hardt & Negri 2005, 193). Under industrial capitalism, the external limits of the labouring body were manifested by fatigue and the expenditure of physical energy, yet cognitive capital produces 'in excess of every traditional political-economic measure of value' (ibid., 192).

Such ideals were shared by both capital and its critics, as each embraced the emancipatory and productive possibilities of the new knowledge economy. For capital, knowledge constitutes a radical and transgressive force that breaks through existing material and spatial constraints and promises ceaseless innovation and territorial expansion. Minds that can innovate and make new products, that are entrepreneurial and can connect with others through digital networks, are valued in a model of capitalism that separates execution (muscle power/goods) from conception (ideas). Capitalism acts as an 'economic-symbolic machine' that glamorises the new forms of capital production, presenting them as liberatory, slick and innovative (De Cock, Fitchelt & Volkmann 2009, 2). Maurizio Lazzarato describes capital as a 'semiotic producer' that creates signs and symbols to legitimise and aestheticise the new forms of capital accumulation (2014). In the world of business, knowledge is subject to a form of 'innovation fetishism' that combines ideals of visionary creativity with globalising reach (Ampuja 2016). Whereas the old forms of capital accumulation were confined within the walls of the factory and constrained by the corporeal limitations of manual labour, the mind produces new boundaries, geometries and temporalities. Discourse on cognitive capital is bound up with that of globalisation and an economic vision that frees corporations to transcend national frontiers, capture new markets and establish unprecedented global influence.

Hence, corporations such as Renault sought to cast off their traditional image as a reliable and predictable producer of standardised cars and to redefine themselves as a catalyst of innovation and creativity that is unpredictable, dynamic and transformative. In setting out its corporate vision, Renault places the principles of innovation and creativity at the centre of its business model:

> In the past, companies used these to open up new markets and satisfy their appetite for rapid growth. But now innovation has become not so much an arm of development as a condition for survival on mature markets where good ideas are copied rapidly and subject to fierce price wars. This has resulted in the present paradox where greater effort is required at the creative stage, at a time when the near future is becoming increasingly uncertain. (Bonnafous 1998, 7)

Corporations project a future world filled with 'glimmerings of utopia' in which knowledge will fulfil all our needs and desires, producing an endless flow of cutting-edge commodities that will reshape our lifestyles. Knowledge gestures to possibilities beyond our current condition and prefigures the shape of a different society, in a 'colonization of the unknown' (De Cock et al. 2009, 1, 2). In a rhetoric not dissimilar to that of a space mission, Renault outlines its business vision in terms of a conquest of the future: 'This approach aims at anticipating customer expectations and imagining the car of tomorrow. Special exploratory teams attempt to work out, seven years ahead of time, what the prevailing trends will be, how values and lifestyles will evolve' (Bonnafous 1998, 27). Knowledge is also identified as a source of instantaneous economic production that can engage simultaneously with other minds and apply itself 'to any context, to any task anywhere' (Ampuja 2016, 26). For corporations such as Renault, the knowledge economy relies on a 'total integration' of expertise, knowledge and ideas through 'human contact and interchange' and therefore represents 'a radical break with the past' (Bonnafous 1998, 57, 34). Networked collaboration enhances and reinforces the resources of the mind through creative synergies which spin outwards creating 'positive externalities' that result in cutting-edge creative products (Moulier Boutang 2011, 55). We will see that the creation of Renault's new emblematic site, the Technocentre, configured a new model of work based not on the Taylorist specialisation of the factory, but on the ideal of pollination and a creative pooling of ideas in the interests of economic innovation, as expressed by the name of its main building: La Ruche (the Beehive).

Such positive claims were also made by leftist critics of capitalism and in particular autonomist Marxists close to the Italian school, including Yann Moulier Boutang, Maurizio Lazzarato, Paolo Virno and Antonio Negri. Drawing on what Marx called the 'general intellect' or the entire range of human capacities such as knowledge, skills and wisdom that are embedded in the general population, they pointed to a new era of cognitive capitalism that opened up new emancipatory possibilities for labour. Unlike the exploited body of manual labour, they saw the brain as a limitless, spontaneous and natural productive force that exceeded the capacity of capitalism to capture it. Hence Moulier Boutang pointed to the rise of a new model of capitalism based on 'collective cognitive labour power, living labour, and no longer simply with muscle-power consumed by machines' (ibid., 37). He starts from the premise that work in the new economy increasingly depends on ideas, knowledge, skills and aptitudes that are cognitive or intellectual rather than labour that is physical, manual or corporeal. Moulier Boutang locates the origins of this new third phase of capitalism in Silicon Valley and the free software movement which is seen to have triggered a revolutionary transformation in the modes of capitalist production. Just as Manchester symbolised the genesis of an industrial era driven by man and machine, California has defined the frontiers of a new phase of capitalism driven by brains and networked computers, a model that Moulier Boutang symbolises by the notion of 'Marx in California' (ibid., 4). The image of the beehive is central to Moulier Boutang's conceptualisation of cognitive capitalism as a productive space in which surplus value is created through continuous cooperation by productive forces: 'Production through human pollination requires the creation and preservation of beehives' (2010, 183). Provided the beekeeper leaves sufficient honey for the bees to survive, these act as a continuous and infinitely reproducible productive force.

The shift from body to mind as the new force of economic production signals a new model of labour that transcends the 'dissipatory energy expenditure' of manual labour under industrial capitalism (Moulier Boutang 2011, 53). Brain power is a form of living capital that is not consumed or destroyed in the production process and contrasts with the dead labour that characterises manual production under industrial capitalism. For Moulier Boutang, intellectual capital does not get used up or depleted in daily work but has the capacity to replenish itself indefinitely: 'Unlike the muscles of the body, the human brain works all the time' (ibid., 73). Indeed, cognitive capital becomes stronger the more it is used, as networked exchange produces new ideas, skills and knowledge in a virtuous cycle of continuous production and reproduction. While Moulier Boutang tends to idealise the new model of cognitive capitalism, he also seeks to elucidate the new forms of exploitation that characterise this new capitalist regime. He thus hints at the dangers of an economic order in which exploitation is no longer limited to the duration of working hours and the space of the factory, but extends to the whole of workers' lives. At the current juncture, the physical exhaustion that characterised manual labour has given way to new forms of nervous exhaustion stemming from the demands of constant attentiveness and a hyperactive mind.

Other theorists are more explicit in pointing to the dangers for the individual of cognitive capitalism. Maurizio Lazzarato refers to a 'restructured worker' who is required to invest his or her subjectivity in work and whose personality and private life are susceptible to organisation and command: 'The capitalist needs to find an unmediated way of establishing command over subjectivity itself; the prescription and definition of tasks transforms into a prescription of subjectivities' (1996, 3). Yet, despite these criticisms, the rise of cognitive labour is conceptualised as a liberating rather than an exploitative transformation that brings new freedoms and possibilities for the worker: 'he is no longer a subordinated dependent worker, or rather his bond of dependence has been considerably loosened' (Moulier Boutang 2011, 92). Where exploitation was the core dynamic underpinning capitalism according to traditional Marxist analyses, in theories of cognitive capitalism, exploitation is treated as a marginal and secondary process to other more central liberatory dynamics.

For some critics, theorists of cognitive capitalism engage in a form of neoliberal apologetics that idealises capitalist transformations and ignores their oppressive and exploitative effects. Hence, according to Steven Shaviro, theories of cognitive capitalism transpose onto labour the qualities that Marx had traditionally attributed to capitalism itself, those of ceaseless productivity, a breaking of taboos and a transgression of all limits. He suggests that theorists of cognitive capitalism are too enamoured of California and of Silicon Valley's libertarian ideas of continual innovation and free software and, as a result, they overlook much that is cruel and repressive about the current capitalist regime. He points to the similarities between the ideals of the new capitalist ideology and those of the leftist theories which set out to challenge them (Shaviro 2008). Similarly, Sarah Brouillette suggests that creative labour is an idealised construct: the creative labour that is presented as a source of liberation and self-realisation is the same one that is nurtured and expropriated by capitalism and this 'is not real creativity, but rather its codified and corrupted appearance in commodity form' (Brouillette 2007, 2). We will see that the celebratory discourses surrounding the knowledge economy helped to legitimise a new management model that treated the mind as an infinitely reproducible resource, with profoundly dangerous consequences.

From Factory to Beehive

Renault's transition from industrial producer, harnessing the productive energies of manual labour, to a symbol of the knowledge economy, driven by cognitive labour, was given spatial representation in the shift between two emblematic sites, the Billancourt factory, site of post-war mass production, and the company's new research centre, the Technocentre, symbolising a new era of globalised connectivity and economic innovation. Each site became for Renault, a core symbol of its economic ambition, strategic vision and corporate identity during a specific historical period. Each site also encapsulates a distinctive spatiality of labour, with a differing impact on workers, specific forms of constraint and differing opportunities for exit from work. The purpose of this section is to analyse and compare the two distinctive models of labour that are encapsulated by these emblematic sites.[14] The Technocentre reflected a transformation in Renault's corporate strategy, as economic and human resources were channelled towards research and design activities in France, whilst manual labour, including car assembly and the production of parts, was increasingly outsourced to countries where labour was cheaper. Today, less than 20 per cent of production activities are carried out on French territory.[15]

14   For an analysis of working conditions in Renault's French production and assembly plants during the 2000s, comparing and contrasting them with conditions at the Fordist factory at Billancourt, see Rot (2006).
15   For Louis Schweitzer, boss of Renault between 1992 and 2005, this outsourcing of production was 'a continuous and irreversible movement' in a

This section draws on a corpus of testimonial material in which workers narrate their own experiences of work and its impact on their bodies and minds. In the factory, the worker confronted the world of work with his or her corporeality and this was both a site of exploitation and a form of natural protection against the dangers of overwork; in the knowledge economy, the individual confronts work with the intimate, complex and subjective resources of the mind. Recent suicides disrupt assumptions about the social progress and modernising transformations that marked the closing of the factory and the rise of a knowledge economy in France. They give material embodiment to the new forms of suffering that transcend the external limits of the physical body and exert intense pressure on the mind.

On the centenary of its creation as a family firm in 1998, Renault inaugurated a new research centre, which would inscribe in ultra-modern buildings of glass and steel a new corporate identity as an innovative and exciting carmaker for the twenty-first century. What was at stake went beyond bricks and mortar; according to Renault's glossy publication that celebrated the new centre, it was about 'the invention of the company of tomorrow' (Bonnafous 1998, 6). The Technocentre was designed to transform Renault's image. From being the nation's cherished and reliable manufacturer of standardised cars, it would become a global multinational, asserting economic power in the world and merging with its international competitors. It was originally intended that the Technocentre would be financed by the sale of lands on Île Seguin, following the closure of the Billancourt factory a few years earlier.[16] Its inauguration would thus mark a symbolic and material rupture with the past and with the grimy and

---

competitive globalised economy (2007, 59). Until the late 1960s, car production was concentrated almost exclusively in France. During the period between 1970 and 1977, factories were opened in Spain, Great Britain, Portugal, Bulgaria and Mexico. From 1999 onwards, new factories were opened in Turkey, Brazil and Argentina. In 2019, the company announced that production of the Clio would be transferred from its production plant in Flins (Yvelines) to factories in Turkey and Slovenia (*Les Echos*, 6 August 2019).

16   Funding was originally to be provided from the closure of the Billancourt assembly plant on Île Seguin, but the property slump of the early 1990s affected prices so badly that a decision was made to postpone the sale. The chief executive Louis Schweitzer decided that the project would be funded by an independent property development company, from which Renault would rent the site (Bonnafous 1998).

obsolete world of the factory. The Technocentre opened up a new chapter in French car history, marking 'a watershed in the history of industrial architecture as much as in the history of the automobile' (ibid., 8). If the Technocentre was a powerbase that symbolised corporate ambition, it also fulfilled a functional purpose: to create the spatial configuration for a new model of work based not on the productive energies of the body but on the cognitive resources of the mind.

The team of architects who won the competitive bid to design the Technocentre and manage a budget of five and a half billion francs had a clear brief: to design a space that would foster a new model of work based on a 'cooperation between brains' that was rooted in principles of creativity, collaboration and networked communication (ibid., 6). The research centre would concentrate in a single site, research and development activities that had previously been carried out across a range of different sites in Paris. The building's design seemed to mirror the connections of the human brain itself, mapping the instantaneous interaction between neurons and synapses that crystallise into creative outputs: 'the Technocentre is more than just an architectural statement: the basis of the layout is the logic governing the creative process itself' (ibid., 11). Unlike the Taylorist specialisation of the factory, which separated workers and confined them to single repetitious tasks, production in the knowledge economy requires collaboration between specialists at different stages of the production process. The layout of the three main buildings (Advance Precinct, the Beehive and the Prototype) reflects the different phases of production from conception to the design of the first prototype ready for the assembly line. Yet the buildings were also designed to facilitate work based on regular interaction and communication. The Beehive is connected to other buildings through a set of interconnected pathways and suspended walkways, allowing engineers, technicians and designers to move easily to different stages of production. At the centre of the Beehive is a grand concourse, the Arcade, covered by a vast undulating glass roof and designed as a place to meet and exchange ideas. The Technocentre seeks to cater for the worker as a whole person, meeting diverse cultural, personal and creative needs and the site provides restaurants, a hairdressing salon, banking and shopping facilities.

The importance of knowledge as a core dimension of Renault's new production model reflects broad structural transformations in the economy and a shift to a post-Fordist and flexible model characterised by a small-scale, just-in-time production of cars that are tailored to consumer demand. A carmaker's success is no longer dependent on being able to produce mass volumes of standardised cars, but on a capacity to innovate and create cutting-edge cars that can capture new markets in a competitive and globalised car industry: 'the strength of a company lies in its capacity to innovate faster than its competitors' (ibid., 22). Like other industrial producers, Renault progressively outsourced manual labour to production sites abroad, where labour costs are lower. Hence the closure of the Billancourt factory in 1992 marked the beginning of a new phase of deindustrialisation and a transfer of assembly line production to newly created sites outside of France.[17] The closure of the Vilvoorde factory in Belgium in 1998 allowed Renault to transfer car production to other sites with the Clio model outsourced to a site in Slovenia and the Mégane to Spain. Once a symbol of French industry, producing cars for domestic consumers alone, fewer and fewer Renault cars are now made on French soil, and the majority of production takes places in plants located in Brazil, Russia, Columbia, India, Morocco, Romania, Slovenia, Turkey and Spain (Cuq 2013). In 2012, Renault opened a new production plant in Tangier, Morocco, to assemble cars designed at the Technocentre. A combination of low wages, long working hours, weak labour laws and low trade union membership made production at the Tangier plant highly profitable.[18]

Since its privatisation in 1996, Renault has sought to expand its market share globally by pursuing a strategy of international mergers and acquisitions. Hence Renault took over Dacia in Romania and Samsung in Korea, allowing it to establish itself in new markets and remove competing producers. It formed an alliance with Japanese carmaker Nissan in 1999 and subsequently with Mitsubishi, so that Renault is now part a vast Franco-Japanese conglomerate that dominates the international market. Yet this international division of labour between research activities based in France and manual production

17   Between 2000 and 2011, Renault saw a 60 per cent decline in the volume of car production in France and a 16 per cent increase in car production in countries outside of France (Cuq 2013).
18   Whilst the minimum wage for a Moroccan worker is 240 euros per month, the gross monthly salary for a Renault worker in France is 1,800 euros (Cuq 2013).

outsourced to other countries has now in turn been reconfigured, as Renault has sought to reduce its research and development costs by setting up new research centres in Romania, Brazil, India and Korea, a development that has caused considerablé uncertainty for the Technocentre's employees (*L'Argus*, 19 September 2019).

If the Technocentre placed the cognitive worker at its centre and sought to liberate and capture creative resources, the Billancourt factory had been built to accommodate machines and to concentrate physical bodies in relation to the exigencies of industrial production. Completed over eight years between 1929 and 1937, the factory had been designed to rationalise production, improve efficiency and reduce costs, transforming Renault into an engine of mass production (Costa-Lascoux & Temime 2004). The structural layout was organised according to functional specialisation, with the assembly line operating on five floors, cars passing to each floor by lift and workshops leading from the main building. Although he visited the Ford factory in Detroit in 1911, Louis Renault initially resisted Taylorisation, and the company made a diverse range of vehicles including luxury cars, trucks, railway equipment and aircraft engines. The creation of Billancourt signalled a gradual integration of Taylorist techniques of scientific organisation based on the assembly line, vertical integration of production, the interchangeability of workers and the standardisation of tools and machines. Photos taken during the early years of the factory depict workers dwarfed by the immensity of the building and huddled in front of a linear row of cars on the iron structure of the assembly line. The production line operated non-stop, requiring workers to take shifts over a 24-hour period, except for the annual summer holiday in August, when the factory would shut down. The opening of the Billancourt factory marked a deterioration in working conditions compared with pre-existing workshop production, with increased recourse to unskilled labour, a lowering of salaries and an intensification of work. Material conditions were poor and work in the factory was noisy, dirty and dangerous. Injuries were common, and in the forgery workshop where car parts were made, most workers died of physical exhaustion, injury or disease before they reached the formal age of retirement (Frémontier 1971; Fridenson 1986). Foremen imposed tight discipline and surveillance, many of them coming to the factory from a military background. Discontent with working conditions would erupt during the 1936 Popular Front strikes, when workers occupied the factory, lending it a reputation as a bastion of trade union militancy, a reputation that was reasserted during strike waves in 1947 and 1968 (Ross 1995).

As France's foremost industrial producer, with the largest concentration of workers on French territory (30,000 at the end of the 1960s), Billancourt became a laboratory for studying the conditions of working-class life under industrialism. From the early twentieth century, intellectuals, researchers and activists flocked through the factory gates to observe working conditions and document industrial society in order to 'understand the worker from the perspective of his/her work' (Touraine 1955, 14). Their testimonial accounts give us compelling first-hand insights into lived experiences of work in the Renault factory. Simone Weil's *La Condition ouvrière* (The Condition of Workers, 1951), which recounts her year spent working on the assembly line in a number of car factories in Paris in the mid-1930s, in the form of letters and diary entries, was the first in a long line of testimonials. She compares factory work to a form of slavery in which the worker's every gesture, word or thought is entirely subjugated to the dictates of the machine and the person is deprived of a capacity to think and thereby live fully. The physical demands of assembly line labour brutalise the worker, reducing him or her to a set of raw productive energies and stultifying the mental faculties:

> There are two elements to this slavery: speed and orders. Speed: to get there, you have to repeat movement after movement, at a rhythm which is quicker than thought and which not only prevents reflection, but also daydreaming. In placing yourself in front of the machine, you have to kill your soul, your thoughts, your feelings, everything for eight hours. Orders: from the moment you come into the factory to the moment you leave, you can at any moment receive any kind of order. And you must always keep silent and obey [...] This situation means that thought shrinks, retracts, like the flesh retracts before a knife. You *cannot* be conscious. (Weil 1951, 28)

For Weil, work is a constant struggle to keep the mind alive and thereby retain a sense of humanity in the face of dehumanising and oppressive conditions. She describes a constant temptation to give up this struggle, to renounce the effort to engage thought, to slip into a state of somnolence and simply obey orders. The most poignant passages describe how the experience of work crushes her sense of human dignity and suppresses any impulse towards resistance or revolt:

> For me personally, this is what working in a factory means. It means that all the external reasons (I used to think they were internal reasons) on which my sense of dignity and self-respect were based, have been utterly destroyed in the space of two or three weeks, under the effects of a brutal and daily constraint. And don't think that this has stirred in me a reaction of revolt. No, to the contrary, it has led to something that I had least expected from myself – docility. The docility of a packhorse resigned to his fate. I seem to have been born to wait, receive and execute orders, that this is all I have ever done and would ever do. I'm not proud to admit this. It's the kind of suffering that no worker speaks of: it hurts even to think about it. (ibid., 27)

Similarly, sociologist Jacques Frémontier in *La Forteresse ouvrière* (The Workers' Fortress, 1971) describes the factory as a space that dehumanises the worker, takes away elementary freedoms and imposes intolerable physical suffering. He aims to examine the concrete conditions of the French working class and the social reality that lay beneath class myths projected during the 1968 events by undertaking detailed interviews with workers at Billancourt. He describes assembly line work as a mechanical physical activity marked by repeated gestures over long hours that even a prehistoric man could do. It contrasts with the more specialised but arduous work in the workshops surrounding the assembly line. Like Weil, he conveys factory work as a form of oppression that kills liberty, thought and the desire for revolt: 'The cadences of work kill freedom. They provoke in the worker a constant nervous tension. They condemn him for seven hours a day to a kind of rumbling daydream. They empty his brain, they take away his taste for life, the desire to fight back' (ibid., 134). He describes the material difficulties and insecurity of work for the majority of semi-skilled workers, who are paid for piecework (monthly pay was only introduced for all workers in 1973) and are plagued by a constant fear of falling ill and losing pay or of being sacked. He interviews a 37-year-old French semi-skilled worker responsible for monitoring the assembly line, ensuring its smooth functioning and replacing any worker who leaves:

For me, the assembly line is a form of slavery […] They constantly push us to do more and more. They stretch the cord, they stretch it more and more. One day it will break […] A worker, to have something in life, to be happy, has to fight, we fight […] I hope there will be a revolution […] For me, I am a slave. The only difference is that they let me go home in the evening and don't put me in chains. We should have more than that. A worker should be able to live. (ibid., 77, 79, 80)

Martine Sonnet's *Atelier 62* (Workshop 62, 2009) provides a biographical account of the working life of her father, a blacksmith who moved from rural Normandy to Paris in the 1950s, to work at the forge workshop at Renault and seek a better quality of life for his family. Her book combines an intimate portrait of her father's life with documentary evidence of work in the factory gleaned from trade union publications, company documents and correspondence. While the forge employed skilled workers who were considered to be 'the nobility', they were consigned to the most arduous work, which involved lifting and depositing steel parts in a furnace, spending long hours in the unbearable heat of this 'last circle of hell' (Sonnet 2009, 27, 35). This was a form of labour that ravaged the body through injury, disease or extreme exhaustion. Sonnet documents the injuries that affected workers, like deafness, blindness, lung disease, cancer, stomach ulcers and burns. Citing a trade union publication, she reports that there were 776 accidents in the forgery in a single year. She describes the effects of work on her father's body. Although he was a giant of a man, strong, robust and physically capable ('a force of nature'), he succumbed to deafness and to a weakened heart and lungs and left the factory at the age of 56 for less demanding work in an aeronautic factory where his son had found employment (ibid., 29). Little attention was paid to the health and safety of the workforce, and the thermometer in the forge that measured safe heat levels was permanently broken and the ventilation system never worked. Sonnet provides details of communication between trade union delegates and management that sheds light on the workers' constant battle to acquire the most elementary of material amenities – protective clothing, boots, changing rooms, showers and soap. In an exchange between management and trade union, she shows how the former stubbornly refused to provide soap to allow workers to wash themselves at the end of their shift, considering this a superfluous luxury.

The Technocentre encapsulates a very different model of labour where the impact of work is registered not necessarily through physical manifestations of exhaustion, but through less tangible, internalised and psychological forms of distress. In *Souffrance en France* (Suffering in France, 1998), Christophe Dejours conceptualises the transformations in working conditions under neoliberalism in terms of a shift from an exploitation of the body to a rise of 'subjective suffering' in which trauma is internalised and manifests itself in the form of extreme anxiety and psychological distress. Dejours's conceptualisation of suffering draws on empirical research he carried out at a Renault production site during the 1990s that analyses changing working conditions in the context of a production system based on 'qualité totale' (total quality) that seeks to eliminate all human error in order to maximise productivity. Contrary to assumptions about progress and improved working conditions, he finds a production model that imposes intense, relentless and debilitating pressure and saps workers of their vital energies: 'The work [...] is hardly any different in qualitative terms to what it was 20 years ago [...] The constraints of work and the cadences are in fact "infernal", but this is no longer said [...] The moral and physical suffering is intense' (Dejours 1998, 54). Workers, who are often recruited young and selected on the basis of positive psychological qualities of motivation, self-discipline and stamina, are soon disillusioned and have 'the macabre impression that the assembly line and the company is draining them of vital substance, vigour and life blood' (ibid., 55). The new forms of suffering stem from both an intensification of productivity rates and an absence of collective representation and forms of social solidarity. Dejours notes that there are fewer workers and foremen and no stop clocks on the assembly line and traditional modes of factory regimentation are no longer in evidence. Instead, workers are required to assume forms of self-discipline and control and Dejours describes 'a diabolical system of self-administered performance that far exceeds the disciplinary performance that could be gained from the conventional forms of control of the past' (ibid., 56). Similarly, in her study of working conditions and management practices in Renault's assembly plants during the 2000s, sociologist Gwenaële Rot points to a shift in modes of disciplinary control which seek to bestow enough autonomy to allow the worker to develop skills and adapt to just-in-time production demands, whilst simultaneously monitoring, controlling and regulating the freedoms given. The result is that the individual worker is subject to intense and relentless pressure as the workplace seeks to capture both external productive activity and intimate subjective resources (Rot 2006).

A large-scale enquiry into working conditions at the Technocentre in the wake of the series of suicides found that the proportion of employees experiencing chronic stress was three times the national average for the same professional category. Levels of stress increased according to career level, with senior managers experiencing the highest levels of stress and longest working hours. The enquiry pointed to a workforce subject to high levels of 'psychosocial risk' experiencing generalised psychological distress (Technologia 2008). In fact, occupational doctors and trade union delegates had repeatedly over many years raised the alarm about the dangers of spiralling workplace pressures, and a 2006 report by a medical doctor referred to systemic 'work overload' that was becoming impossible to manage.[19] The Technologia enquiry found that Renault's employees were victims of 'job strain' stemming from an economic strategy that imposed unattainable productivity goals, using these to measure individual performance. Many suffered from 'cognitive overload syndrome' and found themselves overwhelmed by competing demands, vast quantities of data and information that prevented them from working properly (ibid., 133).

Testimonies by workers gathered in the course of 122 interviews reveal the effects of such intense and sustained pressure on lived experiences of work. One line manager commented, 'We are constantly pushed to do more, we are never quite up to the mark, and we receive negative criticism constantly, even from ourselves. This leads to a situation of chronic overwork. We are always pushing ourselves to work harder' (ibid., 149). Another employee referred to a culture of fear that stems from the terror of failing to meet targets: 'It is not the workload that makes you afraid, it is the fear of not meeting the expected result. I am afraid of being perceived as someone who is not good enough. And it is the same for everyone else' (ibid., 164). Similarly, another employee remarked that fear led to a decline in working standards: 'we are so afraid of being late in completing a project that we are prepared to break certain rules' (ibid., 125). Others point to a working life that increasingly encroaches on private life and takes away any opportunity

19   Tribunal des Affaires de Sécurité Sociale des Hauts de Seine. Jugement du 17 décembre 2009. Dossier 08-01023/N.

for rest. One manager who was responsible for visiting other production sites noted: 'Travel arrangements mean that I have to leave home on a Sunday during the day and return home the following Saturday during the day, with no day of rest. Visits to factories during the day sometimes involve hours on the road alongside a full working day' (ibid., 84).

Suicides are less a consequence of transformations in material conditions of work, linked to the shift to a post–Fordist knowledge economy, than transformations in forms of workplace constraint. Although the Billancourt factory was characterised by physically exhausting work, poor material conditions, job insecurity and poor safety regulations, there are few documented cases of suicide in testimonial accounts of the period. Frémontier alludes to suicide as a possible form of escape from the factory, but without documenting any real-life cases. Describing a typical worker on the assembly line, he observes: 'He is crushed by his own contradictions, he chooses flight. Flight in alcohol, in dreaming, in racism, in violence, in suicide' (Frémontier 1971, 82). Whereas in the factory, constraint was imposed by an external machine or by the dictates of the foreman, against which the worker shielded him or herself, the contemporary knowledge economy is characterised by an internalisation of constraint that transcends the protective carapace of the body. At the Technocentre, employees benefit from excellent material conditions, good salaries, stable jobs and strong social protection, yet this did not protect some workers from suicide. Those who took their own lives shared a similar profile: they were dedicated professionals ('office warriors'), devoted to their jobs and the company, who held meticulous standards and produced work of impeccable quality (Moreira & Prolongeau 2009, 147). Employees pushed themselves to meet prescriptive targets and often blamed themselves for failing to do so. Maurizio Lazzarato describes a shift of constraint from external force to internal imperative:

> Capital wants a situation where command resides within the subject him- or herself, and within the communicative process. The worker is to be responsible for his or her own control and motivation within the work group without a foreman needing to intervene, and the foreman's role is redefined as that of a facilitator. (1996, 3)

The incorporation of authority that used to be imposed from outside has troubling effects on the individual's freedom and capacity to protect him or herself from the demands of work. The physical body no longer provides a form of natural defence, because work traverses this boundary and occupies the inner self. Franz Kafka encapsulates the perverse effects of an economic model in which the employee can no longer escape from the exigencies of work because they have in fact become their own task master: 'The animal wrests the whip from the master and whips itself in order to become master, and it does not know that this is just a fantasy, created by the new knot in the whiplash of the master' (Kafka 1998, quoted by Schaffner 2016, 336).

Monetising the Mind

The knowledge economy is rooted in a belief that 'minds can make or lose money' and have the capacity to open up new sources of economic growth, innovate, generate wealth and opportunities and connect with others through digital networks (Castells 2000, 3–4). This is a phase of capitalism that separates conception from execution and that idealises the former whilst marginalising or occluding the latter. The discourse surrounding the knowledge economy helped to legitimise a new model of management that extends capital's reach beyond the productive energies of the body that were targeted by industrial capitalism and seeks to codify the complex, immaterial and intimate resources of the human mind. For Danièle Linhart, contemporary management no longer resembles a Taylorist model that dehumanises the worker and reduces him or her to raw productive energies alone. Rather, it is characterised by a 'surhumanisation' that seeks to capture the whole person and place thoughts, ideas and creativity at the service of the company: 'The drama of contemporary work doesn't come paradoxically from the fact that it is dehumanising, but on the contrary, the fact that it plays on the most profoundly human dimensions of individuals' (Linhart 2015, 11). Yet the resources of the mind are immaterial and cannot be measured in the same way as the external and physical gestures of the body. This has resulted, according to Vincent de Gaulejac, in a management ideology driven by a 'dictatorship by numbers' and an obsessive need to convert all working activity into abstract mathematical calculus (2005, 7). Management increasingly quantifies all forms of living activity including thoughts, ideas, relationships and emotions, and forms of activity that cannot be quantified are disregarded and treated as worthless. Underpinned by a belief in objective rationality, this culture of numbers tends to dehumanise workers by reducing them to a factor of adjustment, denying their subjectivity and depriving work of meaning.

Renault exemplifies a management model that expropriates value from the cognitive resources of the mind by converting them into the quantifiable ratios that can generate economic value. Its corporate strategy tied the economic fate of a company, its future profits and share value to a potential for economic innovation derived from the cognitive and creative capabilities of its workforce. Introduced by the company's new chief executive, Carlos Ghosn, the Contrat 2009 strategic plan combined the visionary zeal of corporate transformation with a set of prescriptive economic targets to be followed to achieve this ideal. It sought to inspire, motivate and persuade employees to devote themselves to the company, whilst setting strict quantifiable parameters within which they should do so. In an interview with a journalist, Ghosn describes his strategy in terms of a quasi-religious transformative project: 'I want to take Renault into unknown territory. This means by definition that we have to push ourselves to go beyond small improvements, into a new unexplored space where innovation takes place' (quoted by Moreira & Prologeau 2009, 149). The opening lines of the Contrat 2009 plan convey this transformative exuberance, emphasising that the future of Renault rests on each individual employee and their commitment to attaining the collective goal: 'Renault is writing a new ambitious chapter in its history based on a capacity to mobilise the men and women of the company'.[20] With a reputation in corporate circles as a 'star of global business', Ghosn came to Renault following his leadership of Nissan, where he had applied 'shock therapy' in order to turn around the economic fortunes and profit margins of the company through factory closures and mass redundancies (21,000 employees lost their jobs) (ibid., 140). He intended to instigate a similar radical transformation at Renault, not by implementing closures and redundancies, but by pushing the workforce to redouble their efforts and attain vastly increased productivity levels. Renault employees were initially reassured by Ghosn's announcement, as they had feared a process of restructuring and job losses. Yet Ghosn

20   Renault Communiqué de presse, *Renault Contrat 2009*, 9 February 2006.

insisted that if the strategic plan did not succeed and the productivity targets he set were not met, restructuring and job losses would be the inevitable outcome:

> There isn't, for the time being, a plan to cut staff numbers. There are instead plans to improve costs and productivity. And that is because we foresee a period of very strong growth [...] However, we expect employees to develop in response to this growth. If we don't succeed in the products offensive, we will not avoid restructuring, with everything this implies for the company. (quoted by ibid., 142)

The CGT delegation planning a protest outside the press conference and expecting an announcement of mass lay-offs, folded up its banners and returned home. Yet, in retrospect, some employees felt that this sense of reassurance was shaky: 'we didn't understand that work was going to increase exponentially and that there wouldn't be enough of us to do it' (quoted by ibid., 43).

Contrat 2009's inspirational rhetoric was used to frame a set of productivity targets that would reorganise working activity across the company. According to the plan, the company was to achieve a profit margin of 6 per cent by 2009 and an increase in share price to 4.5 euros per share. This was to be achieved by increasing car sales by 800,000 cars, introducing 14 new models within the space of three years without expanding the existing workforce. It was necessary to conceive, develop and build prototypes for double the number of cars, in a shorter space of time, without expanding the workforce and at a cheaper cost. This would require an intensification of the productivity and workload of each individual employee, by setting tight deadlines that must be adhered to 'as an absolute priority' (Technologia 2008, 112). The closing statement of the plan summarises its strategic ambition: 'With a clear strategic vision and prioritised, precise and measurable objectives, I am convinced that Renault will become in the context of its alliance with Nissan, a great global car company that performs in the long term'. The increase in productivity outputs was to be achieved alongside a reduction in production costs across all sectors. The strategic plan was accompanied by a reorganisation of management structures and the introduction of new auditing techniques. Line managers who had technical expertise and could support employees were replaced with 'transversal managers' whose principal role was to audit, measure and monitor work across different sectors and report to the company's executive. New systems of measuring work according to individual performance were introduced that graded work according to numerical indicators. The enquiry into workplace conditions at the Technocentre found that many employees were completely destabilised by the new management structures and found themselves both lacking managerial support and subject to close surveillance and scrutiny.

Contrat 2009 tied the fate of the company to the success of specific models of car, such as the Laguna, which was due to be launched in 2008 and was to become one of the leading cars of its kind in quality and service. The time between the conception of a new design and the production of the first prototype was to be considerably reduced. At the Technocentre, productivity targets were imposed on a workforce characterised by 'a culture of excellence' and high professional standards in which highly skilled and committed employees worked long hours, went beyond formal requirements and identified themselves with the goals of the company (Moreira & Prolongeau 2009, 48). One trade union representative suggested that the strategic plan was particularly punitive for those employees who worked hardest: 'The whole system applies pressure. And you get this absurd paradox where the person who gets on best is the one who cares the least about the work' (ibid., 146). Under Contrat 2009, the Technocentre was transformed into a kind of pressure cooker which would eventually have explosive and tragic consequences. It triggered a toxic situation in which highly committed employees pushed themselves to the limit to achieve Renault's redefined goals, in some cases, by working themselves to death.

Interviews with employees about the impact of the strategic plan point to a gap between what Christophe Dejours describes as 'travail prescrit' (prescribed work) and 'travail réel' (real or concrete work). For Dejours, the suffering that characterises the contemporary workplace stems from the introduction of targets that are completely disconnected from the realities of work and real human capacity, so that employees are forced into a situation of being permanently inadequate and failing to attain the objectives set (Dejours 1998). A survey carried out when Contrat 2009 was introduced found that whilst 91 per cent of employees identified with the objectives set, only 62 per cent believed that they were achievable (Technologia 2008). In the words of an engineer:

It's a very negative way of operating. It is much easier to set unrealistic objectives and to see what happens than to set realistic objectives that make sense. From a human perspective, it's a catastrophe. It is not a good way to manage human beings. It's not by systematically receiving negative messages that you are going to feel proud of your work. (ibid., 123)

Another employee remarked:

The fact that the bar is set very high means that we only meet 10 per cent of the objectives; every week we receive emails telling us that it isn't good enough. It's never good enough. If you treat it as a game, it's okay, but if you take it personally, things can go wrong. I struggled to cope with a situation where you're always failing. You become used to being borderline and to scoring badly according to all the indicators. (ibid., 123)

Others criticised an authoritarian culture of numbers that endangers the quality of work produced: 'Today, everything must be quantified, we're in a culture of numbers. It is a very top-down form of management that categorises according to the results achieved. You don't get the impression that any discussion is allowed' (ibid., 122). Similarly: 'Work has less and less meaning; we are no longer engaged in anything concrete. We manage indicators [...] Many of us came to the company to exercise a professional skill and this creates a problem' (ibid., 146). In each of the legal cases taken against Renault, Contrat 2009 was identified as the main source of work intensification that created the dangerous working conditions leading to the suicides.

Vital Exhaustion

In *The Human Motor* (1990), Anson Rabinbach notes that fatigue and bodily exhaustion became core preoccupations within industrial society during the late nineteenth and early twentieth century and were bound up with a wider concern about the productivity of the working classes. Fatigue was defined as a physiological condition that encompassed both physical and nervous strain and which manifested itself externally on the body in the form of objective, visible and measurable symptoms. On the one hand, fatigue was considered to be an obstacle to productivity and a form of resistance to the exigencies of economic progress and social modernity. European scientists and social reformers developed sophisticated techniques to measure the expenditure of productive energy, in an effort to resolve what they saw as an endemic disorder of fatigue. If physical exhaustion could be predicted, gauged and subsequently eliminated, this opened up the prospect of revitalised productivity and economic growth. On the other hand, fatigue was conceived as a form of natural defence, acting as the worker's protection against the dangers of overwork or exploitation. Exhaustion generated external physical symptoms, affecting the muscles and sinews and signalling the necessity to stop working, to recuperate and replenish productive energies: 'Fatigue obeys its own dictates – a fatigued body refuses work until sufficient rest and nutrition replenishes its supply of energy' (Rabinbach 1990, 136).

In the knowledge economy, work generates different forms of fatigue to those of industrial society, with a shift from physical tiredness to various symptoms of mental exhaustion. The notion of burnout signifies a shift in the physiological site of exhaustion, from the physical body with its external and visible symptoms, to the inner and hidden reserves of the mind. In his historical study of conceptions of fatigue in the workplace, Marc Loriol suggests that the contemporary economic order generates new forms of emotional exhaustion and cognitive weariness that are disconnected from physical or material conditions of work. Mental fatigue tends to be prevalent amongst skilled or intellectual professions, where there are fewer external structural constraints determining working activity. Unlike the physical fatigue of the factory worker, mental exhaustion cannot be easily measured and objectified, as it is conditioned both by structural determinants and the individual's subjective engagement in work (Loriol 2000).

This section examines suicides as a manifestation of vital exhaustion, a fatigue that transcends the defences of the physical body and engulfs the whole person, sapping mental, emotional and subjective energies and, in some cases, the will to live. Because such forms of exhaustion may not leave external traces and are often internalised and unseen, their existence is often denied.

In the post-war industrial period the Billancourt factory generated a form of exhaustion that depleted the energies of the labouring body, as a consequence of a daily subjugation to the exigencies of production. Jacques Frémontier describes the factory as a 'universe of fatigue' that ravages the body and strips away autonomy (1971, 13). He notes that in 1969 12 workers died of exhaustion in the factory's forge workshop. The cadences of the assembly line forced the worker to meet a productivity target of 400 pieces per hour or 3,200 pieces over the course of an eight-hour shift. The assembly line also pushed the worker into a state of nervous tension, as he or she must concentrate on the cadences, tightly control physical movements and move as quickly as possible from one gesture to the next. Frémontier suggests that exhaustion is the key source of a worker's alienation because it makes it impossible for them to live a meaningful life outside of the factory. Such is the scale of fatigue at the end of a shift that the worker is obliged to seek rest or sleep and thereby renew labour power in the time spent away from the factory. The worker is reduced to the level of a machine 'incapable of reading, incapable of watching television, incapable of having a family life, incapable of engaging in struggle to improve his lot' (ibid., 136). Similarly, Simone Weil describes an exhaustion that is particular to factory work and unlike anything she has ever experienced before. The physical drudgery of work is combined with a sense of deep-seated humiliation and indignity that induces a state of 'moral depression' in the worker (Weil 1951, 199). This was a fatigue that tended to leave the cognitive faculties untouched, as the mind was considered either superfluous to the requirements of work or an obstacle to the physical effort of muscular movements. She describes her experiences at the end of a day's shift, when she is broken by exhaustion, drained of all vital energy and racked with pain. Whilst her heart is full of rage against the indignities of work, a pervasive sense of powerlessness and submission quells any impulse towards revolt: 'Tiredness. Overwhelming, bitter tiredness, sometimes so painful that one wishes for death. Every person in whatever situation knows what it means to feel tired, but this tiredness belongs in a category of its own' (ibid., 226).

For Albert Hirschman (1970), the individual has two options in the face of oppressive conditions, either 'exit' and a flight from the social situation or 'voice', whereby the individual confronts the social conditions and seeks to improve them. The factory offered the worker various means of escape from the physical drudgery and subjugation of work. The act of finishing a shift, clocking off and returning home in the evening or at the weekend was thus a way to separate oneself physically and symbolically from the factory and to extricate the body from the demands of work. The return home allowed the worker to break the chains that tied him or her to the machine, to occupy a familial space and affirm a different kind of social identity to that of the factory worker. Simone Weil observes that it was only on Saturday afternoons and Sundays that she reconnected with a sense of her own humanity, becoming once again someone who could think and reflect and not simply execute orders. Without the weekend break from work, she notes that she would have been completely destroyed by the factory and reduced to the level of a docile brute. Martine Sonnet describes her father's elaborate ritual when he returned home from the factory in the evening, of changing clothes, washing and shaving. This was not a physical necessity – he had already washed and changed before leaving the factory – but was a symbolic gesture, a means to cleanse all traces of the factory from his body, to keep the factory out of his home and away from his family. She describes how he would spend his Sundays on long walks across Paris, as the act of strolling freely seemed to liberate him from the controlled movements and confines of the factory workshop. In August, when the factory shut down for four weeks, the family would move back to their old house in rural Normandy, reconnecting with the habits of their old life and to the rituals of collecting apples, making cider, going to mass and socialising with others in the community (Sonnet 2009).

Workers also engaged in forms of individual and collective resistance to working conditions. Hence, historian Patrick Fridenson notes that workers engaged in individual strategies of escape through absenteeism or voluntary departure as a means to reject the dictates of Fordism. In the face of growing mechanisation, some workers responded by slowing their output or by deliberately engaging in bad workmanship (Fridenson 1986). Others pursued less salubrious forms of escape through alcoholism. In the forgery workshop, where workers spent the day in unbearable heat, alcohol offered a form of flight and a means of suppressing pain, and some workers consumed a litre of wine before the start of their shift. Yet Billancourt was also a site of trade union militancy and collective mobilisation. Jacques Frémontier set out to examine the possibilities for class struggle that lay behind the myth of a unified workers' movement that had come to the fore during the events of 1968. He finds in the factory the reality of a deeply atomised workforce divided by oppressive working conditions, social stratification and linguistic and cultural barriers. Only a third of workers were unionised, and Frémontier observes that political consciousness was a luxury reserved for the factory's skilled workers, whose conditions were less severe. Among immigrants, who constituted 39 per cent of the workforce and were allocated the worst-paid and most difficult jobs and 'brutalised by fatigue', union militancy was non-existent (Frémontier 1971, 49). On the assembly line, the noise, language barrier and accelerated cadences made any form of social interaction impossible. At the end of their shift, workers hurried home and had no reserves left for collective organisation. Yet, even if concrete conditions of work made collective action difficult, class struggle and the possibility of mass protest or a strike still survived as an ideal that offered workers a glimpse of an alternative future and the hope of social progress. Trade union activism was a means to channel individual grievances into a collective movement and to assert a sense of social agency and belonging in the face of a factory system that tended to alienate and dehumanise them.

Some critics have reconceptualised fatigue in the post-Fordist era not as a wearing of the physical body but as a psychological state caused by broad structural transformations in society. Mental exhaustion is no longer an individual pathological state but a social condition that reflects the impact of contemporary capitalism on the individual. Hence sociologist Alain Ehrenberg in *La Fatigue d'être soi. Dépression et société* (*The Weariness of Self: Diagnosing the History of Depression in the Contemporary Age*, 2010) situates this new exhaustion in broad social transformations and, in particular, the shift from a class-based social order that created stable social identities, authoritative rules and moral conformity, to an individualised society where everything is permitted and where the person is responsible for defining his or her own subjectivity. Depression is a consequence of this weariness of being oneself and the pressure constantly to perform a version of an entrepreneurial self. For Ehrenberg, the individualisation of work has triggered an exponential rise in psychosomatic disorders and transformed the workplace into what he describes as 'the antechamber of the nervous breakdown', a space that is literally driving us mad and making us ill (2010, 184). Similarly, Christophe Dejours in *Travail, usure mentale* (Work, Mental Weariness, 2008) describes the effects of work on the individual in terms of mental attrition, exhaustion and weariness. This exhaustion is a consequence of a model of work that transforms social conditions, by both isolating the individual and intensifying the demands of work. This new model of work has destroyed the workplace as a space of social relationships, value and belonging, and signals an irreversible civilisational crisis:

> The exacerbation of mental pathologies linked to work and the macabre surge in suicides [...] sounds the death knell of culture. The new forms of workplace organisation driven by powerful imperatives have succeeded in deeply destabilising the foundations of the relationship between the human being and work. By dismantling the connections between work, communal living and culture across the entire western world, our civilisation, it is to be feared, may have entered a new era of decadence. (Dejours 2008, 16)

At the same time, occupational specialists, including sociologists and psychologists, have produced a new lexicon to describe workplace fatigue in terms of the syndrome of professional exhaustion or burnout. The proliferation of new information and communication technologies including email, social networks and the mobile phone no longer allow us properly to disconnect or relax, so that experience itself is restructured by the demands of constant productivity. In February 2018, Jean-Luc Mélenchon presented a bill to the National Assembly that called for burnout to be legally recognised as a work-related illness for which companies could be held responsible, and stated: 'Who can tolerate the fact that in this country people are dying because of professional exhaustion?' (*Le Figaro*, 1 February 2018).[21]

The Technologia enquiry into working conditions at Renault's Technocentre found that some employees were experiencing exhaustion as a consequence of prolonged and intense stress and that this gave rise to symptoms including physical pain, extreme anxiety, nervous tension, poor concentration, violence, insomnia or poor appetite. The enquiry defined exhaustion as a distinctive pathological condition arising from excessive workplace pressures that produces wide-ranging physiological symptoms: 'If the stressful situation continues or intensifies, the organism's capacities can become overwhelmed. The organism enters a phase of exhaustion characterised by hyperstimulation of the corticotropic axis' (Technologia 2008, 241). Each of the suicides at the Technocentre was associated with a period of intense and chronic overwork that pushed

---

21   The majority in the National Assembly voted against the bill and burnout is still not legally recognised as a work-related phenomenon in France.

the employee into a phase of terminal exhaustion immediately preceding the suicidal act. In the first legal case, the employee was described on the morning of his suicide as being so exhausted after two hours' sleep that he could barely stand up. One of the key measures introduced in the aftermath of the suicides was a reduction in daily working hours in order to prevent overwork, and the Technocentre's opening hours were reduced from 5.30am to 10.30pm, to between 7.00am and 8.30pm. Another initiative proposed was to help employees to manage their exhaustion better and take responsibility for their own symptoms of fatigue by taking powernaps or 'micro-siestes' (Goussard 2016).

The knowledge economy offers limited opportunities for physical or symbolic escape from the demands of work. At the Technocentre, the majority of employees work more than nine hours a day (compared with the eight-hour day at the factory), and 40 per cent work over ten hours per day. An occupational doctor at the Technocentre observed in his 2004 annual medical report that it was crucial to 'protect managers from themselves as they are particularly invested in their work and do not recognise their own limits' (TASS 2009, 19). These hours are not enforced by the company but are deemed necessary by the employee in order to meet the prescriptive targets set by the former. Testimonies by employees reveal a working life in which both professional and private spheres are overtaken by work. One engineer who was interviewed described his working day in the following terms:

> I start at 6.30 in the morning to avoid traffic and leave work at 6.00 in the evening to pick up my children, which involves a one-hour commute. I start working again at 9.00 in the evening and continue until 11.00 or midnight. This is my working pattern every day. I am obliged to work every weekend. (Technologia 2008, 82)

One project manager remarked: 'The workload is such that you have to work every evening during the week (on average between 9.00 and midnight). It is the only means of keeping up with your projects. This results in a completely destabilised personal life' (ibid., 83). Another employee observed that long working hours are no longer exceptional, but have become the norm:

> I have no problem working 12 hours a day when it is a temporary situation. However, these hours have now become routine,

which means I no longer have the capacity to absorb additional tasks which would push me to 14 or 16 hours a day, and this creates acute stress when problems arise. (ibid., 83)

Conclusion

This chapter has situated the suicides at Renault in relation to a broad historical shift to a knowledge economy that treats the mind as an inexhaustible and limitless economic resource that transcends the physical limitations of the body. Suicides are the end point of a model of labour that is no longer constrained by the spatial and temporal limits of the workplace or by the labouring body, that pushes employees to work continuously and devote every fibre of themselves to the economic goals of the company. Workers enter a state of 'permanent hyperactivity' in which dead time is eliminated and every minute and second, including nocturnal time, must be harnessed towards profitable activity (De Gaulejac & Hanique 2015, 165). Suicides took place not in the dehumanising and oppressive conditions of the factory but in the slick, modernist and airy spaces of the research centre, where employees enjoyed excellent material conditions, good salaries, job security and formal social protection. We have seen that suicides were not the consequence of a deterioration in formal and material conditions of work but reflect an internalisation of constraint, in which authority is increasingly imposed on workers from within themselves. Renault's strategic plan, in its visionary corporate rhetoric, exhorted workers to redouble their efforts, to work harder and devote themselves to achieving production targets. The future of the company and its stature in the global economic order rested on the dedication and commitment of each individual employee.

Franco Berardi reminds us of the dangers of idealising the mind and treating it as a free-flowing, ethereal and disembodied force that somehow exists separately from the body. The rise of cognitive capitalism was marked by a forgetting of the body and an erasure of the corporeal, with profoundly dangerous consequences:

But the social existence of cognitive workers cannot be reduced to intelligence: in their existential concreteness, the cognitarians are also body, in other words nerves that stiffen in the constant strain of attention, eyes that get tired staring at a screen. Collective intelligence neither reduces nor resolves the social existence of the bodies that produce this intelligence, the concrete bodies of male and female cognitarians. (Berardi 2005, 57)

The Renault suicides were victims of a vital exhaustion that transcends the physical body and engulfs the whole self, sapping physical, mental and emotional resources and, in some cases, the will to live. Workers were pushed into a state of extreme cognitive exhaustion in which their subjective reserves were depleted, emptied and used up. In a situation in which work offers limited opportunities for escape or recuperation and in which the home no longer acts as a physical and symbolic refuge from the constraints of work, the individual is left with no means of exit. Suicide can be interpreted as a desperate form of escape from the relentless pressures and deadening exhaustion of cognitive work. Indeed, for Cederström and Fleming, suicide is a form of exit from a workplace in which we have become our own boss and in which work consumes our entire lives: 'Because, ultimately, we *are* the boss; we are the embodiment of the corporation. To kill ourselves, symbolically, is to kill the boss function' (2012, 66).

Conclusion

My aim in this book has been to use subjective, lived and narrated experiences of suicide as a prism for investigating the changed relationship between capital and labour at the contemporary neoliberal juncture. I have used suicide letters as a lens to shed light on some of the extreme effects of systemic economic processes on flesh-and-blood bodies within the fixed spaces of the French workplace. Emile Durkheim demonstrated that suicide is a historically contingent and cyclical phenomenon that reflects broad socio-economic transformations in society at a given moment in time and, in particular, the impact of economic crisis on the individual. Suicide acts as a mirror onto society that reveals the fundamental tensions and dysfunctions of the social order itself (Durkheim 1897). We have seen that work suicides in France appear to be a new phenomenon in historical terms, and documented cases prior to the 1990s are rare (Bourgoin 1999; Dejours & Bègue 2009). While Marx and Engels recorded in exhaustive detail the ravages of industrial capitalism on labour and the 'social murder' perpetrated within the factory system, they gave scant attention to the phenomenon of suicide (Engels 2009, 127). For Marx, suicide was a private tragedy that occurred within the confines of the bourgeois family and resulted from an absence, rather than an excess of society in the life of the individual (Plaut & Anderson 1999).

As historians of suicide have shown, suicide in industrial society was prevalent outside of the workplace, amongst those on the margins of society, such as the jobless, destitute and infirm (Chevalier 1973; Chesnais 1981). Work and occupation, despite physical hardship and poor material conditions, protected the individual from suicide, and the most physically arduous jobs had the lowest rates of occupational suicide (Anderson 1987; Baudelot & Establet 2006). I situate suicides in recent historical transformations and, in particular, the shift to neoliberal capitalism which has radically altered the status and perceived value of the individual worker within a system of capital accumulation. From a source of productive value and economic profit under industrial capitalism, the worker is increasingly treated within neoliberal management regimes as a material encumbrance whose salaried existence interferes with rational, logical and external financial goals.

In the contemporary economic order, which tends to conceal the labour processes that bring products and services to us, suicide pushes extreme suffering to the surface and forces it into the open. Suicides occur at what Saskia Sassen (2014) defines as the systemic edge, a space where abstract economics comes into contact with human bodies and gives rise to extreme elementary brutalities. In the act of suicide, economic processes are given material embodiment in the form of corporeal suffering that leaves external and deleterious traces on the body. In the suicide cases examined in this book, the act of self-killing does not constitute a leap into the unknown, an eruption of the uncontrollable or a loss of bearings, but rather a premediated, self-determined and communicative social act. As Costica Bradatan observes, suicide can be a self-determined and performed mode of agency: 'death ceases to be a mere biological occurrence, a moment in the history of one's body, and starts to count as something with a distinct cultural, political and social significance' (2015, 162).

The suicide letter constitutes an urgent testimonial form that bears witness to suffering in the quotidian and universal spaces of work. Suicide voices make visible a workplace in which everyday order and routine overlap with exceptional violence and brutality. Suicide letters subvert a top-down order of economic value that measures costs and benefits in quantifiable and monetary terms. How do we evaluate an economic strategy that subjects workers to such intense pressure that some choose to take their own lives? How do we quantify the productive value of workers as dead bodies? Is extreme human suffering an acceptable price to pay for increased shareholder value? Work is a place characterised by the 'utterly ordinary' and underpinned by hierarchical order, scientific rationality, undifferentiated sameness and cyclical routines (Kaplan & Ross 1987, 3). Yet this everydayness has a profound quality because it can make visible conditions of violence that lie beneath the surface of routine and institutionalised social life. Suicide is a profoundly personal tragedy, but it is also a social accusation that calls on us to question the social structures and economic order which determine the universal conditions of everyday life. It raises urgent questions about the nature and demands of work within the familiar spaces of the neoliberal workplace.

Suicides might be seen to manifest the rise of a form of necropower whereby it has become economically expedient and even profitable to eliminate workers from the social and productive spaces of the company (Mbembé 2003; Bargu 2014; Haskaj 2018). Unlike Foucault's 'biopower', which governs from the perspective of the production and regulation of life, necropower regulates life from the perspective of a production and regulation of death: 'necropower is the exercise of power to let live and make die' (Gržinić 2010, 40). In such an order, the vitality and productivity of the whole is dependent on classifying, segregating and excluding those who are deemed to be worthless or superfluous. Value is no longer generated from extending control over productive bodies but in determining who should die or be exposed to death through a construction of 'death worlds' (Mbembé 2003, 40). For Achille Mbembé, power is bound up with this capacity to determine life and death:

> the ultimate expression of sovereignty resides, to a large degree, in the power and the capacity to dictate who may live and who must die. Hence, to kill or to allow to live constitutes the limits of sovereignty, its fundamental attributes. To exercise sovereignty is to exercise control over mortality and to define life as the deployment and manifestation of power. (ibid., 11–12)

In the contemporary workplace, both life and death have become an issue of economic power, and each is inscribed within a regime of value. Fatmir Haskaj observes that the contemporary 'necroeconomy' embodies a new logic of capital in which living labour, embodying productive value, coexists alongside dead labour, which is valued only in terms of its negation (2018, 1149). In the neoliberal workplace, it is not simply a question of abandoning, neglecting or forgetting about workers, but of actively expelling them in order to generate economic value. Death has become a central activity in the creation of value, through the activity of killing and through death itself, as profit is squeezed out of dead bodies (Haskaj 2018).

In French corporations that are increasingly driven by the need to generate shareholder value, labour is often treated as a surplus cost whose value is determined by its elimination from the balance sheets. Companies must demonstrate their credit worthiness to external financial investors by producing favourable statistics in which lower labour costs signify higher stock price values. The dead worker in a shareholder company therefore becomes a 'quantum of value' whose economic worth is linked to his or her non-existence within the company (ibid., 1150). After France Télécom's privatisation, the company's strategic goal was no longer to produce cutting-edge telecommunications by fostering its workforce's knowledge and technological skills, but to push a maximum of employees to leave. The figure of the manager was replaced by that of the 'cost-killer', whose primary purpose was to shed jobs in order to maximise profitability. Managerial success is measured according to a killing capacity and rewarded financially according to the number of heads that roll. When Carlos Ghosn became chief executive of Renault, he had earned a reputation as a cost-killer, a visionary business leader whose aggressive restructuring of Nissan in Japan, involving factory closures and mass job cuts, was heralded as an extraordinary success story. Renault workers, who were initially relieved to find out that their jobs were safe, soon experienced such intense productivity pressures that some chose to take their own lives. In the film *Corporate* (2016), human resources director Emilie joins a group of Japanese businessmen, fellow cost-killers, in a bar and together they drink a round of shots to toast their brilliant and effective job-cutting methods. Yet alcohol cannot numb Emilie to the horror of the role she has assumed in the corporation, where she uses orchestrated psychological violence to push workers out.

I have suggested in this book that suicides are a tragic but logical fulfilment of expulsionary dynamics within the financialised economic order that creates value by expelling labour from the workplace. This is not to suggest that these suicides were a deliberate or intended outcome of managerial policies (although bosses at France Télécom and Renault have been accused in the courts of knowingly endangering their workers' lives). Suicide might instead be seen as a form of collateral damage in a system driven by exclusionary tendencies (Bauman 2011). In the neoliberal workplace, the individual worker is subject to two overarching and differentiated management dynamics (Christiaens 2019). The first requires workers to increase their productivity in a context in which their individual economic value has been diminished. Individuals must recoup the cost of their reduced value in a finance-orientated system by redoubling their productive efforts, by pushing themselves to work longer and harder and by becoming exceptional. Work is no longer an activity limited to the time and space constraints of the workplace but requires total devotion, belief and self-sacrifice. The second dynamic requires workers to accept their status as surplus cost and remove themselves from the workplace in the interests of economic profitability. At France Télécom, management integrated a psychological model based on the 'grieving curve' designed to track the emotional stages experienced by employees and identify when they were most likely to accept a proposal for redundancy. In their suicide letters, some workers portray their self-killing as a perverse means both to subvert and fulfil a company strategy orientated towards eliminating salaried costs.

This process of segregating, classifying and expelling workers is given representation in Tatiana Arfel's satirical novel *Des Clous* (The Nails, 2010), set in the fictional company Human Tools, where a group of employees have been selected for corrective training ('the non-conformists') because they are too meticulous, too generous, too fragile or they don't look or behave the right way. The boss of the company, Frédéric, opens the first training seminar by presenting the process as a form of bloodletting that drains away bad blood in order to revitalise the company:

> It sometimes happens in a healthy and strong organism that bad blood accumulates, stagnates, blackens and takes hold of the entire mechanism, and in this case, it is necessary to respond with gut instincts and act, as I have always done. The six colleagues in front of you [...] are today this bad blood, and as in traditional medicine, we need to drain away this blood and replace it with clear, red, vital blood like that in the rest of Human Tools. (Arfel 2010, 27)

Employees are forced to engage in pseudo-psychological tasks that include completing self-evaluation questionnaires that will allow them to incriminate themselves and legitimise their formal dismissal from the company. Here management methods do not seek to improve employees' skills, knowledge and capabilities, but to extract information that can be used to push them out (Christiaens 2018).

Marc, a young employee believes unquestioningly in the company's methods, and when he is forced to accept a contract without any pay, he internalises a sense of inadequacy, worthlessness and shame. His suicide at the end of the training programme is a culmination of an orchestrated managerial process in which he has arguably been selected to die.

Yet to argue that work suicides are a product of necropower and killing techniques is problematic in that the act of self-killing is not a death imposed by others, but an end that is chosen and self-inflicted. Suicide is a deeply conflicted act that combines a surrender of life with a form of self-assertion, a silencing of voice with speaking out and a rupture of social ties with their rehabilitation. I have suggested that in the contemporary workplace, suicide has become an extreme mode of protest against working conditions which are deemed to be intolerable and where other channels of mediation have been foreclosed. In the absence of mediating structures to channel and externalise individual grievances, such grievances may be internalised and manifest themselves in the form of violence by the self, against the self. Grievances that stem from structural conditions of work are reconfigured as personal inadequacies or failings and are directed inwards. Suicide is an expression of rage in a situation in which the individual finds him- or herself powerless, disenfranchised and without voice. In the face of remote and disembodied capital and where channels of collective representation are shut off, suicide becomes a perverse means of asserting power. In Marin Ledun's novel *Les Visages écrasés* (Smashed Faces, 2011), suicide and extreme violence are represented as a deadly language of resistance in the face of a silent, programmed and orchestrated violence exerted by the company. When the lead character, Carole Matthieu, an occupational doctor who works at a call centre, decides to murder one of her patients who has been targeted by a vicious management campaign, this is presented as a constructive act and a means to restore his dignity, autonomy and self-control in the face of a slow death at the hands of the company:

> This guy was going to die. He was no longer in charge of his own destiny. In any case, it wasn't him that would choose. His torturers had planned the date and time of his execution, by means of a kind of random and deadly software. They would decide instead of him. I am talking about murder here. Programmed, controlled and organised homicide. (Ledun 2011, 32)

She kills him in a perverse attempt to make visible a structural violence that is hidden and denied by management. Ledun's novel skilfully represents the extreme human consequences of official expulsionary practices, making visible the connections between objective structural violence and subjective violence in the everyday. Matthieu reflects that suicide is not a response to a single dramatic incident, but the consequence of a slow, pernicious and organised violence:

> An employee doesn't take his or her own life because of an overzealous boss or a bullying colleague. That is not enough. Suffering stems from the gradual disappearance of all the minuscule, yet necessary and vital spaces of freedom that senior management destroys in order to increase its productivity margins: one minute less break, customer calls timed to the precise second, cigarette breaks reduced by half, the phone line connected to a manager, the script delivered to the customer set out word for word or the programmed smile. (ibid., 223)

Instead of organised labour as a symbol of resistance, the individual turns his or her body into a deadly and embodied weapon of protest. By destroying the body, the individual resists the power of the company that is inscribed on the corporeal and subjective self. Suicide as protest has emerged under conditions of neoliberal capitalism that have repressed and marginalised structures of representation and solidarity in the workplace. Whereas exploitation under industrial capitalism generated for some workers the conditions for collective resistance, in the contemporary economic era, exploitation isolates, alienates and disenfranchises the individual (Dejours 1998; 2008). Suicide may signal the rise of a new 'politics of the body' which reveals the presence and evidence of the body as both a site of structural violence and subjective resistance (Fassin 2011). Mbembé notes that under conditions of necropower, 'the lines between resistance and suicide [...] are blurred' (2003, 40). In her study of death by fasting amongst Turkish political prisoners during the 2000s, Banu Bargu points to the rise of new self-destructive forms of political struggle, which she defines in terms of necroresistance or a 'weaponization of life':

> *Necroresistance* is an emergent repertoire of action that is based on the appropriation of the power of life and death into the hands of those who resist. The predominant characteristic of

necroresistance is its negation of life through a technique of self-destruction, transforming death into a 'counterconduct,' with a whole range of rituals and discourses that theologize its politics. (Bargu 2014, 14 and 272)

In France, work suicides were an act of nihilism that emerged out of the detritus of a failed trade union movement, but also one final and desperate attempt to make oneself heard and to assert agency. In an open letter to the boss of France Télécom that was published in the French press at the height of the suicide crisis, an employee reflects that suicide is a product of the systematic destruction of the trade union movement and the forms of democratic representation and expression that it provided:

You wanted weakened unions and you have won. Your courtship with financial markets and shareholders has pushed you to destroy insidiously a counter-power that ensured a social equilibrium. You have exceeded your ambitions [...] Yes, for years the lack of significant collective struggle made you think that you had won [...] Those years of terror that you organised were of an unprecedented violence. History will one day be your judge. And now this violence is coming back at you like a boomerang. You think you have won, but you have lost [...] In suppressing democratic expression, collective struggle, organised resistance and in treating trade union representation with contempt [...] you didn't see or didn't wish to see a new form of insidious, subterranean struggle: suicide. (*L'Humanité*, 15 September 2009)

Bibliography

Agamben, Giorgio 1998 *Homo Sacer: Sovereign Power and Bare Life* (Stanford: Stanford University Press).

Alemanno, Sylvie P. & Cabedoche, Bertrand 2011 'Suicide as the Ultimate Response to the Effects of Globalisation? France Télécom, Psychosocial Risks and Communicational Implementation of the Global Workplace', *Intercultural Communication Studies* (XX: 2), 24–40.

Améry, Jean 1999 *On Suicide: A Discourse on Voluntary Death*, translated by D. Barlow (Bloomington and Indianapolis: Indiana University Press).

Ames, Mark 2005 *Going Postal. Rage, Murder and Rebellion: From Reagan's Workplaces to Clinton's Columbine and Beyond* (New York: Soft Skull Press).

Ampuja, Marko 2016 'The New Spirit of Capitalism, Innovation Fetishism and New Information and Communication Technologies', *Javost: The Public* (23: 1), 19–36.

Anderson, Olive 1987 *Suicide in Victorian and Edwardian England* (Oxford: Clarendon Press).

Anizon, Emmanuelle & Remy, Jacqueline 2016 *Mon Travail me tue* (Paris: Flammarion).

Ardagh, John 1990 *France Today* (London: Penguin).

Ariès, Paul 2014 'En finir avec la centralité du travail', *Réveil-mutin*, 16 November, https://reveilmutin.wordpress.com/2014/11/16/en-finir-avec-le-travail-aliene-paul-aries/.

Austin, Guy 2015 'Political Depression and Working Practices in Recent French Cinema', *Studies in French Cinema* (15: 2), 156–67.

Balbastre, Gilles 2002 'Un service public metamorphosé en commerce', *Le Monde diplomatique*, October.

Balibar, Etienne 2015 *Violence and Civility: On the Limits of Political Philosophy* (New York: Columbia University Press).

Balthazard, Louis 2007 *De 'l'amputation psychique' des fonctionnaires. Les 'placardisés' de la République* (Paris: L'Harmattan).

Barba, Thomas 2013 *Le Livre noir de la Poste* (Paris: Jean-Claude Gawsewitch).

Barber, Alan 2018 'The Future of our Public Postal Service', Presentation for the Center for Economic and Policy Research, http://cepr.net/publications/briefings/testimony/the-future-of-our-public-postal-service.

Bargu, Banu 2014 *Starve and Immolate: The Politics of Human Weapons* (New York: Columbia University Press).

Barthes, Roland 1966 'Introduction à l'analyse structurale des récits', *Communcations* (8), 1–27.

Baudelot, Christian & Gollac, Michel 2006 *Suicide. L'envers de notre monde* (Paris: Seuil).

Baudelot, Christian & Gollac, Michel 2015 'Que peuvent dire les suicides au travail?', *Sociologie* (2: 6), 195–206.

Bauman, Zygmunt 2005 *Liquid Life* (Cambridge: Polity Press).

Bauman, Zygmunt 2011 *Collateral Damage: Social Inequalities in a Global Age* (Cambridge: Polity Press).

Beinstingel, Thierry 2018 'Ecrire sur le travail: être dedans et dehors – oeuvres emblématiques et histoires singulières', *Modern & Contemporary France* (6: 3), 323–33.

Bell, Daniel 1973 *The Coming of Post-Industrial Society* (New York: Basic Books).

Bellos, David 1999 'Tati and America: Jour de fête and the Blum-Byrnes Agreement of 1946', *French Cultural Studies* (10: 29), 145–59.

Benach Joan, Vives, Alejandra, Amable, Marcelo et al. 2014 'Precarious Employment: Understanding an Emerging Social Determinant of Health', *Annual Review or Public Health* (35), 229–53, http://www.annualreviews.org/doi/full/10.1146/annurev-publhealth-032013-182500.

Benquet, Marlène, Marichalar, Pascal & Martin, Emmanuel 2010 'Responsabilités en souffrance. Les conflits autour de la souffrance psychique des salariés d'EDF-GDF (1985–2008)', *Sociétés contemporaines* (3: 79), 121–43.

Berardi, Franco 2003 'Market-Ideology, Semiocapitalism and the Digital Cognitariat', *Public database. Non Stop Future*, http://nonstop-future.org/txt?tid=57c26a6cc2bae24a2e71c3f8a3da5ca4.

Berardi, Franco 2005 'What Does Cognitariat Mean? Work, Desire and Depression', *Cultural Studies Review* (11: 2), 57–63.

Berardi, Franco 2012 *The Uprising: On Poetry and Finance* (Los Angeles: Semiotext(e)).

Berardi, Franco 2015 *Heroes: Mass Murder and Suicide* (London: Verso Books).

Béroud, Sophie 2018 'French Trade Unions and the Mobilisation against the El Khomri Law in 2016: A Reconfiguration of Strategies and Alliances', *Transfer: European Review of Labour and Research* (242), 179–93.

Biggs, Michael 2012 'How Suicide Protest Entered the Repertoire of Contention', *Sociology Working Papers* (Paper no. 2012–03), University of Oxford.

Blaize, Aurelie 2011 'Suicide: la liste noire des entreprises et métiers à risques', *Médisite*, 28 November, https://www.medisite.fr/deprime-et-depression-suicide-la-liste-noire-des-entreprises-et-metiers-a-risque.138740.110.html.

Blanchot, Maurice 1987 'Everyday Speech', *Yale French Studies*, special issue on Everyday Life (73), 12–20.

Boismont, Brière de 1856 *Du suicide et de la folie suicide, considérés dans leurs rapports avec la statistique, la médecine et la philosophie* (Paris, Germer-Baillière).

Boltanski, Luc & Chiapello, Eve 1999 *Le Nouvel Esprit du capitalisme* (Paris: Gallimard).

Bon, François & Stéphani, Antoine 2003 *Billancourt* (Paris: Editions Cercle d'Art).

Bonnafous, Gilles 1998 *Le Technocentre Renault* (Paris: Renault, Boulogne-Billancourt).

Bossard, Claire, Santin, Gaëlle, Lopez, Vincent, Imbernon, Ellen & Cohidon, Christine 2016 'Mise en place d'un système de surveillance des suicides en lien avec le travail. Étude exploratoire' *Revue d'Epidémiologie et de Santé Publique* (64: 3), 201–10.

Bourgoin, Nicolas 1999 'Suicide et activité professionnelle', *Population* (1), 73–101.

Bradatan, Costica 2015 *Dying for Ideas: The Dangerous Lives of the Philosphers* (London & New York: Bloomsbury).

Brillet, Emmanuel 2004 'Le service public "à la française": un mythe national au prisme de l'Europe', *L'Economie politique* (4: 24), 20–42.

Brouillette, Sarah 2007 'Creative Labor', *Mediations* (24: 2), 140–9, http://www.mediationsjournal.org/articles/creative-labor.

Brun, Thierry 2013 *Qui veut tuer La Poste? Chronique d'un démantèlement* (Paris: Politis).

Brunel, Valérie 2008 *Les Managers de l'âme. Le développement personnel en entreprise, nouvelle pratique de pouvoir?* (Paris: La Découverte).

Burgi, Noëlle 2012 'Anomie néolibérale et suicide au travail', *Interrogations* (14), https://www.revue-interrogations.org/Anomie-neoliberale-et-suicide-au.

Burgi, Noëlle 2014 'Societies without Citizens: The Anomic Impacts of Labor Market Restructuring and the Erosion of Social Rights in Europe', *European Journal of Social Theory* (17: 3), 290–306.

Burgi, Noëlle & Postier, Antoine 2013 'A La Poste, "des gens un peu inadaptés"', *Le Monde diplomatique*, July.

Camus, Albert 1955 *The Myth of Sisyphus*. Translated by Justin O'Brien (New York: Random House).

Canetto, Silvia & Lester, David 2002 'Love and Achievement Motives in Women's and Men's Suicide Notes', *The Journal of Psychology* (136: 5), 573–6.

Castells, Manuel 1996 *The Rise of the Network Society: The Information Age: Economy, Society and Culture* (Cambridge, MA & Oxford: Blackwell).

Castells, Manuel 2000 *The Information Age: Economy, Society and Culture* (Oxford: Blackwell).

Catala, Sylvie 2010 *Rapport de l'inspectrice du travail au procureur de la République du 4 février 2010* (Référence SC no. 22.). Objet: Signalement en application de l'article 40 du code de procedure penal.

Cazes, Séverine & Hacot, Valérie 2015 *La Face cachée de La Poste. Enquête sur un service public en péril* (Paris: Flammarion).

Cazi, Emeline 2014 France Télécom, la mécanique de la chaise vide', *Le Monde*, 12 December, http://www.lemonde.fr/societe/article/2014/12/12/france-telecom-la-mecanique-de-la-chaise-vide_4539636_3224.html.

Cederström, Carl & Fleming, Peter 2012 *Dead Man Working* (Alresford: Zero Books).

Chabrak, Nihel, Craig, Russell & Daidj, Nabyla 2016 'Financialization and the Employee Suicide Crisis at France Telecom', *Journal of Business Ethics* (139), 501–15.

Chambers, Ross 2002 'Orphaned Memories, Foster-Writing, Phantom Pain: The *Fragments* Affair', in Nancy Miller and Jason Tougaw, 92–111.

Chan, Jenny & Ngai, Pun 2010 'Suicide as Protest for the New Generation of Chinese Migrant Workers: Foxconn, Global Capital, and the State', *The Asia-Pacific Journal* (18: 37), 1–33.

Chesnais, Jean-Claude 1981 *Histoire de la violence* (Paris: Robert Laffont).

Chevalier, Louis 1973 *Labouring Classes and Dangerous Classes in Paris during the First Half of the Nineteenth Century* (London: Routledge & Kegan Paul).

Christiaens, Tim 2018 'Financial Neoliberalism and Exclusion with and beyond Foucault', *Theory, Culture & Society* (36: 4): 95–116.

CHSCT 2014 'Synthèse de 60 expertises CHSCT menées à La Poste entre décembre 2007 et avril 2014', June.

Clegg, Stewart, Pina e Cunha, Miguel & Rego, Arménio 2016 'Explaining Suicide in Organizations: Durkheim Revisited', *Business and Society Review* (121: 3), 391–414.

Clot, Yves 2015 *Le Travail à Coeur. Pour en finir avec les risques psychosociaux* (Paris: La Découverte).

Clot, Yves & Gollac, Michel 2017 *Le Travail peut-il devenir supportable?* (Paris: Armand Colin).

Cobb, Richard 1978 *Death in Paris: The Records of the Basse-Geôle de la Seine October 1795–September 1801 Vendémiaire Year IV–Fructidor Year IX* (Oxford: Oxford University Press).

Cohen, Stanley 2001 *States of Denial: Knowing about Atrocities and Suffering* (Cambridge: Polity).

Costa-Lascoux, Jacqueline & Temime, Emilie 2004 *Les Hommes de Renault-Billancourt. Mémoire ouvrière de l'Ile Seguin 1930–1992* (Paris: Editions Autrement).

Coupechoux, Patrick 2009 *La Déprime des opprimés. Enquête sur la souffrance psychique en France* (Paris: Seuil).

Critchley Simon 2015 *Notes on Suicide* (London: Fitzcarraldo Editions).

Crocker, Lester G. 1952 'The Discussion of Suicide in the Eighteenth Century', *Journal of the History of Ideas* (13: 1), 47–72.

Crouch, Colin 2011 *The Strange Non-Death of Neoliberalism* (Cambridge: Polity).

Cullen, John 2014 'Towards an Organizational Suicidology', *Culture and Organization* (20: 1), 40–52.

Cuq, Benjamin 2013 *Le Livre noir de Renault* (Paris: First Editions).

Cushen, Jean 2013 'Financialization in the Workplace: Hegemonic Narratives, Performative Interventions and the Angry Knowledge Worker', *Accounting, Organizations and Society* (38) 314–31.

Dalglish, S. L., Melchior, M., Younes, N. & Sukan, P. J. 2015 'Work Characteristics and Suicidal Ideation in Young Adults in France', *Social Psychiatry and Psychiatric Epidemiology* (50), 613–20.

Danford, Andy, Richardson, Mike & Upchurch, Martin 2003 *New Unions, New Workplaces: A Study of Union Resilience in the Restructured Workplace* (London: Routledge).

Davis, Elizabeth 2015 "We've toiled without end": Publicity, Crisis and the "Suicide epidemic" in Greece', *Comparative Studies in Society and History* (57: 4), 1007–36.

Decèze, Dominique 2008 *La Machine à broyer. De France Télécom à Orange: quand les privatisations tuent* (Paris: Gawsewitch).

De Cock, Christian, Fitchett, James A. & Volkmann, Christina 2009 'Myths of a Near Past: Envisioning Finance Capitalism anon 2007', *Ephemera. Theory and Politics in Organization* (9: 1), 8–25.

De Gastines Clotilde 2016 'Suicides à France Télécom. Pourquoi la prévention n'a pas fonctionné', *Santé et Travail* (96), 6–9.

De Gaulejac, Vincent 2005 *La Société malade de la gestion. Idéologie gestionnaire, pouvoir managérial et harcèlement social* (Paris: Seuil).

De Gaulejac, Vincent & Hanique, Fabienne 2015 *Le Capitalisme paradoxant. Un système qui rend fou* (Paris: Seuil).

Dejours, Christophe 1998 *Souffrance en France. La banalisation de l'injustice sociale* (Paris: Seuil).

Dejours, Christophe 2005 'Nouvelles formes de servitude et suicide', *Travailler* (91: 13), 53–73.

Dejours, Christophe 2008 *Travail, usure mentale. Essai de psychopathologie du travail* (Paris: Bayard).

Dejours, Christophe 2009 *Travail vivant.* Tome 1: *Sexualité et travail* (Paris: Petite bibliothèque Payot).

Dejours, Christophe & Bègue, Florence 2009 *Suicide et travail. Que faire?* (Paris: Presses universitaires de France).

Dejours, Christophe & Duarte, Antoine 2018 'La souffrance au travail: révélateur des transformations de la société française', *Modern & Contemporary France* (26: 3), 233–44.

Delézire, Pauline, Gigonzac, Virginie, Chérié-Challine, Laurence & Khireddine-Medouni, Imane 2019 'Pensées suicidaires dans la population active occupée en France en 2017', *Bulletin Epidémiologique Hebdomadaire* (3–4), 65–73, http://invs.santepubliquefrance.fr/beh/2019/3-4/2019_3-4_5.html.

Derrida, Jacques 1993 *Spectres de Marx* (Paris: Editions Galileé).

Derrida, Jacques 2000 'A Self-unsealing Poetic Text: Poetics and Politics of Witnessing', in Michael P. Clark (ed.) *Revenge of the Aesthetic: The Place of Literature in Theory Today* (Berkeley, Los Angeles & London: University of California Press), 179–207.

Dervin Yonnel 2009 *Ils m'ont détruit! Le rouleau compresseur de France Télécom* (Paris: Michel Lafon).

Desriaux, François & Magnaudeix, Mathieu 2009 'Le Jour où France Télécom a lancé son crash programme', *Santé et Travail* 23 December.

Diehl, Bruno & Doublet, Gérard 2010 *Orange: le déchirement. France Télécom ou la dérive du management* (Paris: Gallimard).

Douglas, Jack D. 1967 *The Social Meanings of Suicide* (Princeton: Princeton University Press).

Douglas, Jack D. 1971 'The Sociological Analysis of Social Meanings of Suicide', in Anthony Giddens (ed.), *The Sociology of Suicide* (London: Frank Cass), 121–51.

Dressen, Marnix & Durand, Jean Pierre (eds.) 2011 *La Violence au travail* (Toulouse: Octarès).

Du Roy, Ivan 2009a *Orange stressé: le management par le stress à France Télécom* (Paris: La Découverte).

Du Roy, Ivan 2009b 'Suicides à France Télécom: hypocrisie sur toute la ligne', *Bastamag*, 1 September, http://www.bastamag.net/article627.html.

Duménil, Gérard & Lévy, Dominique 2011 *The Crisis of Neoliberalism* (Cambridge, MA: Harvard University Press).

Durkheim, Emile 1971 'From Durkheim's Suicide', in Anthony Giddens (ed.), *The Sociology of Suicide* (London: Frank Cass), 11–27.

Durkheim, Emile 2002 (1897 reprinted 1930) *Le Suicide* (Paris: Félix Alcan). English translation *Suicide: A Study in Sociology*, translated by John A. Spaulding (London & New York: Routledge Classics).

Ehrenberg, Alain 2010 *The Weariness of the Self: Diagnosing the History of Depression in the Contemporary Age* (Montreal & Kingston: McGill-Queen's University Press).

Engélibert, Jean-Paul 2011 'Que faire du novlangue de l'entreprise? Quelques exemples contemporains (Beinstingel, Caligaris, Kuperman, Massera)', *Raisons publiques* (15), 51–65.

Engels, Friedrich 2009 *The Condition of the Working Class in England* (London: Penguin Books).

Epstein, Gerald A. (ed.) 2005 *Financialization and the World Economy* (Cheltenam & Northampton, MA: Edward Elgar).

Etkind, Marc 1997 *Or Not To Be: A Collection of Suicide Notes* (New York: Riverhead Books).

Evans, Brad & Giroux, Henry A. 2015 *Disposable Futures: The Seduction of Violence in the Age of Spectacle* (San Francisco: City Lights Books).

Fassin, Didier 2011 'The Trace: Violence, Truth and the Politics of the Body', *Social Research* (78: 2), 281–98.

Faverjon, Claire & Lantin, François 2011 'La notation financière et les stratégies des firmes multinationales', in Ulrike Mayrhofe (ed.), *Le Management des firmes multinationales* (Paris: Vuibert), 87–106.

Fayner, Elsa 2010 'Suicides à France Télécom: dossier à charge', *Santé et Travail*, 19 March.

Felman, Shoshana & Laub, Dori 1992 *Testimony: Crises of Witnessing in Literature, Psychoanalysis and History* (Abingdon: Routledge).

Fincham, Ben, Langer, Susanne, Scourfield, Jonathan & Shiner, Michael 2011 *Understanding Suicide: A Sociological Autopsy* (New York: Palgrave Macmillan).

Florida, Richard 2012 *The Rise of the Creative Class, Revisted* (New York: Basic Books).

Fontenelle, Sébastien 2013 *Poste stressante. Une entreprise en souffrance* (Paris: Seuil).

Forrester, Viviane 1996 *L'Horreur économique* (Paris: Editions Fayard).

Foucault, Michel 1981 *Histoire de la Sexualité*, Vol 1 (Paris: Editions Gallimard).

Foucault, Michel 1985 'Sexuality and Solitude', in Marshall Blonsky (ed.), *On Signs: A Semiotic Reader* (Oxford: Blackwell), 365–72.

Foucault, Michel 1991 *Discipline and Punish: The Birth of the Prison* (London: Penguin).

Foucault, Michel 2002 *The Essential Works of Foucault 1954–1984* (London: Penguin).

Frémontier, Jacques 1971 *La Forteresse ouvrière. Une enquête à Boulogne-Billancourt chez les ouvriers de la régie* (Paris: Fayard).

Fridenson, Patrick 1986 'Automobile Workers in France and Their Work 1914–83', in Steven L. Kaplan and Cynithia J. Koepp (eds.), *Work in France* (Ithaca and London: Cornell University Press), 514–47.

Froud, Julie, Haslam, Colin, Johal, Sukhdev & Williams, Karel 2000 'Restructuring for Shareholder Value and Its Implications for Labour', *Cambridge Journal of Economics* (24), 771–97.

Géhin, Michel & Raoult-Monestel, Muriel 2013 'Geste suicidaire et travail: enquête aux urgencies psychiatriques du CHU de Caen (France)', *Archives des Maladies Professionnelles et de l'Environnement* (74), 359–68.

Giddens, Anthony 1971 'The Suicide Problem in French Sociology', in Anthony Giddens (ed.), *The Sociology of Suicide* (London: Frank Cass), 36–51.

Goeschel, Christian 2009 *Suicide in Nazi Germany* (Oxford: Oxford University Press).

Goldberg, Jonah 2018 *Suicide of the West: How the Rebirth of Tribalism, Populism, Nationalism, and Identity Politics Is Destroying American Democracy* (New York: Crown Forum).

Gollac, Michel et al. 2011 'Mesurer les facteurs psychosociaux de risque au travail pour les maîtriser', Rapport du Collège d'expertise sur le suivi des risques psychosociaux au travail, faisant suite à la demande du Ministre du travail, de l'emploi et de la santé (Paris: INSEE).

Gournay, M., Lanièce, F. & Kryvenac, I. 2004 'Etude des suicides liés au travail en Basse-Normandie', *Travailler* (2: 12), 91–8.

Goussard, Lucie 2016 'Une expertise CHSCT pour faire face aux suicides au travail? Les usages limités d'une expertise pour risque grave dans l'industrie automobile', *Sciences de la société* (95), 9–24.

Groupe de la Poste 2014 'La Poste 2020. Conquérir l'avenir', communiqué de presse, Paris, 4 April.

Gržinić, Marina 2010 'From Biopolitics to Necropolitics and the Institution of Contemporary Art', *Pavilion: Journal for Politics and Culture* (14), 9–93.

Halbwachs, Maurice 1978 *The Causes of Suicide* (London and Henley: Routledge & Kegan Paul).

Hamon, Hervé 2013 *Ceux d'en haut. Une saison chez les décideurs* (Paris: Seuil).

Hanique, Fabienne 2014 *Le Sens du travail. Chronique de la modernisation au guichet* (Paris: Editions Erès).

Hardt, Michael & Negri, Antonio 2000 *Empire* (Cambridge, MA: Harvard University Press).

Hardt, Michael & Negri, Antonio 2005 *Multitude* (London: Penguin).

Harman, Chris 2009 *Zombie Capitalism: Global Crisis and the Relevance of Marx* (London: Bookmarks).

Haskaj, Fatmir 2018 'From Biopower to Necroeconomies: Neoliberalism, Biopower and Death Economies', *Philosophy and Social Criticism* (44: 10), 1148–68.

Hatzfeld, Nicolas, Rot, Gwenaële & Michel, Alain 2006 'Filmer le travail au nom de l'entreprise? Les films Renault sur les chaînes de production (1950–2005)', *Entreprises et Histoire* (44: 3), 25–42.

Hayes, Graeme 2012 'Bossnapping: Situating Repertoires of Industrial Action in National and Global Contexts', *Modern & Contemporary France* (20: 2), 185–201.

Hazel Routley, Virginia & Ozanne-Smith, Joan E. 2012 'Work-related Suicide in Victoria, Australia: A Broad Perspective', *International Journal of Injury Control and Safety Promotion* (19: 2), 131–4.

Hermann, Christoph 2007 'Neoliberalism in the European Union', *Studies in Political Economy* (79), 61–89.

Hermann, Christoph 2014 'Deregulating and Privatizing Postal Services in Europe: The Precarization of Employment and Working Conditions', *Global Research* (1 January), https://www.globalresearch.ca/deregulating-and-privatizing-postal-services-in-europe/5363277.

Hirschman, Albert O. 1970 *Exit, Voice and Loyalty: Responses to Decline in Firms, Organizations, and States* (Cambridge MA: Harvard University Press).

Institut de veille sanitaire 2010 'Suicide et activité professionnelle en France: premières exploitations de données disponibles', 10 May (Paris: IVS).

Jacobs, Jerry 1967 'A Phenomenological Study of Suicide Notes', *Social Problems* (15: 1), 60–7.

John, Matthew 2019 'Cinematic Work as Concentrationary Art in *Ressources humaines* (Laurent Cantet, 1999)', in Griselda Pollock & Max Silverman (eds.), *Concentrationary Art: Jean Cayrol, the Lazarean and the Everyday in Post-war Film, Literature, Music and the Visual Arts* (New York & Oxford, Berghahn Books), 145–71.

Jones, Evan 2012 'The Privatization from Hell', *Counterpunch* 23 July.

Kaplan, Alice & Ross, Kristin 1987 'Introduction', *Yale French Studies*, special issue on Everyday Life (73), 1–4.

Kaspar, Jean 2010 'Radicalisation des conflits sociaux', *Revue Projet* (315), 17–25.

Kaspar, Jean 2012 'Rapport de la Commission du Grand Dialogue de La Poste', September, http://www.rds.asso.fr/RapportKaspar_enligne02.pdf.

Kawanishi, Yuko 2008 'On Karo-Jisatsu (Suicide by Overwork): Why Do Japanese Workers Work Themselves to Death?', *International Journal of Mental Health* (37: 1), 61–74.

Kilby, Jane & Rowland, Anthony (eds.) 2014 *The Future of Testimony: Interdisciplinary Perspectives on Witnessing* (London: Routledge).

Laanani, Moussa & Rey, Grégoire 2015 'Impact of Unemployment Rate and the Economic Crisis on Suicide Mortality in Western European Countries (2000–2010)', *European Journal of Public Health* (25: 3), https://academic.oup.com/eurpub/article/25/suppl_3/ckv168.049/2578031.

Lallement, Michel, Marry, Catherine, Loriol, Marc, Molinier, Pascale, Gollac, Michel, Marichalar, Pascal & Martin, Emmanuel 2011 'Maux du travail: dégradation, recomposition ou illusion?', *Sociologie du travail* (53), 3–36.

Lane, Jeremy F. 2018 'From "moule" to "modulation": logics of Deleuzean "control" in recent reforms to French Labour Law', *Modern & Contemporary France* (26: 2), 245–59.

Lapavitsas, Costas 2011 'Theorizing Financialization', *Work, Employment and Society* (25: 4), 611–26.

Lapavitsas, Costas 2013 'The Financialization of Capitalism: "Profiting without producing"', *City* (17: 6), 792–805.

Lapavitsas, Costas, Mason, Paul, Mazzucato, Mariana, Milne, Seumas & Chew, Ben 2014 'How to Change the Post-crash Economy', *City* (18: 2), 175–90.

La Poste 2006 *Facteurs en France. Chroniques du petit matin* (Paris: Textuel).

Larcher, Gérard 2003 'La Poste: le temps de la dernière chance', Rapport d'information no. 344 (2002–2003) fait au nom de la commission des affaires économiques (Paris: Le Sénat).

Laub, Dori 1992 'Bearing Witness or the Vicissitudes of Listening', in Felman & Dori, 57–74.

Lazonick, William & O'Sullivan, Mary 2000 'Maximising Shareholder Value: A New Ideology for Corporate Governance', *Economy and Society* (29: 1), 13–35.

Lazzarato, Maurizio 1996 'Immaterial Labour', http://www.generation-online.org/c/fcimmateriallabour3.htm.

Lazzarato, Maurizio 2014 *Signs and Machines: Capitalism and the Production of Subjectivity* (South Pasadena: Semiotext (e)).

Ledun, Marin & Font Le Bret, Brigitte 2010 *Pendant qu'ils comptent les morts. Entretien entre un ancien salarié de France Télécom et une médecin psychiatre* (Paris: La Tengo Editions).

Leenaars, Antoon 1988 *Suicide Notes* (New York: Human Sciences Press).

Lefebvre, Henri 1987 'The Everyday and Everydayness', *Yale French Studies*, special issue on Everyday Life (73), 7–11.

Legifrance 1990 Loi no 90-568 du 2 juillet 1990 relative à l'organisation du service public de la poste et des télécommunications.

Lerouge, Loïc 2014 'Etat de la recherche sur le suicide au travail en France: une perspective juridique', *Travailler* (31), 11–29.

Levé, Edouard 2008 *Suicide* (Paris: Gallimard).

Lhuilier, Dominique 2002 *Placardisés. Des exclus dans l'entreprise* (Paris: Seuil).

Liberman, Lisa 1991 'Romanticism and the Culture of Suicide in Nineteenth-Century France', *Comparative Studies in Society and History* (33: 3), 611–29.

Linhart, Danièle 2015 *La Comédie humaine du travail. De la déshumanisation taylorienne à la sur-humanisation managériale* (Paris: Erès).

Loriol, Marc 2000 *Le temps de la fatigue. La gestion sociale du mal-être au travail* (Paris: Anthropos).

Lyon, David 2006 *Theorizing Surveillance: The Panopticon and Beyond* (Cullompton: Willan).

Macdonald, Michael & Murphy, Terence R. 1990 *Sleepless Souls: Suicide in Early Modern England* (Oxford: Clarendon Press).

Manokha, Ivan 2018 'Panopticism, and Self-discipline in the Digital Age', *Surveillance & Society* (16: 2), 219–37.

Manzerolle, V. R. 2010 'The Virtual Debt Factory: Towards an Analysis of Debt and Abstraction in the American Credit Crisis', *Triple C* (8: 2), 221–36.

Marcelo, Coralie 2011 'Suicides à France Télécom. Réactions de la bourse', *Réseau financité*, https://www.financite.be/fr/reference/suicides-france-telecom-reactions-de-la-bourse.

Marsh, Ian 2010 *Suicide: Foucault, History, Truth* (Cambridge: Cambridge University Press).

Mathieu, Lilan 2010 *Les années 70, un âge d'or des luttes?* (Paris: Textuel).

Mazzucato, Mariana 2018 *The Value of Everything: Making and Taking in the Global Economy* (Allen Lane).

Mbembé, Achille 2003 'Necropolitics', *Public Culture* (15: 1), 11–40.

McClelland, L., Reicher, S. & Booth, N. 2000 'A Last Defence: The Negotiation of Blame within Suicide Notes', *Journal of Community & Applied Psychology* (10), 225–240.

McGuire, Kelly 2012 *Dying to Be English: Suicide Narratives and National Identity, 1721–1814* (London: Pickering & Chatto).

McKercher, Catherine & Mosco, Vincent (eds.) 2007 *Knowledge Workers in the Information Society* (Lanham: Lexington Books).

Merriott, Dominic 2017 'Factors Associated with the Farmer Suicide Crisis in India', *Journal of Epidemiology and Global Health* (6: 4), 217–22.

Miller, Nancy K. & Tougaw, Jason (eds.) 2002 *Extremities: Trauma, Testimony and Community* (Urbana & Chicago: University of Illinois Press).

Mills, China 2018 'Dead People Don't Claim: A Psychopolitical Autopsy of UK Austerity Suicides', *Critical Social Policy* (38: 2), 302–22.

Milner, Susan 2017 'Employment and Labour Market Policy under the Hollande Presidency: A Tragedy in Three Acts?', *Modern & Contemporary France* (25: 4), 429–43.

Miner, Susan & Mathers, Andrew 2013 'Membership, Influence and Voice: A Discussion of Trade Union Renewal in the French Context', *Industrial Relations* (44: 2), 122–38.

Minois, Georges 1999 *History of Suicide, Voluntary Death in Western Culture*, translated by Lydia G. Cochrane (Baltimore & London: Johns Hopkins University Press).

Molinier, Pascale 2012 'Le Suicides liés au travail: un indice de sa précarisation?', in Sabine Fortino, B. Tejerina, B. Cavia & J. Calderón, *Crise sociale et précarité* (Paris: Champ social), 152–69.

Monahan, Torin & Fisher, Jill A. 2019 'Sacrificial Labour: Social Inequality, Identity Work, and the Damaging Pursuit of Elusive Futures', *Work, Employment and Society*, https://doi.org/10.1177%2F0950017019885069.

Moreira, Paul & Prolongeau, Hubert 2009 *Travailler à en mourir. Quand le monde de l'entreprise mène au suicide* (Paris: Flammarion).

Moulier Boutang, Yann 2001 'Richesse, propriété, liberté et revenue dans le "capitalisme cognitive"', *Multitudes* (2: 5), 17–36.

Moulier Boutang, Yann 2010 *L'Abeille et l'économiste* (Paris: Carnets nords).

Moulier Boutang, Yann 2011 *Cognitive Capitalism*, translated by Ed Emery (London: Polity).

Musée de la Poste 2015 'Philatélie: La Poste rend hommage à Roland Barthes à l'occasion du centième anniversaire de sa naissance', https://ladresseip. wordpress.com/2015/10/21/philatelie-la-poste-rend-hommage-a-roland- barthes-a-loccasion-du-centieme-anniversaire-de-sa-naissance/.

NETPoste 2018 'Transformations and Bargaining of Work and Employment in the European's Postal Services', financed by the European Commission (DG Employment, Social Affairs and Inclusion), http://netposte.ulb.be/spip. php?article24&lang=fr.

Oblet, Thierry & Villechaise-Dupont, Agnès 2005 "Les Guichetiers de la Poste à l'épreuve du marché: service public et 'bureaucratie libérale'", *Cahiers internationaux de sociologie* (119), 347–66.

Observatoire national du Suicide (ONS) 2014 *Suicide. Etat des lieux des connaissances et perspectives de recherche, premier rapport, novembre* (Paris: ONS).

Observatoire national du Suicide (ONS) 2016 *Suicide. Connaître pour prévenir: dimensions nationales, locales et associatives* (Paris: ONS).

Office of National Statistics (ONS) 2017 *Suicide by Occupation, England: 2011 to 2015*, https://www.ons.gov.uk/peoplepopulationandcommunity/ birthsdeathsandmarriages/deaths/articles/suicidebyoccupation/england 2011to2015.

Oliver, Kelly 2004 'Witnessing and Testimony', *Parallax* (10: 1), 79–88.

O'Shaughnessy, Martin 2007 *The New Face of Political Cinema: Commitment in French Film since 1995* (New York & Oxford: Berghahn Books).

O'Shaughnessy, Martin 2018 'Putting the Dead to Work: Making Sense of Worker Suicide in Contemporary French and Francophone Belgian Film', *Studies in French Cinema* (19: 4), 314–34.

Palpacuer, Florence & Seignour, Amélie 2019 'Resisting via Hybrid Spaces: The Cascade Effects of a Workplace Struggle against Neoliberal Hegemony', *Journal of Management Inquiry*, https://doi.org/10.1177%2F1056492619846408.

Parisot, Eric 2014 'Suicide Notes and Popular Sensibility in the Eighteen-Century British Press', *Eighteenth-Century Studies* (47: 3), 277–91.

Parsons, Nick 2012 'Worker Reactions to Crisis: Explaining "Bossnappings"', *French Politics, Culture & Society* (30: 1), 111–30.

Peters, John 2011 'The Rise of Finance and the Decline of Organised Labour in the Advanced Capitalist Countries', *New Political Economy* (16: 1), 73–99.

Plaut, Eric A. & Anderson, Kevin 1999 *Marx on Suicide* (Evanston: Northwestern University Press).

Pollock, Griselda & Silverman, Max (eds.) 2019 *Concentrationary Art: Jean Cayrol, the Lazarean and the Everyday in Post-war Film, Literature, Music and the Visual Arts* (New York & Oxford, Berghahn Books).

Puggioni, Raffaela 2014 'Speaking through the body: Detention and Bodily Resistance in Italy', *Citizenship Studies* (18: 5), 562–77.

Pun, Ngai, Shen, Yuan, Guo, Yuhua, Lu, Huilin, Jenny, Chan & Mark, Selden 2014 'Worker-Intellectual Unity: Trans-border Sociological Intervention in Foxconn', *Current Sociology* (62: 2), 209–22.

Rabatel, Alain 2010 'Le traitement médiatique des suicides à France Télécom de mai–juin à mi–août 2009: la lente émergence de la responsabilité du management dans les suicides en lien avec le travail', *Studia Universitatis Babes-Bolyai, Philologia* (LV: 1) 31–52.

Rabatel, Alain 2011 'La levée progressive du tabou des responsabilités socio-professionnelles dans les suicides en lien avec le travail à France Télécom (fin août–octobre 2009)', *Questions de communication*, 175–98.

Rabinbach, Anson 1990 *The Human Motor: Energy, Fatigue and the Origins of Modernity* (Berkeley and Los Angeles: University of California Press).

Renou, Gildas 2009 'Les laboratoires de l'antipathie. A propos des suicides à France Télécom', *Journal du Mauss*, 29 September, http://www.journal-dumauss.net/./?Les-laboratoires-de--l-antipathie-A.

Rolo, Duarte 2015 *Mentir au travail* (Paris: Presses universitaires de France).

Ross, Kristin 1995 *Fast Cars, Clean Bodies: Decolonization and the Reordering of French Culture* (Cambridge, MA & London: MIT Press).

Rot, Gwenaële 2006 *Sociologie de l'Atelier. Renault, le travail ouvrier et le sociologue* (Toulouse: Editions Octarès).

Rothberg, Michael 2000 *Traumatic Realism: The Demands of Holocaust Representation* (Minneapolis & London: University of Minnesota Press).

Rowland, Antony & Kilby, Jane 2014 *The Future of Testimony: Interdisciplinary Perspectives on Witnessing* (New York & London: Routledge).

Sanger, Sandra & McCarthy Veach, Patricia 2008 'The Interpersonal Nature of Suicide: A Qualitative Investigation of Suicide Notes', *Archives of Suicide Research* (12), 352–65.

Sassen, Saskia 2014 *Expulsions: Brutality and Complexity in the Global Economy* (Cambridge MA & London: Harvard University Press).

Sassen, Saskia 2016 'Expulsions: Brutality and Complexity in the Global Economy', *Trajectories* (27), 362–84.

Sassen, Saskia, 2017 'Predatory Formations Dressed in Wall Street Suits and Algorithmic Math', *Science, Technology & Society* (22: 1), 1–15.

Schaffner, Anna Katarina 2016 'Exhaustion and the Pathologization of Modernity', *Journal of Medical Humanities* (37) 327–41.

Schweitzer, Louis 2007 *Mes années Renault. Entre Billancourt et le marché mondial* (Paris: Gallimard).

Selly, Aude 2013 *Quand le travail vous tue. Histoire d'un burn out et de sa guérison* (Paris: Maxima).

Sénat 1996 'Pour réussir France Télécom doit devenir une société anonyme à majorité détenue par l'Etat', Rapport au Sénat no. 260 (Paris: Sénat). https://www.senat.fr/rap/r95-260/r95-26056.html.

Shaviro, Steven 2008 'Cognitive Capitalism: The Pinocchio Theory', http://www.shaviro.com/Blog/?p=620.

Shneidman, Edwin (ed.) 1976 *Suicidology: Contemporary Developments* (New York, San Francisco & London: Grune & Stratton).

Shneidman, Edwin 1996 *The Suicidal Mind* (Oxford: Oxford University Press).

Siblot, Yasmine (2006) *Faire valoir ses droits au quotidian. Les service publics dans les quartiers populaires* (Paris: Presses de sciences Po).

Silverman, Max 2006 'Horror and the Everyday in Post-Holocaust France: *Nuit et brouillard* and Concentrationary Art', *French Cultural Studies* (17: 1), 5–18.

Silverman, Max 2019 'Introduction: Lazarus and the Modern World', in Pollock & Silverman, 1–28.

Standing, Guy 2011 *The Precariat* (London: Bloomsbury Academic).

Stuckler David & Basu, Sanjay 2013 *The Body Economic: Why Austerity Kills* (New York: Basic Books).

Taylor, Chloë 2015 'Birth of the Suicidal Subject: Nelly Arcan, Michel Foucault, and Voluntary Death', *Culture, Theory and Critique* (56: 2), 187–207.

Technologia 2008 *Technocentre Renault de Guyancourt. Rapport d'expertise CHSCT* (Paris: Technologia).

Teissier, Claude 1997 *La Poste: Logique commerciale / logique de service public. La greffe culturelle* (Paris: L'Harmattan).

Thompson, Paul 2003 'Disconnected Capitalism: Or Why Employers Can't Keep Their Side of the Bargain', *Work, Employment and Society* (17: 2), 359–78.

Tiesman, Hope M., Konda, Srinivas, Hartley, Dan, Chaumont Menéndez, Cammie, Ridenour, Marilyn & Hendricks, Scott (2015) 'Suicide in U.S. Workplaces 2003–2010', *American Journal of Preventative Medicine* (48: 6), 674–82.

Tilly, Charles 1986 *The Contentious French: Four Centuries of Popular Struggle* (Cambridge, MA: Belknap Press).

Touraine, Alain 1955 *L'Evolution du travail ouvrier aux usines Renault* (Paris: CNRS).

Tribunal Administratif de Rennes 2016 Jugement No. 1302767. Audience du 31 mars 2016.

Tribunal des Affaires de Sécurité Sociale des Hauts de Seine (TASS) Jugement du 17 décembre 2009. Dossier No. 08-01023/N.

Vatin, François 2011 'La question du suicide au travail', *Commentaire* (134), 405–16.

Vezinat, Nadège 2012 *Les Métamorphoses de la Poste* (Paris: Presses universitaires de France).

Vincent, Stéphane 2018 'Suicides à France Télécom: dix ans d'enquête', *Santé et Travail*, 18 June.

Virno, Paolo 2004 *A Grammar of the Multitude* (Los Angeles: Semiotext(e)).

Waters, Sarah 2014a 'A Capitalism that Kills: Workplace Suicides at France Télécom', *French Politics, Culture & Society* (32: 3), 121–41.

Waters, Sarah 2014b 'Capitalism's Victims: An Interview with Patrick Ackermann', *Jacobin*, 13 February.

Waters, Sarah 2017a 'Suicidal Work: Work-related Suicides Are Uncounted', *Hazards Magazine*, March, http://www.hazards.org/suicide/suicidalwork.htm.

Waters, Sarah 2017b 'Workplace Suicide and States of Denial: The France Télécom and Foxconn Cases Compared', *Communication, Capitalism and Critique* (15: 1), 191–213.

Webster, Edward, Lambert, Rob & Bezuidenhout, Andries 2008 *Grounding Globalization: Labour in the Age of Insecurity* (Oxford: Blackwell).

Weil, Simone 1951 *La Condition ouvrière* (Paris: Editions Gallimard).

Weil, Simone 1997 *Gravity and Grace*, translated by Arthur Wills (Lincoln, NE: University of Nebraska Press).

Wieviorka, Annette 1998 *L'Ère du témoin* (Paris: Plon).

Wieviorka, Michel 1998 'Un nouveau paradigme de la violence', *Cultures & Conflits* (29–30), https://journals.openedition.org/conflits/48.

Yaegar, Patricia 2002 'Consuming Trauma; Or, The Pleasures of Merely Circulating', in Miller & Tougaw, 25–51.

Yamauchi, Takashi, Yoshikawam, Toru, Takamoto, Masahiro, Sasaki, Takeshi, Matsumoto, Shun, Kayashima, Kotaro, Takeshima, Tadashi & Takahashi, Masaya 2017 'Overwork-related Disorders in Japan: Recent Trends and Development of a National Policy to Promote Preventive Measures', *Industrial Health* (55: 3), 293–302.

Zemmour, Eric 2014 *Le Suicide français* (Paris: Albin Michel).

Žižek, Slavoj 2008a *Violence: Six Sideways Reflections* (London: Profile Books).

Žižek, Slavoj 2008b 'Use your Illusions', *London Review of Books*, 14 November.

Novels

Arfel, Tatiana 2010 *Des Clous* (Paris: Librairie José Corti).

Beinstingel, Thierry 2010 *Retour aux Mots sauvages* (Paris: Fayard).

Claudel, Philippe 2010 *L'Enquête* (Paris: Stock).

Filhol, Elisabeth 2010 *La Centrale* (Paris: Folio).

Ledun, Marin 2011 *Les Visages écrasés* (Paris: Seuil).

Levé, Edouard 2008 *Suicide* (Paris: P.O.L).

Sonnet, Martine 2009 *Atelier 62* (Paris: Le Temps qu'il fait).

Films

Carole Matthieu (Louis-Julien Petit, 2016).
Corporate (Nicolas Silhol, 2016).
En guerre (Stéphane Brizé, 2018).
Jour de fête (Jacques Tati, 1949).
La Question humaine (Nicolas Klotz, 2007).
Near Death experience (Benoît Delépine & Gustave Kervern, 2015).
Ressources humaines (Laurent Cantet, 1999).

Documentaries

Ils ne mouraient pas tous mais tous étaient frappés (Sophie Bruneau & Marc-Antoine Roudil, 2005).
La Mise à mort du travail (Jean-Robert Viallet, 2009).
Le Grand Incendie (Samuel Bollendorff & Olivia Colo, 2013).
Les Impactés (Thibault Dufour, 2008).
Orange amère (Patricia Bodet & Debord Bernard, 2011).
Poste restante (Christian Tran, 2005).
Une tournée dans la neige (Hélène Marini, 2016).

Theatre

Au Pays des (Sylvain Levey, 2011).
Les Impactés (Compagnie Naje, 2011).
Très nombreux, chacun seul (Jean-Pierre Bodin, 2012), http://jeanpierrebodin. com/spectacles-parent/tres-nombreux-chacun-seul-2012/.

Index

Ackermann, Patrick 161–2
Améry, Jean 13, 16
Ames, Mark 107–8
Anderson, Olive 35, 37–8
Anizon, Emmanuelle 94–5
'anomie' 28–9, 57–8, 109
Arendt, Hannah, 'banality of evil' 78
Arfel, Tatiana, Des Clous 219–20

Bailly, Jean-Paul 102–3, 120, 123,
    131, 135
Balibar, Etienne 62–3
Balthazard, Louis 46
Barba, Thomas 119
Barberot, Olivier 162, 167
Bargu, Banu 61, 221–2
Barthes, Roland 18, 112
Baudelot, Christian 15, 34
Bauman, Zygmunt 27, 28
Bayatrizi, Zohyreh 14
Beaudeau, Marie-Claude 159–60
Beinstingel, Thierry 142
    Retour aux mots sauvages 88, 155
Benjamin, Walter 36
Benquet, Marlène 30n1
Berardi, Franco 38–9, 68, 185
Bernard, Debord 151
Bertrand, Xavier 102
Bodet, Patricia 151
Bodin, Jean-Pierre, Très nombreux,
    chacun seul 90n4
Boismont, Brière de 74n1
Bokanowski, Maurice 172

Bollendorff, Samuel, Le Grand Incendie
    17, 87–8, 103
Boltanski, Luc 63–4
    Le Nouvel Esprit du capitalisme 117
Bon, Michel 147
Bradatan, Costica 82, 216
    Dying for Ideas 69
Breton, Thierry 148, 160
Brizé, Stéphane, En guerre 3–4, 66–7
Brouillette, Sarah 190
Bruneau, Sophie 91–2
    Ils ne mouraient pas tous, mais tous
        étaient frappés 91–2
Brunel, Valérie, Les managers de
    l'âme 50
Burgi, Noëlle 58
'burn out' 94–6

Camus, Albert, Myth of Sisyphus 13
Cantet, Laurent, Ressources humaines
    78
Carole Matthieu (film) 142, 156–7
Castells, Manuel 184
Cederström, Carl 213
Chesnais, Jean-Claude 32
Chevalier, Louis 31
Chiapello, Eve 63–4, 117
China 9, 62, 158n6
    Foxconn 62, 141, 158n6
Claudel, Philippe, L'Enquête 43–4
Clot, Yves 48, 60
Cobb, Richard 83n3
    Death in Paris 32

Colo, Olivia, *Le Grand Incendie* 17,
    87–8, 103
Contrat 2009 strategic plan, Renault
    173–4, 176, 180, 202–5
Corporate (Nicolas Silhol) 3, 49–50,
    80, 142
Critchley, Simon, *Notes on Suicide* 73,
    175

Darcos, Xavier 47–8, 101
De Gaulejac, Vincent 58–9, 201
De Staël, Madame 13
Decèze, Dominique, *La Machine à*
    broyer 156
Dejours, Christophe 29, 54–5, 65–6,
    78, 176, 204–5
    Souffrance en France 198
    Travail, usure mentale 209–10
Delépine, Benoît, *Near Death*
    Experience 56–7
Derrida, Jacques 81, 104
    Spectres of Marx 76
Dervin, Yonnel 142
    Ils m'ont détruit 86–7
Disneyland Paris 1–2n2
Douglas, Jack 16, 72, 75
Du Roy, Ivan 146, 159
Dufour, Thibault, *Les Impactés* 152n4–3
Duménil, Gérard 39
Durkheim, Emile 8, 29, 33–5, 37,
    57–8, 74n1, 77–8, 99, 109, 215
    Suicide 14–15, 25, 33–5

Ehrenberg, Alain, *La Fatigue d'être soi*
    209
Engels, Friedrich 215
    Condition of the Working Class in
    England 35–6
Esquirol, Etienne 99
Establet, Roger 15, 34
Etkind, Marc, *Or not to be* 73–4
Evans, Brad 27

Felman, Shoshana 76
Filhol, Elisabeth, *La Centrale* 53–4

'financialisation' 39–40, 67–8, 104–5,
    142–50, 168–9
commodification of knowledge
    184–201, 212–13
as driving force of economic
    power 26–7, 215–27
shareholder value 140–69
Fincham, Ben 74, 75
Fleming, Peter 213
fonctionnaires 46–7, 52–3, 112, 113,
    146, 153
Font Le Bret, Brigitte 149–50
Fontenelle, Sebastien 116
Foucault, Michel 14, 21–2, 110,
    123–5, 127, 128–9, 137, 217
    History of Sexuality 125
Foxconn (China) 62, 141, 158n6
France
    Disneyland Paris 1–2n2
    economic restructuring 9–10n9,
        171–4
    Labour reforms 10, 43, 47, 51,
        64–5, 98
    public service companies 46
    see also France Télécom; La Poste;
        Renault
France Télécom (Orange) 1–2, 5–7n8,
    11, 17, 22
    collective denial of damage caused
        by management restucturing
        157–63, 222
    emblematic crisis symbolising
        excesses of finance capitalism
        141, 218
    employees' legal cases 163–8, 219
    executives charged with driving
        employees to suicide 5–6, 86,
        101, 141n2, 151, 163–8, 219
    'financialisation' 42–3
    'management terror' 6, 44–7, 162,
        167, 183–4
    rebranding as Orange 139–69
    restructuring 72–3, 93–4, 109,
        139–69, 150–7, 218
    see also NExT restructuring plan

Fraysse, Monique 161
Frémontier, Jacques, *La Forteresse ouvrière* 196–7, 200, 206–7, 208–9
Fridenson, Patrick 208

Ghosn, Carlos 180, 202–4, 218
Giddens, Anthony 63, 85, 99
gilets jaunes movement 10–11n10, 61
Giroux, Henry 27
Goeschel, Christian de 75n2
'going postal' phenomenon 107–38
Goldberg, Jonah, *Suicide of the West* 4n5
Gollac, Michel 60
Guéant, Claude 2, 101–2

Halbwachs, Maurice 34, 78, 89
    Les Causes du suicide 15, 89
Hamon, Hervé 102
Hanique, Fabienne 58–9, 110, 116, 126, 129
harcèlement moral (psychological bullying) 6, 45, 47, 98, 162, 167, 183–4
Haskaj, Fatmir 217
Hermann, Christophe 119
Hirschman, Albert 207–8
Holbach, Baron de 13
Hollande, François 10, 64

India 9

Japan 9n9
karo-jisatsu 93–4
John, Matthew 78

Kafka, Franz 201
Kervern, Gustave, *Near Death Experience* (film) 56–7
Klotz, Nicolas, *La Question humaine* 78–9
knowledge economy 171–4, 190–201, 212–13, 218

La Poste 1–2, 11, 21–2, 58, 72, 86, 102–3, 137–8

change from public service ethos to commercialisation 109–16
    Facteurs en France corporate text 113–14
    'going postal' phenomenon 107–38
    restructuring framed as freedom narrative 116–23
    traditional and unique status of postman used for rebranding 111–16
    warnings from health professionals about working conditions 108–9, 130–1, 135–7
Lagarde, Christine 160
Lapavitsas, Costas 39–40, 143
Larcher, Gérard 159
Laub, Dori 76
Lazzarato, Maurizio 116, 186, 188, 189, 200
Ledun, Marin 142, 149–50, 152, 156
    Les Visages écrasés 220–1
Lefebvre, Henri 79
Les Impactés (play) 142, 152n4–3
Levé, Edouard, *Suicide* 76
Levey, Sylvain, *Au pays des* 1–2n2
Lévy, Dominique 39
'licenciements boursiers' (stock market redundancies) 43
Linhart, Danièle 201
Lombard, Didier 7, 100–1, 148–9, 151, 160, 162–3, 167
Loriol, Marc 206

Macdonald, Michael, *Sleepless Souls* 32n3
Macron, Emmanuel 10–11, 43, 64
management bullying (*harcèlement moral*) 6, 45, 47, 162, 167, 183–4
Marichalar, Pascal 30n1
Marini, Hélène, *Une tournée dans la neige* 128
Marsh, Ian 14
Martin, Emmanuel 30n1
Marx, Karl 36–7, 188, 215

Mbembé, Achille 217, 221
Mélenchon, Jean-Luc 210
Mercier, Jean-Baptiste 31
Milner, Susan 64
Minois, Georges 33
Molinier, Pascale 55–6
Montesquieu 13
Moulier Boutang, Yann 188–9
Murphy, Terence R., *Sleepless Souls* 32n3

necropower 217, 220
    emergence of 23, 68–9
Negri, Antonio 188
neoliberalism 104–5
    changing management methods
        8–10, 20–1, 26–9, 39–40, 117,
        215–22
    commodification of knowledge
        184–201, 212–13
    expulsionary dynamics 26–7, 140
    'licenciements boursiers' (stock
        market redundancies) 43
    status of labour under globalised
        capitalism 77, 104–5, 216–17
    subjective violence 38
    see also 'financialisation'
NExT restructuring plan (France
    Télécom) 11, 22, 46n6, 92–3,
    148–9, 151–7
    forced redeployment 153–7

Orange amère (documentary) 151,
    161

Paddock, Stephen Craig 107n1
Padieu, René 3
Parisot, Laurence 2n4
Petit, Louis-Julien, *Carole Matthieu*
    156–7
Peuchet, Jacques 36
Peugeot 1–2, 17
'placardisation' (closeting/sidelining)
    48–50, 96–8
Pollock, Griselda 78
privatisation 142–50

Rabinbach, Anson, *The Human Motor*
    205–6
Raffarin, Jean-Pierre 147
Raynal, Cathy 142
    Les travailleuses sans visage
        154–5
Reagan, Ronald 117
    economic changes 107–8
Remy, Jacqueline 94–5
Renault 1–2, 11, 17, 18, 22–3, 50–1,
    72
    Contrat 2009 strategic plan
        173–4, 176, 180, 202–5
    legal cases 176–84
    Technocentre 172–4, 190–201,
        210–12
    transition to knowledge economy
        171–4, 190–201, 212–13,
        218
Renou, Gildas 160
Richard, Stéphane 46, 160, 162–3
Rolo, Duarte 127
Ross, Kristin 41
Rot, Gwenaële 198–9
Rothberg, Michael 77
Roudil, Marc-Antoine, *Ils ne
    mouraient pas tous, mais tous étaient
    frappés* 91–2
Rousseau, Jean-Jacques 13

Sarkozy, Nicolas 156
Sassen, Saskia 27, 79–80, 91, 143, 216
Schweitzer, Louis 190–1n15
Selly, Aude, *Quand le travail nous tue*
    95–6
Shaviro, Steven 189–90
Sherrill, Patrick 107n1
Shneidman, Edwin 74–5, 94
sidelining ('placardisation') 48–50,
    96–8
Silhol, Nicolas, *Corporate* 3, 49–50,
    80, 142
Silverman, Max 78
Sonnet, Martine 208, 218
    Atelier 62 197

suicide
  as final act of agency and
    empowerment 167, 169, 220
  final act of desperate communi-
    cation 81–9, 104–5, 222
  inversion of individual's biography
    175
  object of censorship 19–20
  social significance of notes and
    letters 74–89, 110, 130–7,
    163–4, 216

Tati, Jacques, *Jour de fête* 111, 127
Teissier, Claude 113, 115–16
Thatcher, Margaret 117
trade unions, attempts to expose
  work stress 161–2, 199–201
Tran, Christian, *Poste restante* 122n3

United States
  Amazon workplace 'suicide wave'
    9
  postal service 107–8, 137

Vatin, François 2–3
Viallet, Jean-Robert
  La Dépossession 40–1
  La Mise à mort du travail 17, 40, 65
Virno, Paolo 188
Voltaire 13

Wahl, Pierre 120, 121
Weil, Simone 76–7, 207, 208
  La Condition ouvrière 195–6
Wenes, Louis-Pierre 100, 148, 167
work patterns
  company restructuring 91–3
  forced redeployment 150–7, 165
  intensified surveillance of daily
    work activity 22, 27–8, 83,
    110, 123–9, 137–8
  knowledge economy 22–3,
    212–13
  restructuring leading to increased
    precarity 9–10, 42–3, 52–3

underwork ('placardisation')
  96–8
work intensification (overwork)
  93–6, 174, 205–12
work suicide
  affecting specific sectors
    30–1n1
  definition 1–2n1
  emerging social phenomena 7–8,
    15–16, 29–52, 217
  form of protest 61–9, 220–1
  gender patterns 55–6
  historical link with social class
    31–3, 51–3
  hypermediatisation 3, 51–2
  lack of statistical research 4–5
  legal cases 176–84
  loss of social integration and
    group solidarity 34–5, 38–9,
    57–8, 62–5
  negotiation of blame 89–91,
    99–104
  neoliberalism and changing
    management methods 8–10,
    20–1, 27–9, 39–51, 215–16
  notes and letters as testimony
    16–19, 21, 71–105, 110, 130–7,
    163–4, 216
  official narrative of minimisation
    2–3, 5–6, 71–3, 99–104,
    130–1, 157–63, 183–4
  reframing as act of autonomous
    individual 1–7, 14, 130–2
  research around causality 4–6, 17,
    25–6, 175–84
  social order and the individual
    12–14, 28–9, 55–6, 59–60,
    110, 219–21

Yaegar, Patricia 20, 81

Zanati, Frédéric 7
Zemmour, Eric, *Le Suicide français*
  4n5
Žižek, Slavoj 38, 79, 99